Approaches to Discourse in Dementia

Jacqueline Guendouzi
University of South Alabama, Mobile

Nicole Müller
University of Louisiana at Lafayette

Psychology Press
Taylor & Francis Group

New York   London

First published 2006 by
Lawrence Erlbaum Associates, Inc., Publishers

This edition published 2012 by Psychology Press

Psychology Press
Taylor & Francis Group
711 Third Avenue
New York, NY 10017

Psychology Press
Taylor & Francis Group
27 Church Road, Hove
East Sussex BN3 2FA

First issued in paperback 2014

Psychology Press is an imprint of the Taylor and Francis Group, an informa business

Cover design by Kathryn Houghtaling Lacey

Cover art by Tom Thomson. "Soft Maple in Autum," 1914. Collection
of Tom Thomson Memorial Art Gallery, Owen Sound, Ontario,
Canada. Gift of Louise (Thomson) Henry, sister of Tom Thomson.

Library of Congress Cataloging-in-Publication Data

Guendouzi, Jacqueline A.
  Approaches to discourse in dementia / Jacqueline A. Guendouzi,
  Nicole Müller.
      p.   cm.
  Includes bibliographical references and index.
ISBN 0-8058-4594-1 (cloth : alk. paper)
1. Dementia. 2. Communicative disorders. I. Muller, Nicole, 1963-
  II. Title.
RC521.G84   2006
616.8'3—dc21

2005040072
CIP

ISBN 13: 978-0-8058-4594-5 (hbk)
ISBN 13: 978-1-138-00386-6 (pbk)

Contents

Preface and
Acknowledgments

This book is written from an interdisciplinary perspective with an interdisciplinary readership in mind. We are linguists and investigators of discourse, and our primary sphere of action is defined by our employment in university departments of communicative disorders. Thus, part of our job description is the education of future speech-language pathologists in both undergraduate and graduate degree programs. An important element of our teaching involves instructing students in the analysis of various aspects of discourse produced by persons with various diagnoses of communicative disorders. To these students, we offer this book as an aid in their investigations of disordered discourse and the discourses of disorders and hope that the discussion of the approaches to discourse we selected will better enable them to choose appropriate tools for various analytical tasks. Another part of our teaching is concerned with neurogenic disorders of communication, such as aphasia, and with dementia. The teaching and clinical practice in these areas has experienced a salutary, in our opinion, shift away from a sole focus on "disorder" or "disease" toward a model of care and intervention that views the individual and the individual's skills and impairments as embedded in multiple social contexts and focuses on functional skills in interaction. As a contribution to this growing tradition, this book centers around conversational interactions between persons with dementia and without and finds its focus not in the dementia but rather in the evolving interactions and their context-bound successes and failures. Thus, readers working either in clinical practice as speech pathologists or with caregivers in nursing home settings or in the community may find this book useful as a source of perspectives on interaction.

We are both active observers of and consultants on clinical cases in our own university settings. In addition, our interest in dementia has led us to get involved with support organizations for persons with dementia and their caregivers and with various residential care facilities. To better understand the challenges involved in communicating with people who have dementia, we regularly visit nursing homes and assisted-living facilities observing and interacting with residents who have dementia and their caregivers and families. This book would not have been possible without the goodwill, help, and assistance of the residents and staff of these institutions. First and foremost, we wish to honor our participants in the conversations in this book. Special thanks also go to the students who have over the years ventured into dementia country with us, in particular, Melanie Bartmess, Megan Hurst, Ruixia Yan, and Brent Wilson and to facilitators and members of dementia support group meetings, especially Ray and Marilyn Yandle. We also wish to thank Morris, Brian, Carol, Garnette, Shirley, Jeanne, Peter, and other members of DASNI (Dementia Advocacy and Support Network International) for their many valuable insights and contributions to the thought processes that underpin Chapter 7. We also thank the anonymous reviewers who supported this project and the reviewers of the typescript for their constructive comments and advice in the final stages of this book as well as Cathleen Petree at Lawrence Erlbaum Associates, Inc. Finally, thanks go to Anne Perry, who is still fighting a long battle with Alzheimer's disease and who was the inspiration for this book.

Jacqueline Guendouzi is an Associate Professor in the Speech Pathology and Audiology Department at the University of South Alabama and is a research member of ASHA (American Speech-Language Hearing Association), a member of the International Clinical Phonetics and Linguistics Association (ICPLA) and International Pragmatics Association. Before moving to South Alabama, Dr. Guendouzi worked in the Communications Sciences Department at Southeastern Louisiana University and prior to that in the Speech Therapy Department at the University of Central England. She was consultant to a language unit for children with developmental language delays in the United Kingdom and coordinator of the Alzheimer's Support Group in Hammond, Louisiana until 2004 and was a member of the Patient/Family/Education Committee for the Greater New Orleans Alzheimer's Association Regional Advisory Board. Guendouzi's data collection was funded with the aid of research grants awarded to her through the Office of Faculty Excellence at the Southeastern Louisiana University.

Nicole Müller is an Associate Professor and Doris B. Hawthorne/BoRSF Endowed Professor in Communicative Disorders at the University of Louisiana at Lafayette. She is a research member of ASHA and a founder member of ICPLA. Dr. Müller moved to Louisiana from the Centre for Language and Communication Research at Cardiff University in Wales. She volunteers with the Alzheimer's Association of Acadiana as a cofacilitator for caregivers of persons with dementia, and with a local nursing home.

1

Dementia and Its Discourses

THIS BOOK AND ITS CONTEXT

In recent years, there have been steady advances in the neurology, neurophysiology, and neuropathology of dementing diseases and in experimental studies probing their communicative and cognitive consequences. There is also a growing body of work, in dementias and other neurogenic communicative disorders (such as aphasia following focal brain injury or traumatic brain injury), that uses qualitative methods to analyze naturally occurring interactions between persons with a communicative disorder and persons without. The focus of our own work, and of this book, is this comparatively young, although by now well-established, tradition of qualitative research in communicative disorders. Our approach to the analysis of interaction or discourse brings with it certain assumptions and practices, which we revisit repeatedly and in some detail as we progress through the book:

1. Our focus on communication disorder could be described as contextualized and emergent. The object of analysis is the interaction between two or more human beings as it unfolds. Order or disorder, success or breakdown in communication, arise out of the unfolding interaction in its context. Communicative interaction is a joint, collabo-

1

rative, distributed, and contextually situated activity. Disorder, in this perspective, is not primarily concerned with the limitations of an individual person's communicative faculties but with the mutually perceived success or lack thereof of a communicative interaction. This also implies that communicative disorder, for our purposes, needs to be described, analyzed, and understood within the realm of real communicative events: the prototypical such event being conversation.[1]

2. Our attempts to analyze naturally occurring interaction are interdisciplinary in nature. Researchers and teachers in clinical communication studies have some scavenger-like characteristics: Promising-looking methods from linguistics, pragmatics, anthropology, sociology, various branches of psychology, and more recently, complexity theory and network theory are ruthlessly adopted, adapted, and applied. As we discuss further later on in this chapter and throughout this book, this interdisciplinary approach holds both a great promise and some danger. On one hand, having multiple descriptive frameworks and analytic methods available makes for a rich tool kit, and thus, it should in theory become easier to capture at least some of the complexity of human interaction. On the other hand, if frameworks and methods are divorced from their philosophical backgrounds, understood imperfectly, and applied inappropriately, the resulting picture will be less than illuminating (see Perkins, 2000, 2002). There is of course some degree of overlap between the various approaches, methods, and theories that make up the umbrella category of discourse analysis (DA). However, one must not assume that the differences are superficial and consist only of different sets of labels for the same phenomena. Rather, terminologies and categories bring with them the legacies of different methodological preferences, theories, and philosophical orientations. These legacies determine how different schools of discourse analysis approach (and indeed construct) their data, which in turn will determine which questions can usefully be answered by any given approach and which conclusions can sensibly be drawn.

In writing this book, we have pursued three main goals. First of all, we wished to provide readers with an interest in the analysis of spoken discourse with an overview of the main approaches and theories in DA. Second, we aimed to show how these approaches and theories can be applied to data from clinical contexts by offering detailed analyses of data extracts from conversations with persons with dementia. Third, in presenting these analyses, we wished to illustrate some of the characteristics and challenges inherent in interaction in the context of dementia. The title, and to a lesser extent the structure of this book, are a deliberate echo of Schiffrin's (1994) admirable work, *Approaches to Discourse*, which over the years has been an

---

[1]See also the special issue of *Clinical Linguistics and Phonetics* (vol. 19, issue 5), edited by M. Perkins, which is centered around an emergentist perspective on impairments of interaction.

invaluable resource to many researchers, students, and teachers in discourse studies. In the remainder of this chapter, we discuss notions of discourse, discourses, and interaction before moving on to a brief introduction to dementia and communication in and with dementia.

DISCOURSE IN DEMENTIA STUDIES

The terms *discourse* and *discourses* mean many different things to different people. It is not our intention here to survey the many existing definitions; for such a survey, the reader is directed to, for example, the opening chapter of Jaworski and Coupland (1999).[2] Schiffrin, Tannen, and Hamilton (2001) distil three major definitional strands from the literature, namely, "(1) anything beyond the sentence, (2) language use, and (3) a broader range of social practice that includes nonlinguistic and nonspecific instances of language" (p. 1). The definition of discourse used in any analysis of language or language use, whether spoken or written, depends of course on the theoretical and analytical framework adopted. Schiffrin (1994) draws a basic distinction between formalist and functionalist approaches to the analysis of discourse. Formalist, or structural, frameworks focus on the relations between constituent elements of discourse "(1)" as defined by Schiffrin et al. (2001) (see Grimes, 1975; Stubbs, 1983; van Dijk, 1985a, 1985b, 1997), whereas functional approaches analyze language in use including the purposes and functions of linguistic form in human interaction: in other words, Schiffrin et al's discourse "(2)" and/or "(3)" (see Brown & Yule, 1983; Fasold, 1990). Discourse "(3)" underlies critical discourse studies, which presuppose language and its use as a part of society and reciprocally, society as constructed through linguistic and nonlinguistic (discursive) practices (see Fairclough, 1989).

The field of clinical discourse studies is truly multidisciplinary in nature, but typically the frameworks used are adapted from nonclinical contexts to clinical ones. Each theoretical bias, or approach, brings with it its own framework for description, categorization, and analysis and crucially, its own understanding of the nature of its data. Thus, what makes up discourse differs as widely in clinical as in nonclinical discourse studies. The explicit or implicit definitions of discourse in published work on dementia are on a continuum that spans elicited spoken or written discourse in experimental settings on one end and free conversation or narrative on the other end. This continuum partly overlaps with an analysis continuum in which quantification of predetermined discourse characteristics occupies one end and qualitative methods attempting to describe, rather than count patterns, the other. It comes as no surprise that elicited discourse in experimental set-

---

[2]See also Duchan (1994) for a summary of the historical development and theoretical underpinnings of various approaches to discourse.

tings tends to team up with quantitative analyses, whereas qualitative research tends to insist on naturally occurring language data.

At the experimental end of the continuum, there are studies on discourse data that fall squarely under Schiffrin et al.'s (2001) definition "(1)," and the classic studies carried out and reviewed by Ulatowska and colleagues (see, e.g., Ulatowska, 1985; Ulatowska & Chapman, 1995) may serve as useful illustrations and recommended reading here. Ulatowska and Chapman's (1995) definition of discourse and their view on the use of discourse data in dementia studies, is worth quoting here:

> Although discourse may be composed of a single word, a phrase, a sentence, or a combination of all the above, discourse typically consists of a sequence of connected sentences. The coherence of discourse is determined by how well this sequence of sentences is related. Discourse provides a promising avenue for investigating behavioral changes in dementia, because discourse can be manipulated to explore how cognitive impairment impinges on linguistic functioning and communicative competence. This approach is possible because of the inherent nature of discourse, which entails a complex interaction among *linguistic, communicative,* and *cognitive* processes. Precisely, discourse is expressed linguistically (i.e. via words and sentences) and is defined communicatively (i.e., a unit of language that conveys a message). Moreover, complex cognitive processes (e.g. memory, attention, perception, and retrieval) underlie discourse comprehension and production. (p. 115)

Studies in this tradition typically use elicitation procedures for connected spoken and written language in controlled experimental settings. In their review of discourse studies in dementia, Ulatowska and Chapman (1995, p. 116ff) list the use of oral and written picture description tasks using various stimuli, orally presented narratives for retelling, delayed story retelling, self-generated narrative, the elicitation of summaries and morals for stories, and interview dialogue. Students and researchers working in, for example, the assessment of aphasia or brain injury will be familiar with various assessment materials and techniques that use these tools, and there is no need to go into detail here discussing them.

Among Bayles and Kaszniak's (1987) "recommendations for evaluating the communication deficits of dementia patients" (p. 174), we find the following important passage:

> Analyze Communication Beyond the Sentence Level. The third basic principle in testing the dementia patient is to include an analysis of a unit of language larger than the sentence, namely, discourse. Discourse is the most natural and common type of communication and requires the integration of all types of linguistic knowledge. It is a medium through which the social, psychologic, and linguistic aspects of communication can be studied. With discourse analysis, the clinician can quantify the emptiness of language associated with dementia, the fragmentation of thought, and anomia. (pp. 174–175)

Again, discourse is essentially understood as language structure beyond the sentence level, discourse is elicited in a testing situation, and the analysis of discourse is primarily seen as a means of quantifying deficits associated with disorder. One may of course question the naturalness of language produced through a picture elicitation task or in a story retelling, but the research questions we pursue here are explicitly not questions of naturalistic communicative functioning but questions of underlying competences and knowledge and their impairment through the effects of dementing conditions.

A middle ground between experimental-quantitative and naturalistic-qualitative studies is occupied by work that uses more naturally occurring language but analyzes the data thus gathered by means of predetermined categories in an attempt to quantify the characteristics of discourse produced by persons with dementia (see, e.g., Garcia & Joanette, 1994; Hamilton, 1994b).

At the end of the clinical discourse studies continuum opposite the experimental-quantitative end, we find work that is explicit in using naturally occurring, interactive language, often in the form of conversations or self-generated narratives. In this tradition falls the groundbreaking work by Hamilton, Ramanathan, and Sabat (e.g., Hamilton, 1994a; Ramanathan, 1997; Sabat, 2001) in Alzheimer studies. Hamilton (1994a, p. 18) discussed an important point of test situations in which participants are asked to produce "spontaneous" language on a specific, very narrow topic: The participants may consider the task trivial (or maybe even demeaning?) and may not see the need to communicate about, for example, a button, an envelope, a nail, or a marble placed in front of them (as in, e.g., Bayles, 1982). As Hamilton (1994a) puts it, "There must be a need for the patient to communicate before we can be sure that our statements regarding the patient's ability to communicate are valid" (p. 19). In fact, we could say that in testing situations, we have at a minimum two levels of discourse happening at the same time: The actual "experimental" utterances, that is, instructions given by the tester, and responses by the test participant, which are embedded into the surrounding test situation, a discourse including all nonverbal, situational, and so forth factors as well as all utterances not directly pertaining to the experiment. That is, we have an instance of discourse "(1)," as defined by Schiffrin et al. (2001), embedded into an instance of discourse "(2)"/"(3)."

Hamilton's (1994a, 1994b) work is strongly data driven; her data consist of naturally occurring conversations with a single participant. Hamilton (1994a) herself adopted the role of the participant observer, using a "personal research approach which is meant to supplement the technical approach normally taken in studies of Alzheimer's disease" (p. 31). The term "personal research approach" is from Kitwood (1988); the approach contrasts with that of the objective, depersonalized observer of traditional experimental science in that "at its core, it works interpretively and empathetically, going far beyond the measurement of indices or the codification of behaviour. In all of this the researcher takes a personal risk " (Kitwood 1988, p. 176, as cited in Hamilton, 1994a, p. 31.). A crucial point in Hamilton's (1994) work is that the analytical tools and categories emerge out of the data rather than being given a priori, in the form of an analytical framework superimposed on the data gathering and analysis processes. Hamilton describes her approach thus:

> Sense-making difficulties and unusual moments in the conversations would pique my linguistic curiosity along the way and lead me to wonder about possible interrelationships in the data. But it was not until after the final conversation examined in this study that I began to use these observations and considerations to form the analytical tools and frameworks which would allow me to carry out quantitative analyses which seemed to be true to the data. (pp. 30–31)

Ramanathan (1997), in discussing Hamilton (1994) and Sabat (1991), draws attention to the jointly distributed character of face-to-face interaction and the changing role of the interlocutor over time as dementia progresses. Thus, here, the interviewer or conversational partner is seen as a facilitator, accommodating to the partner's interactive needs (see also Sabat, 1991). Ramanathan uses life narratives rather than interviews or conversations as primary data, although the narratives were collected in face-to-face interactions, thus incorporating an interactive element. Indeed, the interactional processes or schemas are a major focus of analysis in a work that "examines how particular interactional features inhibit extensive and meaningful talk from the patient, whereas others facilitate it.… A close examination of language as a social product and process can be another fruitful approach to understanding the Alzheimer experience" (Ramanathan, 1997, p. 6).

It is not our intention here to make a case that discourse elicited under experimental conditions represents "worse" (or indeed "better") data than conversations or narratives collected under circumstances that are as "natural" and spontaneous as possible. Rather, we wish to point out that we are dealing with different types of data, and approaches to analysis, in each case, and that ideally, experimental-quantitative and naturalistic-qualitative studies should complement each other. A brief mention of Sabat's (2001, p. 3ff) discussion of classical and romantic science, following Luria (1987a), may be useful at this point. Researchers working within the tradition of reductionist classical science in experimental settings "look upon events in terms of their constituent parts. Step by step they single out important units and elements until they can formulate abstract, general laws." (Luria 1987a, as cited in Sabat, 2001, p. 3).

As Sabat (2001, p. 3ff) points out, the focus on generalization is crucial here. Classical science aims to distil the general, the average, out of typically large amounts of data gained in experimental settings and subjected to various processes of quantification. Equally important in classical science is the focus on the reduction of complex organisms, functioning in a complex environment, to their constituent parts, which in turn are examined separately and the results expressed in terms of test scores. Hence, the use of standardized tests and controlled settings, elicitation procedures for discourse that are kept as constant as humanly possible across participants, and the quantification of discourse characteristics as in the work discussed in, for example, Ulatowska and Chapman (1995), or Bayles and Kaszniak (1987). Aggregates from these separate examinations are combined into averages and compared with average scores from other groups (in dementia research, typically normally aging participants) who have undergone the same tests. Thus, an individual's functioning is not only compartmentalized but grouped with and matched against the compartmentalized functioning of others. The aim is to identify the general, typical bundle of symptoms of dementing conditions, such as Alzheimer's disease (AD) as evidenced in certain types of language use, in comparison to persons without these conditions. This is of course a necessity in the search for the abstract, general laws of classical science, and in research efforts aimed at the improvement of clinical diagnosis of AD and other dementing diseases, which require the establishment of a reliable, recognizable, and at least to an extent generalizable symptom complex, this approach is of great value and indeed necessary (Sabat, 2001, p. 4).

Our concern in this book is not, however, the clinical diagnosis of dementing conditions, nor, in the first instance, their pathological symptom complexes. The diagnosis of, for example, AD as experienced by persons with AD and their carers, and certainly the presence of AD and its effects on human interaction, are of course part of the universe in which we collected our data and carried out our analysis. However, our starting points and primary concerns in this book are not with the quantification of symptoms or typical traits. In terms of data, we begin with naturally occurring conversations or as natural as conversations can be while they are being recorded on video or audio tapes. In terms of analysis, our aim is to examine various approaches to language use or discourse. One of our concerns here is a meta-analysis, in that we aim to investigate what questions can sensibly be asked from which approach, and what we can learn about our assumptions concerning language, language use, and linguistic interaction by applying methods developed on the implicit basis of "normal" discourse practices to "disordered" data. In terms of dementia, persons with dementia, and their carers, our focus of investigation lies with individuals functioning and interacting more or less successfully within the complexity of their environments. Thus, our ideological home, if one may use the term, is closer to what Luria (1987b) calls "romantic science," than to classical, reductionist science. In Luria's words (1987b, as cited in Sabat, 2001), "Romantics in science want neither to split living reality into its elementary components nor to represent the wealth of life's concrete events in abstract models that lose the properties of the phenomena themselves. It is of utmost importance to romantics to preserve the wealth of living reality, and they aspire to a science that retains this richness" (p. 14).

Principles of Qualitative Research and Discourse as a Metacategory

At this stage, we need to ask ourselves whether it is really possible to achieve Luria's romantic (1987b) science and to genuinely preserve the "wealth of living reality."

Rempusheski (1999) draws a distinction between realists and idealists in scientific inquiry, defining the realist as conducting research in the tradition of logical positivism, following a "deductive approach and quantitative research methods wherein phenomena are viewed objectively and reduced to numerical configurations" (p. S45). The idealist on the other hand "explores a world known through perceptions and the subjectivity of humans," in the tradition of "postpositivist philosophy of science," which "follows an inductive approach and qualitative research methods wherein the context is maintained and the subjectivity is acknowledged" (Rempusheski, 1999, p. S45).

Qualitative approaches to inquiry have found increasing numbers of followers in neurogenic disorders of communication in recent years. The philosophy and objectives of qualitative research make it a paradigm (or maybe rather a bundle of paradigms) that is attractive in areas in which the researcher is not or cannot be certain from the very beginning exactly what questions need to be asked, or can sensibly be asked from a certain constellation of raw data, such as a communicative, interactive context between persons with and without communicative disorders.

What follows is our reading of some major principles of qualitative inquiry as applied and applicable in clinical communication studies or clinical discourse studies; other researchers in this tradition may phrase their own priorities somewhat differently (see also Creswell, 1997; Damico, Oelschlaeger, & Simmons-Mackie, 1999; Damico, Simmons-Mackie, Oelschlaeger, Elman, & Armstrong, 1999; Lincoln & Guba, 1985; Rempusheski, 1999; Silverman, 2000 for more detailed explorations of qualitative research approaches).

   1. The main function of the researcher in qualitative research is that of a learner, although not necessarily that of a seeker after objective, un-

changing truth. The researcher is not the a priori expert, although she or he may very well be the person who "asks the questions." Ideally, though, she or he will be, to the same or a greater extent, the person who listens to what others have to say in their own words, their own terminology, their own language. This also means that our approach to our participants has to be one of partnership and collaboration.

2. In order to be able to do this, a qualitative researcher has to be willing to enter into real-life contexts with an open mind as to what might emerge in these contexts. The focus has to be wide at least initially; precise foci of observation and analysis will emerge during a cyclical process of observation, data gathering, and analysis. Focused research questions will emerge from very broad research agenda. Thus, the context of observation is of great importance in our research, and this context includes the researcher with her or his own biases, abilities, training, assumptions, and preferences such as the assumptions with which we opened this chapter. A crucial point in qualitative research is that these subjectivities are embraced and have to be made explicit.

3. As the researcher attempts to enter the world of the participants and the research agenda, she or he needs to acknowledge that the reality constructed collaboratively, socially, and (as stressed by Rempusheski, 1999, p. S46), subjectively really consists of multiple realities constructed through multiple voices. These realities concern normal (or indeed disordered) life, as it unfolds from day to day; in other words, we strive to "understand the mundane" (Damico et al., 1999, p. 645).

4. Our broad research agenda is communication, and therefore, our interest lies with processes more so than products; how a communicative interaction unfolds is of greater interest than the ratio of accurate versus inaccurate responses, for example. This also implies that our starting point is always the individual in her or his social and communicative environment rather than, for example, the "average" person with AD.

5. Because our starting point is that of a learner who does not have, cannot have, a predetermined list of precisely formulated research questions to ask, our approach to data gathering and analysis has to be open minded and flexible enough to accommodate, when necessary, the unexpected. Indeed, within a qualitative research paradigm, it makes perfect sense to ask where the disorder in communication actually lies and to question traditional clinical assumptions that a disorder of communication is a simple manifestation of, for example, a neurological impairment or cognitive deterioration in a person and thus a necessary, somehow linear, consequence of said impairment or deterioration. It is necessary to observe and closely describe patterns that emerge from interactions, and the tools we use to categorize these patterns have to be, on one hand, precise enough to provide a rich description that allows us to formulate questions of underlying mechanisms contributing to the patterns we find. On the other hand, our tool kit has to be flexible and adjustable such

that, for example, terminologies may have to be readjusted or redefined when necessary, and such readjustment has to be explicit.

6. Our "macro" research context is a clinical one, which includes many different types of "micro" contexts, or contexts of individual interactions, between many different individuals and many categories of individuals. However, under the umbrella category of clinical qualitative research or clinical discourse studies, researchers have to understand themselves as carrying out applied research. It is our view that clinical discourse study cannot afford to "do discourse" for its own sake. The process of research will typically be motivated by the perception of a clinical need; someone will always ask, "What can I do with this?," or, to put it more bluntly, "What's the use of this?" It is, we think, a salutary process to keep these questions in mind, as they remind of the responsibility we ultimately have to our participants-be they persons with dementia, or their family members, or other carers-namely, to contribute, if we possibly can, to their quality of life.

We opened this section with the question whether any research approach could really achieve the ideal of capturing the wealth or complexity of living reality. It would appear that research in the qualitative tradition at least attempts to move toward such a goal, and in keeping with a preference for processes over products, the journey toward such an end, the questions that arise on the way, and the process of questioning the realities constructed is as important as the goal itself. However, qualitative research should also embrace a healthy wariness of its own ability to capture said complexity in its entirety, which we consider an unrealistic goal. Indeed, we should guard against the assumption that the results from our case analyses are widely and unqualifiedly generalizable to "dementia discourse" overall. Although good qualitative research will always check its results against reality (see, e.g., Silverman, 2000, on generalizability), the question of how any reality is filtered through our methodological preferences and theoretical biases should never be far from our minds. Similarly, a personal preference or "take" on the processes underlying interaction must never replace a detailed analysis (see Verschueren, 2001, for further discussion of this point).

Every description, however open minded, data driven, or inclusive, imposes categories on the object of description. Thus, any framework of analysis, any method of data gathering, even, is necessarily selective. We must not lose sight of this selectivity in our efforts but again, in keeping with the principles of qualitative research, make it explicit. This brings us to our definition of discourse for the purposes of this work. We view discourse as a metacategory, an analytic level of interaction. People interact, talk to each other, tell stories; researchers do discourse. Of course, one could argue that every interaction contains an element of analysis, as in, for example, the mutual monitoring of the interlocutors' communicative intentions or of the developing common ground between them (see Clark, 1996, for this latter concept). However, discourse analysts construct the discourse as an object of description and analysis. This construction of the discourse begins with the gathering of data and includes the process of transcription. We deal with this in more detail in chapter 2.

DEMENTIA AND DEMENTING DISEASES

The literature, both "lay" and "specialist," on dementing diseases is clearly dominated by AD. This is not surprising because AD is the most common brain pathology leading to the progressive cognitive and behavioral symptoms summarized by the term *dementia*. Indeed, it appears that in everyday language usage, *Alzheimer's* and *dementia* have become more or less synonymous. Evidence for this common conflation of terms comes from encounters at support group meetings for caregivers of persons with dementia where it is not uncommon that new members arrive with the question, "So what's the difference between Alzheimer's and dementia?" or for one caregiver to say, "I'm X, and my father was diagnosed with Alzheimer's a couple of months ago," which might prompt another someone else to comment, "My mother's got dementia. Is that the same thing?" We do not intend to insinuate here that neurologists, family physicians, or anyone else involved in the diagnostic process are not doing their job of informing the family members of a person newly diagnosed with a dementing condition such as AD. Rather, from the perspective of anyone working with persons with dementia and their caregivers, it is very important to keep in mind that this process can be a rather overwhelming time in a family's life and that there is much information to take in and to come to terms with. Therefore, a terminological confusion as regards the technicalities of a brain pathology and its cognitive and behavioral sequelae is more than understandable. Further, the foregrounding of the "disease" in the thinking of a caregiver or a person afflicted with symptoms of dementia is a natural result of the search for an explanation or cause of the experienced gradual decline of cognitive functions.

There are many sources available that present a detailed account of the neurological, neuropsychological, and behavioral symptoms of variously caused dementias. We restrict our discussion on this point to the minimum necessary to inform a lay reader of the basic facts and focus on cognitive and behavioral aspects rather than possible etiologies. Incidentally, this puts a reader in a position similar to that of many who are confronted with the disease as nonspecialists, which includes most caregivers and indeed persons with dementia.

Diagnostic Features of Dementia

The Diagnostic and Statistical Manual of Mental Disorders (4th ed., text revision, DSM–IV–TR; American Psychiatric Association, 2000) summarizes the diagnostic features of dementia as regards cognitive deficits and resulting impairment as follows:

A. The development of multiple cognitive deficits manifested by both
   (1) memory impairment (impaired ability to learn new information or to recall previously learned information)
   (2) one (or more) of the following cognitive disturbances:
      (a) aphasia (language disturbance)
      (b) apraxia (impaired ability to carry out motor activities despite intact motor function)
      (c) agnosia (failure to recognize or identify objects despite intact sensory function)
      (d) disturbance in executive functioning (i.e. planning, organizing, sequencing, abstracting).
B. The cognitive deficits in Criteria A1 and A2 each cause significant impairment in social or occupational functioning and represent a significant decline from a previous level of functioning. (pp. 147–150, 157)

Various types of dementia can be distinguished based on their etiologies.[3] However, identifying causes of dementing symptoms is far from straightforward, especially for Dementia of the Alzheimer's type (DAT). DAT dominates discourses of dementia in the public sphere as well as much of the available research due to its higher prevalence and incidence and also due, in part, to the remaining uncertainties of premorbid diagnosis and ultimate cause. Therefore, we devote the bulk of our discussion below to DAT but also include brief descriptions of some characteristic features of other dementias, again based on DSM–IV–TR (American Psychiatric Association, 2000, pp. 147–171) unless otherwise specified.

Dementia of the Alzheimer's Type

The diagnosis of DAT in a living human being is problematic. The brain pathology underlying the symptoms of DAT, first described by Alois Alzheimer (Alzheimer, 1907), cannot be diagnosed with absolute certainty in the absence of evidence from an autopsy or a brain biopsy. A likely diagnosis of DAT is made first and foremost on the basis of behavioral and psychological indices and through a process of elimination of other conditions that can cause a similar symptom complex. Sabat (2001) discusses in some detail the

[3]We only discuss irreversible dementias here. For a description of reversible dementias, see, for example, American Psychiatric Association (2000, pp. 147ff) and Molloy and Lubinski (1995).

complex issues surrounding the identification and classification, and ascription of symptoms in DAT. The margin of perceived uncertainty, however infinitesimal, that is left by a thorough and ethically responsible diagnosis is worth stressing in a book on the discourse and discourses of dementia because this margin plays a considerable role in how a family may come to terms with the course of the disease.

Typically, the onset of DAT is gradual, with a steady decline in functioning. Patterns of decline may vary, although a common pattern is a gradually developing decline in recent memory; memory loss increases in severity over the course of several years, with other symptoms developing and increasing in severity several years after the onset of memory problems. Many, although not all, persons with DAT experience changes in their personality and behavior patterns, such as frequent agitation for no reason immediately apparent to a carer, increased irritability, or wandering. Motor disturbances tend to develop in the later stages of the disease, and commonly, persons with DAT become "bedbound" and eventually lose the ability to speak. DSM–IV–TR distinguishes between two subtypes of DAT: with early onset, specified as onset at age 65 or below, and DAT with late onset (after 65 years of age). Age of onset is of course one key factor in the likely impact of DAT (or any other type of dementia) on the life, life expectancy, and functioning as a social person of the person diagnosed. The social sequelae of a progressive brain pathology are different for a person who preonset was the main wage earner in a family as opposed to a person who is already in retirement. Similarly, the possible constellations of caregiving are different depending on whether the primary caregiver is, for example, a child of a person with dementia who may have to reconcile caregiving for a parent with being a spouse, a parent, and a wage earner, or an elderly spouse with possible physical infirmities.

The Neuropathology and Neurobiology of (Senile) DAT. In AD, there are patterned occurrences of an abnormal protein, so-called plaques of beta-amyloid, and abnormal neuronal tissue, so-called tangles of axonal material, in the cerebral cortex and the hippocampus. The presence of these abnormal structures has been found to be significantly higher in the brains of persons who during their lifetime showed the classic behavioral symptoms of DAT in comparison to persons not exhibiting these symptoms. Further, shrinkage of the cortex by up to 30% of its volume has been observed as well as a reduction in certain neurotransmitters (dopamine, serotonin, acetylcholine, and norepinephrine; see Blessed, Tomlinson, & Roth, 1968; Reisberg, 1983; and Tomlinson, Blessed, & Roth, 1970, for much more detailed descriptions of the neuropathology of AD; also Snowden, 2001, for a report on a large epidemiological study; and Shenk, 2001, for a discussion aimed at the informed lay reader). Some studies state that AD is more commonly found in women than in men (Gurland et al., 1983), whereas others explain the higher number of female AD patients by the generally longer life span of women (Ogden, 1996).

While the "plaques and tangles" associated with AD have made their way into the AD (and dementia) folklore, there are voices in AD research who point out that a causal link between the neuropathological deterioration thus described and the symptoms of DAT during a person's lifetime is far from unproblematic. Sabat (2001, p. 8ff) points out that in the classic autopsy studies (Blessed et al., 1968; Tomlinson, Blessed, & Roth, 1968; Tomlinson et al., 1970), a considerable number of persons who during their lifetime had been diagnosed with dementia showed no cerebral atrophy, or no plaques, or no neurofibrillary tangles. Therefore, Sabat (2001) states "it was surmised that it is the combination of these indicators that is key to AD" (p. 8f). In addition, Sabat referred to work by Collerton and Fairbairn (1985), Kitwood (1988), and Albert, Naeser, Levine, and Garvey (1984) that showed a considerable overlap in the range of postmortem brain states of persons with dementia and persons without. Therefore, although a prototypical (for the purposes of postmortem confirmation of a diagnosis) state of the AD brain emerges from the research landscape, there is a wide variation in both the postmortem picture and the progression and development during a person's lifetime.

Senile Versus Presenile Dementia: Aging Versus Disease?   Chen and Fernandez (2001) argue that a difference should be maintained between senile dementia and presenile dementia or AD as originally described by Alzheimer. Plaques and tangles, a product of metabolic inefficiency, are, according to Chen and Fernandez (2001), a *"natural* and *necessary* event during aging" (p. 30). They argued that the presence of plaques and tangles themselves does not explain AD, and late-onset sporadic AD, or senile dementia, should be explained through the interaction of *"advanced aging* intensified by *risk factors"* (p. 31). Thus, senile dementia should not be treated as a conventional disease (such as cancer) caused by a clearly identifiable pathogen, whereas AD, or presenile dementia, should appropriately be so labeled.

Goodwin (1991)[4] tracks the metamorphosis from senility as a normal process of advanced aging to a disease process, namely AD (see also Fox, 1989) and examines this transformation in terms of ideology. Goodwin describes the disease view of dementia as "the fundamental tenet of the geriatric belief system" (p. 333). His own view falls squarely within the "aging" side of the debate, formulated in the following hypothesis:

---

[4]Page references are to Gubrium and Holstein's (2000) reprint of Goodwin (1991).

> Alzheimer's disease is the clinical expression of an aging brain. Brain function declines with age.... Thus, true presenile dementia represents the extreme of the normal distribution of decline in brain function with age. The average rate of decline in brain function is such that by age 90 approximately 50 percent of individuals will be clinically demented. External factors, such as nutrition, cardiovascular disease, or drugs, can accelerate the onset of clinical dementia by their additive (or perhaps synergistic) effects with the aging process on decline in brain function. (p. 333)

According to Goodwin (1991), this hypothesis is not acceptable under "geriatric ideology" and therefore is not subjected to due consideration and experimental testing. Thus, the question disease or aging is not a question but research agenda, for a variety of reasons, are predisposed toward the disease bias (see also Lyman, 1989, on the "biomedicalization of dementia").

Stages of DAT.   The progression of DAT is often described by making reference to different stages, to which symptom clusters of increasing severity are ascribed. Examples are the seven-stage Global Deterioration Scale (Reisberg, Ferris, de Leon, & Crook, 1982), described, for example, in materials published by the Alzheimer's Association (2005), including their Web site. The range is from Stage 1, "no impairment," through Stage 7, "very severe decline." More commonly referred to in daily conversations about AD and in handbooks for both family and professional carers is a three-stage scale comprising *mild* or *early stage* AD, *moderate* or *mid stage* AD, and *severe* or *late stage* AD (see, e.g., Santo Pietro & Ostuni, 2003, for a mapping of the three-stage scale onto the seven-stage scale). The stages of AD are another aspect of the evolving folklore of AD, or, as one might put it, of its evolving discourses. We prefer to avoid reference to discrete stages whenever possible and do so only when our sources do. The brain deterioration in AD is a continuous process rather than one that progresses in discrete stages, and the occurrence of behavioral symptoms ascribed to the various stages depend on many factors and not only on the deterioration of the affected brain.

Other Dementias

Vascular Dementia.   Vascular dementia, formerly referred to as multi-infarct dementia, has a lower prevalence than DAT but is another common pattern of dementia in the elderly (Molloy & Lubinski, 1995, p. 6). In addition to the common features of dementia, there is evidence of multiple infarctions of both cortical and subcortical regions of the brain. The onset of vascular dementia is typically abrupt, and functioning deteriorates in a stepwise deterioration fashion. Depending on which brain areas have been affected by infarctions, the pattern of deterioration can be "patchy" (American Psychiatric Association, 2000, p. 158ff). Molloy and Lubinski

(1995, p. 6, quoting from Cummings & Benson, 1983), list the following major symptoms: "abrupt onset, stepwise deterioration, fluctuating course, nocturnal confusion, relative preservation of personality, depression, somatic complaints, emotional lability, history of hypertension and strokes, atherosclerosis, and focal neurological symptoms and signs."

Dementia Due to HIV Disease.   DSM–IV–TR lists forgetfulness, slowness, poor concentration, and difficulties with problem solving as cognitive characteristics of dementia that is associated with direct HIV infection of the central nervous system. Among the behavioral characteristics are commonly apathy and social withdrawal, occasionally accompanied by delirium, delusions, or hallucinations (American Psychiatric Association, 2000, p. 163f).

Dementia Due to Head Trauma.   Significant head trauma can be the "trigger event" for dementia. The constellation of impairments resulting from head trauma, as well as their severity, depends on the location and extent of the brain injury. Posttraumatic amnesia is a frequent characteristic as well as persisting memory impairment. Additionally, aphasia, attentional problems, irritability, anxiety, depression, affective lability, apathy, increased aggression, or other personality changes may also occur (American Psychiatric Association, 2000, p. 164).

Dementia Due to Parkinson's Disease.   According to DSM–IV–TR, Parkinson's disease is a slowly degenerative neurological condition characterized by tremor, rigidity, bradykinesia (abnormal slowness of movement), and postural instability. Not every person with Parkinson's disease develops dementia, but it is reported for approximately 20% to 60% of cases and more likely in elderly persons and those with more severe or advanced Parkinson's disease. Features of dementia in Parkinson's disease are a slowing down of cognitive and motoric functioning, problems with executive function, and problems with memory retrieval. In addition, depression is frequently present. At autopsy, the brains of some persons with Parkinson's disease and dementia show signs indicative of AD or of diffuse Lewy body disease (American Psychiatric Association, 2000, p. 164f).

Dementia Due to Huntington's Disease.   DSM–IV–TR describes Huntington's disease as an inherited progressive degenerative disease affecting cognition, emotion, and movement. Symptoms at onset often include behavior and personality changes such as depression, irritability, and anxiety. Early in the course of the disease, problems with memory retrieval, executive functioning, and judgment are common, increasing in severity as the disease progresses. Some persons with Huntington's disease show problems with spoken language (disorganized speech) and psychotic features (American Psychiatric Association, 2000, p. 165).

Dementia Due to Pick's Disease. Pick's disease, another degenerative disease, primarily affects the frontal and temporal lobes of the brain. Early characteristics are personality changes, deterioration of social skills, emotional blunting, behavioral disinhibition, and marked language problems. Other features of dementia, such as memory problems or apraxia, typically follow later in the course of the disease. Apathy, or on the other hand, extreme agitation, may accompany the progression of the dementia. An assessment of cognitive impairment may be hindered by the severity of language, attention, and behavior problems (American Psychiatric Association, 2000, p. 165f).

Dementia Due to Other Conditions and Dementia Due to Multiple Etiologies. DSM–IV–TR describes other conditions that can cause a symptom complex of dementia; the reader is referred to the manual for details (American Psychiatric Association, 2000, p. 166ff). It is worth drawing attention to the category of dementia due to multiple etiologies, however, as a reminder that medical and life histories of persons with dementia are not necessarily as straightforward as catalogs of diagnostic features might suggest at first sight. For example, DAT does not infrequently co-occur with focal brain damage such as is caused by strokes (see, e.g., Snowden, 2001, for discussion). Furthermore, in particular, many older persons with dementia also have other health conditions that may receive priority both in continued diagnostic efforts and treatment such as, for example, a variety of cancers or diabetes.

Dementia in This Book. The persons with dementia who contributed the data for this book had all received a tentative diagnosis of DAT. All of them also experienced other conditions affecting either their general health or their communicative abilities or both (see chap. 2 for a more detailed description of our participants). Another characteristic they have in common is that at the time of data collection, all exhibited "classic" symptoms of dementia that increased in severity as our acquaintance with them progressed, but none of them had experienced a recent full neurological or communicative assessment. This would have made them unlikely candidates for research aiming at, for example, differential diagnosis or the differential description of symptoms of disease progression. However, it made them excellent candidates for the focus of our work, which is on the individual, and the manifestation of skills and impairments in interactions between persons with dementia and persons without. Molloy and Lubinski (1995, p. 8) estimate that around half the residents in nursing homes have dementia. It is our experience that many of these persons do not receive regular assessments of communicative or cognitive functioning for a variety of reasons. However, for all of them as well as their professional caregivers and any family members, dementia becomes a factor of increasing intrusiveness into their lives as a dementing disease, however

r otherwise diagnosed, progresses. Therefore, although it is
on to construct a guide to "typical" interactions with demen-
texts of our participants and their experiences may be more
..presentative of many persons with dementia, especially of nursing home
residents, than of many participants in dementia research.

LANGUAGE AND COMMUNICATION IN DEMENTIA

The following is intended as a brief overview of some of the communicative and linguistic implications of dementia. As in other areas of dementia
research, the bulk of the available sources focuses on DAT (but see, e.g.,
Salmon, Heindel, & Butters, 1995, on possible differentiations between
DAT and dementia due to Huntington's disease or Parkinson's disease).
This section is not intended to be an exhaustive review of the flourishing
literature on dementia and language and communication but is meant to
prepare the ground for the questions asked in the following chapters of
this book. We restrict our brief summary here to spoken language and do
not enter into discussions concerning dissociations or associations of the
different aspects of the language and communication systems or of
brain–behavior relations, as this would lead us too far afield for the purposes of this book.

Experimental research on the linguistic and communicative implications of dementia has identified a whole catalogue of characteristics (see
Kempler, 1995; Mentis, Briggs-Whittaker, & Gramigna, 1995; Ulatowska
& Chapman, 1995). Word-finding problems (*anomia*) is identified as one of
the earliest difficulties of persons with DAT, and gradually, this difficulty
becomes more severe, with consequent behaviors such as the overuse of
empty vocabulary and of increasingly less comprehensible paraphasias
and circumlocutions. Problems with topic maintenance, digressions,
tangentiality, as well as perseverations (repetition of ideas) have been described in the literature (see also chap. 8) as are disruptions of discourse
coherence and cohesion, for example, with regard to reference, and the inappropriate use of pronouns. Some researchers have noted verbosity or
increased output, possibly due to increased facilitation by conversation
partners (see Ripich & Terrell, 1988). Appropriate use of speech acts becomes increasingly a problem, and the sensitivity toward the needs of the
listener (both affective and informational) decreases progressively.
Turn-taking patterns (although not the information content or the comprehensibility of the language output) are described as preserved until
the moderate stages of DAT, as are syntactic abilities. Even at severe
stages, phonological abilities and speech sound production are often
found to be intact (although we add the caveat here that, as mentioned
previously, many persons with DAT may also have other conditions, for

example, stroke damage, that may interfere with the phonological and motor-speech complex).

This brief sketch can of course not do justice to the large amount of experimental research that has been dedicated to the investigation of the impact of dementia on language and discourse abilities (i.e., discourse "(1)" as defined by Schiffrin et al., 2001, and as operationalized in experimental settings). Rather, this may serve as a scene setting for our own investigations, which have rather a different focus than experimental studies of individuals with dementia and their deteriorating linguistic, communicative, and cognitive faculties. We attempt to analyze communicative acts and events in terms of their collaborative nature, which implies that the effort that goes into achieving communicative success (however this may be defined) is a complex of jointly distributed properties pertaining to all participants and to the context or environment in which communication is situated. Thus, we need to approach the discourse (as defined above, i.e., a metacategory or entity of analysis) of dementia not on the basis of experimental settings but on the basis of day-to-day communication. However, the findings from experimental research serve as a basis on which we can build a loose framework of expectations. We also need to acknowledge that no research effort is ever entirely free of such expectations. Despite the principle of openmindedness that is one key element in qualitative research, and one which we hold dear, we would argue that it would be impossible to undertake any disciplined effort of investigation without at least some guiding questions, a "guided curiosity." Thus we can expect that the balance of collaboration will shift as a dementing disease progresses in that the conversation partner without dementia will take on more and more of the burden of communicative success. Indeed, we may suspect that the ways in which each communication partner identifies and implicitly defines communicative success will change and in different ways for persons with and without dementia. Further, given the progressive nature of cognitive and memory impairments in conditions such as DAT, we can expect that various monitoring mechanisms that are an inherent part of human face-to-face interaction will function less efficiently. Following on from this, we can expect the emergence of various strategies to compensate for these deteriorations.

THE REST OF THIS BOOK

In chapter 2, we discuss data collection, transcription, and presentation of data for publication or at conferences. We view the path from data collection to presentation as an "analytical spiral," which actually starts before the data collection process, namely, with the consideration of data sources, securing required permissions, and consent. Once this initial groundwork is done and recording is under way, we need to turn our thoughts to transcribing. Transcribing is seen here as a cyclical process and as an integral part of the data analysis in that our analytical priorities will determine our selections of what to transcribe and how to transcribe it. At the same time, the discovery-driven nature of qualitative research means that a new focus of analysis may emerge during transcription (or at any other stage of the data collection-analysis-presentation spiral) and lead back to a more detailed transcription of the same piece of data or a new data collection effort altogether.

Adherents to different approaches to discourse tend to insist that an analyst work strictly within that particular paradigm, and indeed, as we pointed out previously, it makes a lot of sense to keep different approaches apart and to be mindful of their theoretical and philosophical heritage. Researchers and practitioners working with clinical populations are typically of a more applied mind-set and may well apply different tools to the same data set to be able to ask (and hopefully answer) different questions and to discover different types of patterns. The choice of method depends on the task at hand: For example, an investigation of a nursing home as a communicative universe is a different animal than the investigation of silence, or deteriorating intelligibility, in a conversation.

In chapter 3, we explore the ethnography of communication (EC) in the context of dementia. Much of qualitative research (one could say all of qualitative research) owes a debt to the ethnographic tradition. The insistence on the description of the patterns of behavior, the norms, beliefs, and so forth of a culture from the perspective of the members of that culture is particularly interesting in the case of dementia because it becomes, not only for persons with the dementing condition but also for their carers, a "way of life," a factor that is a major determinant of what is done and how things are done. EC allows for a systematic investigation of patterns in language use in interaction and provides a very useful descriptive and analytical framework for considering the context in which an interaction takes place and of the participants and their social roles and their impact on the interaction. EC can also serve as a tool to categorize background information concerning clients with communicative disorders or research participants. We apply the principles of EC to interviews in two different contexts, a university-based language pathology clinic and a nursing home.

In chapter 4, we examine interactions, and in particular the roles and goals or ends of the speakers, from the perspective of interactional sociolinguistics (IS). Thus, the IS perspective on context is different from that of EC: In IS, context largely refers to the evolving interaction itself as the environment from which multiple speaker roles and goals emerge. IS includes a very wide range of approaches. Our discussion is informed in particular by the work of John Gumperz (1982a, 1982b) and Erving Goffman (1968, 1981) on the interactive construction of identities and

Charles Goodwin's and Marjorie Harness-Goodwin's (1992, 2000) investigations of embodied practices and participation. Further, we apply the notions of face and face threatening acts to the context of interactions between persons with and without dementia.

In chapter 5, we discuss conversation analysis (CA), its roots in sociology, particularly ethnomethodology, and its application to various types of clinical data. Conversation analysts typically understand their approach more as a method than a theory (although, of course, every well-defined method has equally well-defined, although possibly backgrounded, theoretical or philosophical underpinnings). A central concern is the sequential organization of talk, and CA provides a detailed framework for the description of the turn-by-turn organization of conversations or, in other words, of microcontexts. Some assumptions underlying CA are that conversation is orderly (patterned); that participants rather than an analyst's preconceived notions of disorder, for example, drive the analytic process; and that mutual understanding is arrived at collaboratively as the talk progresses turn by turn. These assumptions have made CA an attractive framework for those wishing to explore interactions between persons with a diagnosed disorder of communication or cognition and those without and who are interested in authentic communicative functioning but who are wary of generalization and quantification. CA, and analyses borrowing from CA, have been well established in the literature on aphasia (see, e.g., Damico, Oelschlaeger, et al., 1999; Damico, Simmons-Mackie, et al.,1999; Simmons-Mackie & Damico, 1999; Simmons-Mackie & Kagan, 1999) and to a lesser extent also in dementia research (see, e.g., Friedland & Miller, 1999; Perkins, Whitworth, & Lesser, 1998).

In chapter 6, we approach the question how interactants make sense of each other's contributions to an interaction from the perspective of pragmatics. We focus on Grice's principle of conversational cooperation and speech act theory. Speaker meaning and listener's understanding are central concepts, and the role of inferencing in the process of the listener arriving at an understanding of the speaker's intended meaning. Speech act and pragmatic theories provide a student, researcher, or clinician with the analytical wherewithal to consider the range of potential meanings of an utterance and to differentiate between propositional content and implicit and inferred meanings. Unlike the approaches to discourse that emerged from ethnography and its sister disciplines anthropology and sociology, pragmatics is firmly grounded in the philosophy of language and tends toward a more context-free consideration of principles. As we discuss in some detail, this has implications for the applicability of principles taken from pragmatics to contextually situated conversational data. We do not argue that such applications are not possible but rather that care needs to be taken in how applications are operationalized.

Chapter 7 is the final "approaches" chapter, and we examine the contributions of critical approaches to the discourse of dementia. We focus on three particular approaches-critical discourse analysis, discursive psychology, and social construction theory-to examine the concept of selfhood within the context of dementia. These approaches are somewhat different from those we discuss in the earlier chapters of this volume. Critical approaches, by and large, do not provide a theory of interaction or methodological framework from which to investigate data; rather, they draw on philosophy to examine how everyday discourses are embedded within larger social discourse practices. For researchers or practitioners in the clinical context, critical approaches present tools to identify and describe those common social discourses that are associated with and frame our encounters with people with dementia. In chapter 7, we raise questions about the way people with dementia are treated within society, and further, we examine how individuals with dementia attempt to construct a coherent version of self within their daily interactions. The data in chapter 7 include excerpts from personal e-mail correspondence between the first author of this book, J. A. Guendouzi, and persons with dementia.

Chapters 8 and 9 are issues chapters, and in each, we take as the centerpoint an issue that is of concern to people living with dementia, and of interest to investigators of interactions with dementia. Frequently, we have to ask ourselves how persons with dementia can make the most efficient use of diminishing cognitive and communicative resources and how both persons with dementia and their interlocutors can develop strategies to maximize these resources. In chapter 8, we discuss repetitive verbal behaviors in conversations with DAT. Much of the experimental literature on DAT and other neurogenic disorders approaches repetitive verbal behaviors in terms of their potential symptomatic or indexical status: the question being whether the occurrence of certain types of repetitive behaviors can be mapped onto certain types and severities of brain pathologies. In own approach, we attempt to situate repetitive behaviors within the demands of a conversational context and view them as a product of many speaker-internal and speaker-external factors that interact with each other.

In chapter 9, we take as the starting point a discussion of the concept of intelligibility. The question of how speakers make sense of each other informs many approaches to discourse, from pragmatics to CA, and indeed is central to many investigations in phonetics and linguistics. We present our notion of intelligibility as the potential for mutual understanding and trace the path of how mutual understanding is signaled as established or disrupted in a conversation. The relative clarity or opaqueness of the speech signal (speech intelligibility in a narrower sense) and the disruption of linguistic structure play a key role here but so do strategies on the part of the interactants to deal with any potential and actual breakdown of mutual understanding.

Chapter 10 is a brief wrap-up and outlook, and we present some concerns for future work on the discourse and discourses of dementia.

As Berrewaerts, Hupet, and Feyereisen (2003) show in their detailed review of the available literature on pragmatic deficits in DAT, the deficit and skills patterns manifested by people with DAT and other dementias (and, by implication, their interlocutors) vary greatly, both across individuals and of course along the path of disease progression. The data we introduce in this book show some of this variability and speak to one of the tensions or dialectics inherent in all qualitative research that is largely case based, as our work is. One strives to identify patterns, knowing that the patterns described and perhaps explained hold for one particular reality and will have to be tested against another reality, that of the next case, in a different context. Thus, our analytical spiral of data gathering, transcription, and analysis advances another turn. We are restricting the scope and variety of our data deliberately to conversations between people with dementia (identified as DAT) and the researchers and several of their students. On one hand, this restriction means of course that of necessity, we remain that much further removed from Luria's (1987a, 1987b) ideal of capturing the rich detail of human existence in an endeavor of romantic science. On the other hand, conversational interaction is at the core of social human existence, and interactions between persons with dementia and without are a prime site for many of the frustrations, but also successes, experienced in these conversational constellations. Some of these successes and frustrations are apparent in the conversations in this book, and maybe the most obvious success is the process of extended interaction itself. None of our conversations are "ideal" interactions, and of course many, especially colleagues working in CA, would argue that there is potentially no such thing as an ideal interaction. Those working in classical pragmatics might object and say well yes, there are models of perfect cooperation and smooth inferencing, but these models remain just that, the theory abstracted from contextualized practice. Most certainly, none of our conversations are intended as a guide on "how to" converse with someone with dementia.

2

Data Collection, Transcription, and Presentation

FROM DATA COLLECTION TO PRESENTATION: AN ANALYTICAL SPIRAL

This chapter is based on our ongoing, collaborative work in qualitative data analysis, and our discussion draws heavily on some of our own publications (see, in particular, Müller & Damico, 2002; Müller & Guendouzi, 2002). This ongoing work has led us to a view of doing discourse as an analytical cycle, or better, an analytical spiral in which each iteration of the analytical path should lead to a higher level of interpretation and mediation of the interactive situation(s) under investigation. The starting point of the spiral is the preparation for data gathering. We like to think that the next step, the actual recording of "raw data," that is, of human social interaction, follows after due thought and preparation; however, one has to admit that the most revealing data can sometimes be the chance interaction, the one that was not planned. Once an audio or video recording of an interaction has been achieved, certain aspects of it need to be transcribed. We approach transcribing as an integral part of the analysis process; rather than preparation for analysis, transcribing is data analysis. Transcription and interpretation typically go hand in hand in our work and feed into each other as a spiral within a spiral: The occurrence of certain patterns noted during the transcribing process, for example a hunch that certain paralinguistic features may be used strategically, will usually heighten one's awareness for such paralinguistic phenomena and will motivate one to return to one's data and reexamine data and transcript anew in light of said hunch. If the pattern holds, we have advanced a step further in our analysis. Theoretical considerations also feed into transcribing. As we discuss below in some detail, transcribing happens for a purpose, and one's theoretical outlook on the interaction observed will color one's perception as to which aspects of the interaction to focus on. In essence, these different perceptions are what this book is all about. Presenting one's data, be it for publication or presentation or for the sake of academic evaluation, is mainly a process of distillation. Typically, we need to be selective because of space constraints; at the same time, we need to be illustrative and therefore select "good" examples that support our arguments without being unfaithful to the complexity of the interactions that were our raw material. In the remainder of this chapter, we briefly discuss the preparatory and data recording stages and focus in greater detail on transcribing. The interpretive and presentational stages of the analytical spiral are the topics of the remaining chapters of this book.

PREPARATION FOR DATA GATHERING
AND GETTING RAW DATA

Although we approach our data gathering with an open mind in terms of exact research questions or narrow research foci (in keeping with the basic principles of qualitative research), certain decisions have to be made even before we gather data. Unless we have the luxury of carrying recording equipment with us at all times in case an interesting situation happens to occur (and even then, we have to take a decision as to its potential interest)[1] or unless we are part of a setup in which all interactions in certain settings, such as, for example, speech-language therapy sessions, are routinely recorded in certain formats, it is useful to expend some thought on preparing a recording session. For many extended studies, one develops routines in data recording that are workable for their particular contexts. Many factors influence an interaction, and depending on the study one is engaged in, the participants and the contexts of data gathering and analysis one has more or less control over some of them. For example, when recording a conversation between a researcher and a person with dementia, ideally one would like to choose a situation for one's data gathering that is neither too distracting for the participant nor too dull. It should both be part of the participant's daily routine and conducive to being recorded; there should not be too much background noise, but one would

---

[1]There is also the issue of whether it would be ethically acceptable to spontaneously record conversations.

wish to avoid a feeling of isolation from the rest of the world. In practice, we often do not have many choices where we carry out our recordings. If we gather data in, for example, nursing homes, a participant's bedroom may be the only place available. Background noise, interruptions (sometimes these can be very revealing!), and the like may be unavoidable.

Preparing the Ground: Getting Permission, Building Relationships, and Gaining Trust

A caveat as regards time may be in order here. Many qualitative studies in human interaction, and indeed in interactions with AD, are based on longitudinal, continuous data gathering efforts, sometimes extending over several years (see, e.g., DeClercq, 2000; Golander & Raz, 1996; Hamilton, 1994a; Müller & Guendouzi, 2005; Ramanathan, 1997; Sabat, 2001). The preparation time invested in a study, that is, the time one spends preparing the ground for actual data recording, can also be considerable. For example, one may spend several months doing fieldwork in a participant observation situation before one has built up enough trust and familiarity with one's participants to begin recording interactions. However, none of this preparation time need be "wasted"; the investment in terms of preparation typically pays off in terms of the authenticity of the data one gathers, and the observations one makes during preparatory fieldwork can turn into one or several studies in their own right.

Furthermore, so-called human subjects research based at universities, hospitals, or similar institutions requires the permission of an ethics committee or institutional ethics review board. Each institution has its own specific regulations; among the commonalities are that a committee or review board will need to ensure that confidentiality of data, the participants' rights to privacy, to freedom from coercion, to withdraw from a study as and when they wish, and to the freedom of threats to their physical, mental, and emotional well-being are safeguarded. A plan for a study-whether it be a grant proposal, a dissertation proposal, an unfunded, ongoing study, or a piece of coursework-will need to budget sufficient time to comply with any relevant regulations.

In terms of the eventual results of a qualitative study, building a trusting relationship with one's participants is crucial.[2] One needs to consider not only the immediate participants (in our case, persons with dementia and their carers) but others that are part of our participants' daily lives, for example, nurses, nursing assistants, administrators in nursing homes, administrators of day-care facilities, and volunteers. Whether during the course of a study one becomes, Margaret Mead style, a part of the community one studies or

---

[2]See DeClercq's (2000) discussion on "getting in" and "getting on" as a participant observer in a nursing home for people with dementia.

whether one remains an occasional visitor, or indeed directs several research-ers in a combined effort, more or less from the sidelines, it is crucial to gain the trust and confidence of the people who collaborate with us in our studies. In qualitative research, the researcher is the most important research instrument, and an instrument needs to be in tune with the orchestra in which it plays.

Setting Up and Recording Interactions

Some thought needs to go into the choice of recording method and equip-ment. Video recordings can give valuable information about nonlinguistic features of an interaction, but on the other hand, video cameras can be per-ceived as more intrusive than audio recordings. Many interaction studies (most of our own work included) rely on audio recordings and the partici-pant researcher's keen observer's memory for details concerning visual as-pects of the interaction captured in field notes.

The choice of equipment is typically constrained by budget limitations. High-quality portable tape recorders, minidisc recorders, CD recorders, or video cameras are all useful depending on one's personal preference and of course, depending on the research focus. We have found that high-quality analog audiotapes are of sufficient quality for the purposes of doing spoken discourse as long as a high-quality microphone is used. Especially in inter-actions in which there is a fair amount of movement, lapel microphones are particularly useful. We generally would not recommend the use of dicta-phone-type recorders unless they are of a very high quality.

The knowledge that an interaction is being recorded can be intimidating for a participant; it can impart a feeling of being "tested." There is typically no point in trying to hide the fact that one is recording a conversation, and in any case, most researchers and certainly most institutions would con-sider clandestine recording unethical. Rather than trying to downplay the recording, it can be a useful strategy to foreground it and make it a function of the fact that the participant has many interesting things to tell (which in fact, they do). Thus, rather than trying to avoid the "observer's paradox," one can assign it a function in one's research and make the observation part of the object of interaction (and thereby of the investigation).

TRANSCRIBING DATA: PRODUCTS AND PROCESSES

Transcribing data is an integral part of research in discourse studies. There are many approaches to transcribing, from handcrafted, multitiered efforts most at home in CA to computer-aided coding of language transcripts more com-monly employed in clinical linguistic assessments. The art and practice of transcribing has in the recent past been the subject of lively discussions. Among the topics under scrutiny are the politics of transcription; transcribing as an analytic and selective process; the relations between data, transcript, transcriber, and consumer (reader); and the potential pitfalls of poor transcription practices (see, e.g., Bucholtz, 2000; Edwards, 1993; Fine, 1983; Ochs, 1979; Psathas & Anderson, 1990; Roberts, 1997; Sherzer, 1994; Tyler, 1986; also see the special issue on transcription of *Clinical Linguistics and Phonetics*, 2002).

Transcripts and Transcribing as a Creative, Analytic Activity

At first sight, a transcript appears to be an innocent, innocuous entity: a graphic representation of an audio or video recording. However, because doing discourse relies heavily on these representations, it is worth probing a little deeper into their nature. First of all, we need to make a distinction between the transcript on one hand and transcription or transcribing on the other. We use the term *transcript* to refer to a product, the record that a reader finds on a page. *Transcription* and *transcribing* refer to the process of translating aspects of the recorded interaction into a graphic format. Edwards (2001) defines a transcript as a "distillation of the fleeting events of an interaction, frozen in time, freed from extraneous detail, and expressed in categories of interest to the researcher" (p. 321). Müller and Damico (2002) offer an operational definition of a transcript that we have found useful in clinical discourse studies and clinical linguistics: "A transcript is an intentional representation of data translated from one medium to another as a necessary and convenient analytic strategy requiring selective interpretations that impact on the targeted phenomena" (p. 301).

Transcribing is a purposeful activity. Even though in qualitative research, in theory, our starting question may be as vague as "What's going on here?," in practice (and especially in discourse studies with clinical populations), one or more foci of research emerge very early on in the research, and these foci will determine the nature of the transcript and will often also determine the data collection stages (e.g., the decision whether to use audio or video recordings). In Ochs's (1979) classic paper on transcription as theory, she discusses the necessarily selective nature of transcribing, making every transcript a record of a researcher's priorities and goals. No transcript can capture "the interaction" as it emerges between interactants. Rather, it is the product of numerous filters of selectivity imposed by, for example, the recording equipment, the skills, training and theoretical outlook of the transcriber, and the purpose of the transcript.

Transcribing can thus be seen as a mediated communicative event not unlike a translation. The mediator (the transcriber translator) bears the responsibility not only for the (relative) authenticity of the representation (transcript) vis-à-vis the original event (the interaction) but also for making the various selective processes employed explicit to the reader. The translation metaphor works on two levels in transcribing: on one hand, there is the medium transfer (from spoken, interactive, fleeting to graphic, noninteractive, permanent), and on the other hand, there is the integration of the data analyzed into a framework of interpretation. Although these two levels are of course closely related, it is still useful to draw a distinction between medium transfer as resulting in the transcript as a product and the process of integration as transcribing as process. The transcript as product is the reader's window into the data, and thus, typically the only way a reader has of verifying a researcher's conclusions. This window is shaped by two dimensions: one of content and one of form (Bucholtz, 2000; Goodwin & Heritage, 1990; Jefferson, 1973; Ochs, 1979).

The dimension of *content* is concerned with what is transcribed, in other words, with the selection of behaviors included in the graphic record. The selection may be very narrow in that one may transcribe only the words spoken in a conversation but ignore details of, for example, pausing or prosody. This type of transcript may feature in an analysis of lexical density or diversity, for example. Or one may select a very broad spectrum of communicative and noncommunicative behaviors to include, for example, pausing, prosody, gestures, changes in body posture, background noise; the possibilities are very far ranging indeed. What exactly is selected will depend, as mentioned previously, on the purpose of the transcript and the focus of analysis.

The *form* of a transcript concerns how the selected contents are presented to the reader's eyes. The final form of the transcript is, again, the product of multiple selections on the part of the transcriber. For example, the layout of the transcript guides the reader's eyes (see Ochs, 1979, for a detailed discussion of different layouts): A "musical score" type layout that devotes different lines to verbal and nonverbal behaviors tends to give more prominence to verbal contents, whereas a column layout may give more space and thus, visual prominence, to nonverbal behaviors. Once a layout is chosen, conventions for transcribing various verbal and nonverbal behaviors come into play. One may, for example, adapt the spoken word to the conventions of written discourse, use standard written orthography only, and use punctuation, and so forth to mark syntactic boundaries. This results in a product that is easy to read, especially for a novice reader of transcripts, but it also means that a wealth of detail of the spoken interaction is lost. To preserve some of this detail, one may employ various systematic ways in capturing some of the characteristics of utterances as spoken. For example, one may employ modified orthography to denote either dialectal or idiolectal features, or one may include phonetic transcription at strategic places to flag up certain pronunciation features and use punctuation to demarkate intonation units. Because the readers' only access to the "real" data, that is, the spoken interaction analyzed, is typically by way of the transcript, they have to rely on the transcriber's competence, judgment and basic academic honesty to give them a representative picture of the analysis process as captured in the transcript as product.

Some Relations That Operate in Creating and Using Transcripts

The relationships operating in the creation and use of transcripts are discussed at some length in Müller and Damico (2002); what follows is a brief summary. The mediated communicative event of creating and using transcripts, which in turn is part of the analytical spiral of doing discourse, involves, minimally, the participants or speaker(s), or informant(s), researcher/transcriber(s), and reader(s). (Although all these participants can of course be groups of people, we restrict our discussion to singular individuals for the sake of simplicity.) Mediation or translation is accomplished through the medium transfer from spoken interaction to audio or video recording to graphic representation.

The (In)Visible Transcriber. Because a transcript is the record of a researcher's dialog with the data, the presence of the researcher in the transcript, the various filters applied through her or his perspective on the data, should be explicitly acknowledged. This may at first seem counterintuitive: After all, we strive for accuracy and consistency in our transcribing efforts. However, accuracy and consistency should not be confused with objectivity (see also Coates & Thornborrow, 1999). There is no such thing as an objective transcript, nor, in our view, is there such a thing as a finished transcript, but there are transcripts that are good enough for the analytic purposes at hand. Involving more than one transcriber in a project will result in differences in the transcripts produced; and although we should indeed look for consistency and accuracy in our transcribing practices, pooling different "hearings" can be a very productive part of the process of categorization and analysis (see also Pye, Wilcox, & Siren, 1988). Thus, the transcriber's presence should be an integral presence of the communicative event rather than being removed from the reader's view.

The Reader and the Transcript. It is the mediation of the transcriber that lays the groundwork for the reader's access to the transcript. The reading of a transcript is in itself a creative act: Readers bring with them their own scholarly background, training, and indeed expectations concerning what they are going to find in a mediated data set such as a transcript. Thus, the visibility of the transcriber's input is especially vital in transcribing for scholarly or publication purposes. In clinical discourse studies, many research traditions, and therefore many traditions of notation and transcribing practice, meet (and sometimes clash). Not all readers will always be familiar with the assumptions underlying various conventions of notation and transcribing, and therefore, notations need to be made explicit; and a transcriber will have to weigh considerations of manageability and readability against potential loss of accuracy or representativeness. Furthermore, scholarly research involves the dissemination of one's results typically in the form of published papers or books. This, in turn, involves restrictions both for the researcher and the reader. Due to limitations of space, the researcher needs to be selective in terms of which good examples are most representative of the research conducted. The reader's access to the original data is severely restricted in that she or he has to rely entirely on the researcher's perspective and selection of said good examples, and thus, selected sections of transcripts may, in the reader's eye, "become" the data. We should keep in mind in our endeavors that the reading of a transcript represents yet another level of abstraction away from the original data.

The Speaker and the Transcript.   In doing discourse for clinical purposes, the representation of the speaker through the transcript is the most important of the relationships discussed here. It seems obvious, after the discussion so far, that it is impossible to transcribe a speaker. Indeed, in clinical discourse studies, we are sometimes in danger of attempting to transcribe a disorder, which is of course equally impossible. At their worst, the multiple cycles of selectivity that go into recording and transcribing lead to a stereotyped misrepresentation of a speaker, masking many individual abilities and impairments. Bucholtz (2000) calls for "reflexive transcription practice" in which the "researcher is conscious of her or his effects on the unfolding transcript, and the effect of the transcript on the representation of speakers whose discourse is transcribed" (p. 1462). This represents not only good research ethics but is crucial in a clinical context in which transcripts are part of the tool kit to advance the knowledge base of communicative disorders, to inform clinical decision making, and to train clinical practitioners.

A MULTILAYERED APPROACH TO TRANSCRIBING

We use a multilayered approach to transcribing, with the layering principle applying to two dimensions: the cyclical, diachronic nature of the transcribing process and the layout of the transcript. Transcribing never happens "all at once": As the analysis of the data becomes more focused and more refined, so does the transcript that represents, in effect, a research log. Therefore, our transcript layout and notation schemes need to be flexible enough and detailed enough to allow for a consistent representation of various aspects of the interaction under analysis and a range of questions asked of the data.

The Basic Layout

The core of the transcript, and the starting point of transcribing, is an orthographic representation of the utterances of all participants as in Example

2.1. All speakers are identified in their turns at talk, and all turns are numbered. When transcribing conversations in which speakers produce extended turns, for example, in narrative episodes, numbering individual lines as opposed to turns is an advantage.[3]

Example 2.1 (see Appendix C)
(J = Guendouzi; F = Lady with dementia)

16 J: did you have a good Christmas
17 F: well alright
18 J: it was alright
19 F: m didn't do anything,
20 J: did you get any presents
21 F: no we've- we're just left here dead
22 J: mhm
23 F: oh wha- what I want is to I don't know, what you call it. I call it when
       something changes or your own brain.
24 J: oh
25 F: (unintelligible)

However, we find that an orthographic transcription of the spoken word is rarely sufficient for our work. Thus, we enrich our base layer with additional detail. We follow a tradition long practiced in CA to add aspects of the spoken interaction to our transcript (see, e.g., Atkinson & Heritage, 1984; Sacks, Schegloff, & Jefferson, 1974). Example 2.2 shows how this is accomplished:

Example 2.2

16 J: did you have a good <u>Chris</u>tmas.
17 F: well. (.) alright,=
18 J: =it was alright.=
19 F: = m:, (.) didn't (x) do anything, (xx)=
20 J: =did you get any presents?
       (4.0)
21 F: ↓no::. (we've- we're just left here dead,)=
22 J: =mhm.=
23 F: =↓oh:: wha- what I want is to (4.5) I don't know, (.) what you call it. (2.0)
       I call it when (something changes or) your own brain.
24 J: [o:h*.
25 F: [(xxx*xxX, xx)=

---

[3]See Damico and Simmons-Mackie (2002) for a detailed discussion of this layer of the transcript.

The details beyond the spoken word encoded in this transcript concern basic prosodic information, pausing, overlapping speech, and levels of intelligibility (Appendix A lists all transcribing conventions used in this book).

Prosodic Information.

.	falling intonation
,	level, or continuing intonation (can be a slight rise or fall)
?	rising intonation
↑↓	a marked rise or fall on the syllable following the arrow
<u>Chris</u>tmas	underlining indicates a marked added emphasis.

Punctuation marks are not used to mark syntactic boundaries. When a more sophisticated analysis of prosody or voice quality is required, we can add a separate layer to our transcript (see below, voice quality; also see Ball & Rahilly, 2002).

Pauses and Silences.

| (.) | brief pause; shorter than 0.5 s (brief pauses at the end of utterances are not indicated) |
| (3.0) | timed pause, 3 s |

We generally find that ½-second increments in the timing of pauses are sufficient for our purposes.

Overlaps and Interruptions and Latched Speech.

[	overlap begins
*	overlap ends
=	Latching, i.e., the end of one utterance is followed immediately by the beginning of another, without overlap, but also without any pause

Levels of Intelligibility.   In nonclinical discourse, intelligibility of speech rarely becomes a focus of analysis. However, in clinical interaction studies, impaired intelligibility can be a central concern in terms of, for example, patterns of deteriorating intelligibility or strategies used to compensate for impaired intelligibility. Clinical transcription frequently has to deal with fluctuating degrees of intelligibility. In our approach to transcribing, we do not impose any measurement of intelligibility on our data, but rather a categorization of intelligibility arises out of the transcribing process (see also Müller and Guendouzi, 2002, and the discussion of intelligibility and how it is managed in conversation in chap. 9):

1. Fully intelligible utterances are transcribed orthographically with the added information concerning prosody, pausing, and overlaps as detailed above. Anything in which there is room for doubt in terms of accuracy is enclosed in single parentheses. The single parentheses are distinct from the double parentheses, as in Example 2.3, used to encode audio material or behaviors other than verbalizations or attempts at verbalizations.

2. When the transcriber is not entirely certain of a speaker's utterance but can make a reasonably confident educated guess as to the content, this is transcribed orthographically within single parentheses as, for example, in turn 21 or 23 in Example 2.2.

3. At times, the transcriber cannot identify words or phrases but is able to give a phonetic transcription of an utterance as illustrated in Example 2.3 from the same conversation. We find that a phonetic transcription is preferable to an attempt at capturing a semantically impenetrable part of an utterance in conventional English orthography because phonetic transcription is a more reliable representation of an auditory impression that cannot make recourse to semantics for an interpretation. When a more detailed analysis of the phonetic properties of an utterance is necessary, a separate layer can be added to the transcript (see Ball & Rahilly, 2002).

Example 2.3 (see Appendix C)

37 F: my brother (.) ([βɪkʃəne]) *((sniffs))* (.) but ə (.) my brother w- would like
        me to come out (xx waiting me) jus bein (.) bein kept well an everything,=

4. When the transcriber cannot make out the segmental phonetic characteristics of an utterance with sufficient confidence to attempt a phonetic transcription, it may still be possible to identify the number of syllables produced, which can be represented as in turns 19 or 24 (Example 2.2) in which each "x" represents one syllable. When a distinction between stressed and unstressed syllables is possible, this can be indicated by using "X" for stressed and x for unstressed syllables (see also Gumperz, 1992).

5. When intelligibility deteriorates to the extent that not even the number of syllables can be identified, we time these unintelligible passages as in, for example, "(3.5 s unintelligible)."

Intelligibility in transcribing is of course not the same as intelligibility in interaction. However, because the participants' mutual perception of the intelligibility of each other's and their own utterances is fleeting and not directly accessible to an observer, the transcriber's perspective is what we have to work with. Indicating levels of intelligibility or interpretability is one of the ways in which we keep the transcriber's perceptions visible in the transcript (see also chap. 8).

Voice Quality. The base layer of the transcript incorporates some indicators of intonation. We may also wish to include more detailed information concerning, for example, fluctuating intensity or details about the use of different voice qualities. Such details can be accommodated on the base layer of the transcript as well; however, when they become a focus of analysis, it is useful to reserve a separate line of the transcript (see Ball & Rahilly, 2002). In our multitiered layout, the voice quality layer is situated above the base or orthographic layer. Example 2.4 illustrates the use of a special symbol indicating the voice quality associated with a light laugh or chuckle overlaid over speech.[4] "LV" denotes the laughing voice quality, and curly brackets are used to mark the beginning and end of the stretch of speech it accompanies. Using a separate line for voice quality and related information does of course increase the space taken up by a finished transcript (which may be a consideration for presentation or publication), whereas on the other hand, incorporating these details into the base layer may make some transcripts too "busy" to be easily read.

Example 2.4
Separate voice quality layer:

                                                        {LV}
189 F: everywhere (x to see some) flower I don't know (where xxx may be),
190 J: did you use to walk up the river? by the T?

        {LV}
191 F: no. ə it was ə wild grass up there, *((light laugh))*

Incorporating voice quality into the base layer:

189 F: everywhere (x to see some) flower I don't know (where {LV xxx may be),}
190 J: did you use to walk up the river? by the T?
191 F: no. ə it was ə {LV wild grass up there,} *((light laugh))*

Gaze and Gesture. The use of video recordings permits the analysis of visual information such as gesture and gaze (see Damico & Simmons-Mackie, 2002). Whereas gestures, such as head nods, shoulder shrugs, and the like, are sometimes integrated in the orthographic layer of the transcript, especially if they constitute a speaker's sole contribution in a turn, gaze is more practically accommodated in a separate layer. Example 2.5 illustrates the use of separate layers for gaze and gesture. Note that only

---

[4]See Ball and Rahilly (2002) for the use of the VoQS, or Voice Quality Symbols; Ball, Esling, and Dickson (1999) for other voice qualities; and Müller and Guendouzi (2002) for a more detailed discussion of the strategic use of what we call the laughing voice (LV).

one participant's gaze and gesture behaviors are tracked here-those of E (M = graduate student; E = a gentleman with dementia):

Example 2.5 (see Appendix D)

```
    „ghd----------------,gm----------------------------------------------------------------
                    ((hands half open))                          ((hn))
19  E:  uh:, (6.0) man. that- that's a good question (.) I was in industrial


        ------------------
        management.=

        --------------,ghd
20  M: =okay, okay,
```

The gaze layer is situated above the gesture layer, and the notation reads as follows (see also Appendix A for a complete list of transcribing conventions and chap. 3).

Gaze layer:

  „   a gaze shift occurs at this point
  ghd   gaze half down (approximately 45°)
  gm   gaze to M

Gesture layer:

  (( ))   any gesture
  ((hn)) head nod

Doing Discourse in a Transcript.   At times, it is helpful to include specific analytic categories in a transcript. Of course, any detail of a transcript can be or become an analytic category such as the length of pauses, or the patterns of overlapping speech, or indeed a participant's gaze behaviors. However, one may also wish to add detail that does not pertain to the translation process of transcribing proper such as, for example, the distribution of illocutionary acts. Such categories can again be accommodated on a separate line of the transcript, adding another layer to the picture, as in Example 2.6 (J = J. A. Guendouzi):

Example 2.6 (see Appendix C for the single-tier transcript)

```
1              F:        (Friday,)=
      IA                 ?A/Q-Cf
      CP                 ?*Qn
2              J:        =It's Friday today.
      IA                 A-Cf
```

3		F:	(really,)=
	IA		Q-Cf
4		J:	=hmm=
	IA		A-Cf

This example contains two separate lines for discourse analytic categories, illocutionary acts (IA) and Grice's maxims of conversational cooperation (CP for cooperative principle; see chap. 6). The abbreviations on the IA layer read as follows: A = assertive; Q–Cf = request for confirmation; A–Cf = assertive, confirmation of content of other's utterance; / = an utterance may be assigned to two categories. The CP line tracks violations of Grice's maxims, and the format reads * = maxim violation; Qn = maxim of quantity. Note that the two discourse lines also allow for the incorporation of analyst's uncertainty; we use a "?" to express this. Where such multilayering is used, it is useful to label at the lines added to the baseline of the transcript as done here.

PRACTICALITIES OF TRANSCRIBING

There can be no doubt that careful transcribing is a time-consuming process. Difficult passages of speech can take upwards of an hour of transcribing time for every minute of speech. The question is justified, then: What warrants this considerable investment in time and effort?; or, to put it another way, who has the time to do this, and who should be left with the task of doing this job?

Our view is that a transcript is the researcher's responsibility. It is of course tempting for those of us lucky enough to have research assistants to let them do the transcribing. However, we find that unless a researcher takes an active part in transcribing from the very beginning (although we certainly do not object to team efforts in transcribing), she or he will not gain the familiarity with her or his data that is desirable in the analysis of clinical discourse. However, one may yet ask whether, in research that is supposed to have a clinical impact-for example, in a collaboration between linguists and speech-language pathologists in an ongoing case in which the latter is hoping to base clinical decisions on the former's analysis of data-the fine-grained, multilayered work of art is the final word in practicality. We need to inject our transcribing efforts with a modicum of common sense. Clinical or research objectives need to be the yardstick, and the general rule always has to be, "Be as detailed as necessary." The multilayered tool kit is there to be used, but in many cases, it may not be necessary to exploit it to its full potential. Our approach has to be open-minded, mindful of the complexities of human interaction, and we need to acquire the descriptive and analytic skills that do this complexity justice.

THE DATA IN THIS BOOK

Participants

As we mentioned in chapter 1, we deliberately focused on conversational data in this book as the prototypical site of human communicative interaction. There are, of course, many other possible types of language and speech data that are of interest to students and researchers of discourse and dementia such as narratives, for example, or even recitations or songs. The conversations featured here involve persons with dementia,[5] ourselves, and several of our students. The conversation partners with dementia had several things in common: All had received a diagnosis of probable DAT. All were several years postdiagnosis, and, with the exception of E, none had experienced regular neurological and cognitive follow-up evaluations.[6] All manifested cognitive and behavioral symptoms consistent with DAT, as described in chapter 1, but the constellation of symptoms was particular to each participant. Again, with the exception of E, all participants with dementia were long-term residents in nursing homes. Due to different policies of confidentiality in different institutions and varying access to other family members, we could not include the same amount of medical background data for each participant.

Mr. E.   At the time of recording, Mr. E was 59 years old. He was a monolingual speaker of American English. He suffered from type-A diabetes and had taken insulin throughout his life. As a result of his diabetes, he had impaired vision and was diagnosed as "legally blind." He was able to identify pictures and texts in magazines with relative ease and could still read with the aid of glasses. E also had a hereditary condition that required him to take testosterone supplements. He lived at home and attended a senior center during the morning. During J's acquaintance with him, he was able to remain in the home unsupervised for short periods of time. His wife (and sole caregiver) worked full-time, and he was therefore used to spending time alone in the afternoons. Because of problems with visual acuity and balance, his gait was tentative and unsteady, but otherwise, he had no difficulties with activities of daily living. He had taken early retirement due to impaired vision and then developed memory problems. He was given the diagnosis of DAT after other possible causes of memory deterioration had been medically ruled out. The conversation with E in this book was chosen because we found it very illustrative of the challenges faced by a person inexperienced in

---

[5]None of the participants with dementia was related to either author or any of the graduate students.

[6]In our experience, this is not an uncommon circumstance, particularly when potentially life-threatening health concerns compete for attention and treatment.

interactions with dementia (E's conversation partner) with regard to adjusting her conversational contributions to her partner.

Ms. F.   When J first met F, F was a resident in a nursing home run by an order of Catholic nuns. She was a monolingual speaker of British English. When the data collection began, she had been in the nursing home for approximately 7 years. Her husband reported that she had had some dizzy spells around and just after the onset of her memory problems. He further stated that functional magnetic resonance imaging and computerized tomography scans showed brain damage consistent with ministrokes and cortical atrophy. Her husband and nurses also reported that F had a long-standing hearing impairment, and as a result of this, had worn hearing aids for the past 20 years. F had a large, supportive family who visited frequently and therefore was used to interacting with visitors on a regular basis. F was unable to walk and used a wheelchair, and she needed assistance with bathing, feeding, and other bodily functions. Her behaviors in conversation showed great variability with regard to responsiveness and participation. At times, she was a very lively participant, whereas at other times, she was virtually nonresponsive. The two conversations we include here were recorded within 2 months of each other, either side of Christmas, and were selected because they are good illustrations of the variability of conversational behaviors within conversations with F, in particular, the marked fluctuations in speech intelligibility (see chap. 8).

Ms. FM.   N. Müller (NM) made FM's acquaintance when the latter was in her mid 90s. As well as a diagnosis of DAT, she had inoperable cancer for which she was receiving palliative care. Her first language was Louisiana French, but she had been a fluent speaker of American English since her early youth. She spent her working life as an elementary school teacher. She was widowed in middle age and never remarried. She had no children, did not have any other family members living locally, and therefore received few visitors. She was unable to walk and used a wheelchair but was only able to propel it herself for a distance of a few feet. She had no roommate in the nursing home, but generally enjoyed having visitors, both other residents and "outsiders." The conversation we selected illustrates behaviors that we consistently found in interacting with her, particularly the use of repetitive questions (see chap. 8).

Mr. MA.   Mr. MA was a resident in the same nursing home as FM. He was also a native speaker of Louisiana French but also a fluent speaker of American English. He had received very little formal education and stated that he had never learned to write. When NM first met him, he was 97 years of age. He had inoperable cancer and was receiving palliative care. His wife, who resided in the nursing home with him, died about 9 months after B, his conversation partner, made his acquaintance. MA had been diagnosed with probable DAT more than 5 years previous to the data collection period. The conversation with him that is included in this book shows strong repetitive tendencies, but their manifestation is different from the ones found in FM's conversations. In addition, this conversation is a good illustration of how a person with dementia projects the role of a "competent" or "wise" elder, giving advice to a young man.

Participants Without Dementia.   J is the first author of this book. She regularly visited F for a period of a year. MB was a graduate student of J's at the time of data collection and interacted with E on several occasions. B, MH, and R were graduate students of NM's. B and R made regular visits to the nursing home for over a year, whereas MH visited over the course of a semester. LB is E's wife and primary caregiver; she worked full-time in a professional setting. The students were all working for advanced degrees in communication sciences and disorders, but none had had extensive experience with dementia prior to their participation in these conversations.

Settings

E's conversation was recorded in a speech and hearing clinic on a university campus (see chap. 2, for a discussion of the potential impact of different settings) and on other occasions in his home environment. All other conversations were recorded in nursing homes, one in Britain (F's) and one in the Southern United States (FM and MA's). MA's conversation was recorded in a common room of the nursing home, which brought with it issues of background noise (a practical problem for the purposes of transcription) as well as potential distraction. FM's conversation was recorded in the privacy of her own room where she spent most of her time. Both nursing homes were very supportive of our visits, they welcomed both us and our students, and after the appropriate consultation with family members (where applicable), gave ready permission to record. The participants with dementia also gave permission to have their conversations tape recorded on each separate recording date.[7] As will be the case in many such undertakings, our commitments to both the institutions and their residents have developed into a long-term relationship.

---

[7]The issue of informed consent is of course potentially tricky when one engages in research with persons with dementia (or any other cognitive impairment). Although other individuals involved (the researchers themselves, their caregivers) and the institutions involved need to safeguard the participants' rights and appropriate levels of confidentiality, researchers also need to ensure that during each data collection event, they respect their participant's wishes whether they wanted to have their conversations recorded or not.

Data Collection and Transcription

Equipment.   The recording equipment we used consisted of good quality audiotape recorders and freestanding microphones or lapel microphones. E's conversation was recorded on 8 mm videotape.

Transcription.   We transcribed all the conversations in this book. Our approach was a joint, consensus undertaking rather than a striving for intertranscriber reliability (see the discussion of different approaches to transcribing earlier in this chapter). Our encounters with F, who was our first participant, are in part responsible for our ongoing interest in transcribing as part of data analysis and interpretation.

Data Selection and Presentation.   As we discussed earlier in this chapter, the preparation of data for dissemination brings with it various, sometimes conflicting, pressures. One motivation behind this book was our experience of the great variety of verbal and nonverbal behaviors that can be encountered in conversations with dementia and of the fluctuations of conversational success and "trouble" within single interactions. Therefore, we wished to include not only a considerable amount of data but also extended samples. In addition, we wished to give our readers the chance to carry out their own analyses and compare our conclusions against their own. This is why the appendices contain the full transcripts of the conversations we discuss throughout this book. On the other hand, the reader will encounter several extracts from the long transcripts several times in different descriptive and analytical guises, as it were, and several times, the same linguistic feature (e.g., the use of questions) is pulled into different analytical frameworks. We chose to do this to underline another aim of this book, namely, to introduce multiple different approaches to the analysis of spoken discourse, each with its own analytical, philosophical, and methodological heritage. Each can be applied to any of the conversations we included, but each asks different questions, and each will produce, in effect, a new data set.

3

Ethnography of Communication in Dementia and Alzheimer's Disease

ETHNOGRAPHY, AD, AND DEMENTIA

Researching the effects of dementia on social interaction is a project that inevitably relies on ethnographic methods. *Ethnography* is a qualitative methodology that attempts to describe a culture from the perspective of the people for whom it is a way of life. Through observation of and interaction with the community they are investigating, ethnographers may be better placed to recognize and record significant patterns of social behavior in a particular culture. As was noted in chapter 1, collecting data from speakers who have dementia is a task that often relies on the researcher becoming actively involved in the AD community.[1] Our interest in pursuing this research has, for example, resulted

---

[1] We use the term *AD community* here for reasons both of expediency and content. The term *AD and dementia community* would be too unwieldy, whereas "dementia community" on its own does not capture the fact that most persons with dementia with whom we interacted (or their carers) have gone through the process that lead to a diagnosis of "probable DAT" or "probable AD." As discussed in chapter 1, AD is the most common cause of irreversible dementia, and Alzheimer's has very much become conflated with dementia in public discourses (especially lay and "media" discourses) of dementias, their causes, and consequences.

in active involvement in support groups, nursing homes, and the lives of the people we have interviewed. Therefore, ethnography has shaped this book and aided in both the collection of the data and in gaining a better "understanding" of the AD speech community. In this chapter, we explore the data from the perspective of a particular type of ethnography, EC.

ETHNOGRAPHY OF COMMUNICATION

EC emerged from the work of anthropologist Dell Hymes (1972a, 1972b, 1974) who has argued that the traditional methods of anthropological research (e.g., participant observation) would prove useful in analyzing the communicative patterns of specific cultures and speech communities. EC reflects

> A concern for holistic explanations of meaning and behavior i.e. explanations that locate particular behaviors (including but not limited to, utterances) in a wider framework of beliefs, actions and norms. Also shared with anthropology is an emphasis on how meanings and behaviors need to be understood in an analytical framework in which comparisons establish not only what is different in different cultures (i.e. the diversity) but also what is the same. (Schiffrin, 1994, pp. 140–141)

The importance of context in language research is not a new idea; early in the 20th century, Malinowski maintained that

> Language is thus dependent on its society in two senses: (1) A language evolves in response to the specific demands of the society in which it is used. (2) Its use is entirely context-dependent: utterance and situation are bound inextricably with each other and the context of the situation is indispensable for the understanding of the words. (as cited in Malmkjaer, 1991, p. 159)

Malinowski (1923/1972) hypothesized that if he were to give a European bystander a word-for-word translation of a Trobriand Islander's utterance, they would not really understand the true illocutionary force of that remark unless they understood the Trobriand culture. Malinowski distinguished between the immediate context of utterance and the more general context of situation, and argued that studying the meaning of a language was impossible without reference to how it functions within a social context. Malinowski's work (along with that of his contemporary J. R. Firth, 1957) provided the theoretical foundation for both Hymes' (1972, 1985) work in EC and the functional approach to language developed by Michael Halliday (1978) and his students.

The influence of the generative syntax program (Chomsky, 1957) had by the 1970s narrowed the scope of syntactic enquiry to sentence and phrase level units in isolation. Chomsky claimed that "performance" (language use) was not the object of enquiry for linguistic research.[2] Thus, at this time, many linguists were looking for linguistic universals, the emphasis being on speaker competence rather than performance. Pragmatics, a second and equally theoretical approach to the study of language, was developing in parallel with syntax. Predominantly coming out of the work in the philosophy of language, pragmatics and semantics attempted to examine language in relation to logical form and sentence meaning (Austin, 1962; Grice, 1975; Searle, 1969). Although this area of study was less influential than generative syntax within the field of traditional linguistics, it became the foundation for many of the ideas developed in interactional sociolinguistics and discourse analysis (see chap. 6).

At the time of this expansion in generative syntax, Hymes (1972b), along with Halliday (1978), argued for research that focused on the appropriate use of language in situated contexts, research that would examine the knowledge speakers and listeners rely on to negotiate their daily social interactions-in other words, communicative competence rather than merely linguistic competence. Halliday (1978) described language as a "social semiotic," suggesting that

> The whole of the culture is meaningful, is constructed out of a series of systems of signs. Language is one of these systems-a particularly important one, because most of the other systems are learnt through, and translatable into, language, and because it *reflects* aspects of the situations in which it occurs. It has been one of Halliday's greatest achievements that he has been able to provide an account of how particular situational aspects are reflected in the linguistic choices made by the participants in those situations, and the notion he invokes in this account, is, again, the notion of function. (Malmkjaer, 1991, p. 160)

Hymes, on the other hand, developed EC, a methodology that enables researchers to systematically incorporate features of the context into their analysis. EC's methods for studying communicative competence are integrative: holistic explanations of meaning and behavior, that is, behaviors as reflections of a person's internalized knowledge about communication. EC aims to establish patterns from observed instances of behaviors; the resulting ethnography then provides a culturally embedded "grammar" of communication (for an overview of EC, see Saville-Troike, 1982; Schiffrin, 1994).

Central to EC is the viewpoint that communication is a process that both reveals and sustains culture. It is useful, at this point, to consider what we mean

---

[2]It is not the case (as has been suggested) that Chomsky (1957) thought performance was not important. He acknowledged its validity as an object of academic enquiry but claimed it was not the focus of a linguistics program. The damage, however, was done, and his opinions led to research programs that completely separated the study of performance (language use) from "competence" (a user's knowledge of their language). In reality, both performance and competence interact at any given time within our everyday interactions, and their separation is merely an academic construct that better enables us to study the phenomenon of language.

when we use the term *culture*. Geertz (1973, chap. 1) notes the following definitions: "the total way of life of a people; the social legacy the individual acquires from his group"; "a way of thinking and feeling"; "a storehouse of pooled learning and a set of techniques for adjusting both to the external environment and to other men"; "a behavioral map" (pp. 4–5). As is evident from this selection, the meaning attached to this term ranges from lifestyles and behaviors to the cognitive mapping of experience. Geertz (1973) suggests culture is "essentially a semiotic" concept, and he compared the methods of anthropologists to those of literary critics "sorting out structures of significance" (pp. 4–5). Pinker (2002) suggests that rather than symbolic pattern, "much of what we call culture is simply accumulated local wisdom" (pp. 63, 67; of course this accumulated wisdom is in itself still an abstraction or symbolic pattern). Pinker appears to be focusing on the ways in which humans acquire skills and habits in adaptive response to the environment. For example, habits that originally arose from daily needs, such as making tools to hunt more efficiently, over time became highly skilled activities that were then transferred to others by more ritualistic routines. Some of these needs-based routines eventually acquired symbolic status (e.g., the symbolic status given to ritualized bathing in many religions). It is arguable whether Pinker's interpretation really matters in the long term; after all, knowing a behavior's evolutionary antecedents does not make its semiotic significance any less symbolic. Culture is not something that has ontological status per se; rather, it is the expression of a social group's shared knowledge and a reflection of their belief system. Culture emerges from the dynamics of human interaction, but it also both contains and constrains that interaction. Thus, paradoxically, culture is both a causal factor in its own emergence and the observable "entity" that emerges from human interaction, and of course, the entity is only ever visible in its reflection, that is, through what people say, do, do not do, and so forth.

A further factor is the role that biology plays in the formation of culture. Over the past 30 years, much of the work in the social sciences has reflected a viewpoint that espouses the concept of the 'blank slate' (Pinker, 2002), that is, the notion that human behaviors are "socially constructed" through their environment and upbringing. This viewpoint proposes that humans' cultural inheritance will determine the adults they become; thus, people are "products" of their own culture. However, we should remember that we are also products of our own individual biology. To give a relevant example, although it is true that people's culture determines the language they speak, for example, Welsh or English, it is not true that culture determines linguistic or communicative potential. Those of us working in the field of communication disorders cannot ignore issues of biology and physiology when dealing with people whose cognitive or communicative problems are caused by a disease rather than cultural or social factors. On the other hand, the level of functioning possible or expected in a person at a given level of impairment has cultural dimensions as well. Beliefs about dementia can be situated within a culture that includes among other things (a) confusion, (b) dependence, and (c) loss of self. These beliefs may affect the way in which a society reacts to and cares for (or alternately does not care for) individuals with dementia. The pathology then gives rise to the culture in the form of stereotypes that include ageing and disorder. However, we should be aware that behaviors that may have physiological causes (such as aggression) can elicit responses from a person without dementia that eventually form the basis of how they then categorize a particular speech community (e.g., the belief that all people with dementia are aggressive). When we interact with people who have dementia, we not only bring our existing cultural expectations about ageing and disease but also begin to form new beliefs based on that particular interaction, an experience that in turn leads to the formation of a new culture of dementia.[3] Thus, an important factor when analyzing interactions involving dementia is to remain aware that culture is both a preexisting and an emergent phenomenon.

The ethnographer's key tool when studying a particular speech community is participant observation; the observer attempts to uncover what knowledge an individual requires to make sense of their experiences,[4] and how they then encode and communicate that knowledge to other members of their speech community (Schiffrin, 1994). It is important to note that EC is not merely a narrative account of a researcher's observations. It also draws on its linguistic roots and includes recorded samples (both written and spoken) that are then analyzed to look for patterns of linguistic form, pragmatic usage, and social function. Hymes (1981) conceptualized this research paradigm as both "etic," in that it seeks to provide a universal typology of observations from outside the system, and "emic," in that it involves interpreting particular functions within both their interactional context and the wider social context. In EC, context becomes a systematic unit of analysis rather than a description of the "background" features. Thus, EC incorporates ethnographic information into the analytical framework. Hymes (1981) saw EC as a methodology that extends the role of ethnography and allows for a more systematic way of examining language and communication. "The essential method ... is simply persistence in seeking systematic co-variation of form and meaning. The spirit of the method is 'structural' in the sense of Sapir's linguistics, 'emic' and 'ethnographic' in the sense of concern for valid description of the individual case" (Hymes, 1981, p. 10).

---

[3]Another context in which physiology has given rise to culture is in the "deaf" community, although the parallels with AD are limited because AD is a progressive, terminal condition.

[4]Making sense of experience may be a moot point in interactions involving dementia. However, although we cannot always know whether we have understood the intentions of the person with dementia, or they ours, we can attempt to achieve some understanding of the ways in which both participants manage their interactions.

Context

As we (Müller & Guendouzi, 2005) noted elsewhere, conversational interaction can be understood as a complex, dynamic, self-regulating system that in turn comprises several subsystems. Müller (2003; drawing in part on Perkins, 2000) draws a rough distinction between three major types of subsystems (themselves consisting of complex, interactive systems): cognitive subsystems, sensori-motor subsystems, and contextual subsystems. Out of the interaction of these multiple systems within systems, order, or the perception of mutual understanding, emerges. Although, for purposes of clarity and ease of analysis, researchers examine features of interactions in isolation, one should always remember that the participants experience the interaction as a "whole" speech event. EC attempts to examine context not as a descriptive "scene setting" device but as a dynamic subsystem of communication, one that not only accompanies an interaction but also affects the dynamics of that interaction.

When discussing the role of *context*, it makes sense to consider what we actually mean by this term. There has been much discussion about the role of context in social interaction (for a comprehensive overview, see Duranti & Goodwin, 1992), and it has long been a key concept in analyzing language and texts of all kinds; yet, like culture, it is a difficult concept to define. For many students (and indeed researchers), the term context simply implies the supplying of background information (e.g., noting the participants involved or the time and place of the interaction), but it has a much wider definition. In our own analyses, for example, we include any phenomena that might have a potential impact on an interaction as being an integral part of that interaction and therefore a legitimate "object" of analysis. In research on AD and dementia, the individual's personal history is one aspect of context that is often overlooked (notable exceptions are the work by Hamilton, 1994a, 1994b; Ramanathan, 1997; and Sabat, 2001). Whereas experimental groups are usually matched for education level, gender, or prior occupation, studies involving persons with dementia often by necessity categorize participants by their pathology rather than individual traits. Although such factors may not affect the progression of the AD (that is, of the brain pathology), there is some evidence to suggest that there is a relation between level of education and the ability to resist the effects of dementia (Snowden, 2001). At this point, it is unknown whether Snowden's findings point to the conclusion that higher levels of education and lifelong learning help to slow down the rate of progression of dementia or whether higher levels of education simply give the individual better access to alternative communication strategies. For example, someone who had a wider vocabulary (acquired through education) may find word-finding problems easier to resolve in the early stages of dementia. For the moment, Snowden's work simply shows that (a) there are correlations between education related language skills and the visible manifestation of symptoms of cognitive loss in one particular population, and (b) it is important not to homogenize a group of people simply in terms of a shared pathology. People with dementia are not starting from a sum-zero position, they are also the products of their biology, life experiences, and social environments. Individual contexts are as important as wider social contexts, and indeed, we could say that wider social contexts are in constant cyclical interaction with individual life contexts.

One of the major aims underpinning EC is the search for features of communication shared by a particular "speech event," but it is equally important to note the features of speech events that differ. The speech event is a "central concept" in EC and is seen as a "culturally recognized social activity … in which language plays a specific" or "specialized role" (Levinson, 1983, p. 279). Speech events then are tied heavily to their contexts and are framed (see chap. 4) through the participants' prior experiences of similar speech events and cultural assumptions about such events (e.g., a sermon in a church or a medical consultation in hospital or clinic). This contextually constrained use of language can "operate to assign functions to utterances partly on the basis of social situation" (Levinson, 1983, p. 279). Thus, a remark such as "how are you?" will have a different function in the context of a medical interview than when it is uttered passing a colleague in the corridor.

EC is concerned with the cross-cultural study of language and the differences manifested in communication routines. Identifying cultural differences has been an important part of work in EC (see work in Bauman & Sherzer, 1974). For example, one might say that in some cultures, gesturing and facial expressions are more important than in others or that voice quality may be used deliberately (e.g., whispering) or may be incidental (e.g., a sore throat). Furthermore, different modes of communication will be more likely (or more socially acceptable) in different speech events; for example, it is often not a good idea to tell jokes in a job interview. Within the speech community of dementia, EC may reveal, among other things, what tools people use to communicate. EC can thus help to (a) categorize the data into a typology of speech situations and speech events occurring in dementia and (b) help to situate those speech events within the norms of culture in which they occur. EC is a methodology that emerges from the interaction between the analyst's "eye," the transcribed data, and the contextual information. We conceptualize AD as both a disorder situated in the individual and as a defining part of the culture of dementia, a culture that is in turn defined and constrained by distinct communicative patterns.[5]

_____

[5]The validity for a typology of speech events in interactions with dementia may potentially appear at odds with our call to treat the AD speech community as a nonhomogenous group of individuals. However, this should not deter us from attempting to view conversations within this speech community within a framework of EC; it is only through the process of analysis that patterns emerge. A comparable example here is casual conversation, a speech event that until recently was portrayed as aimless and unstructured yet when examined (Cheepen, 1987; Eggins & Slade, 1997), turns out to be highly structured talk with similarities and patterns of use that hold across diverse populations and contexts.

SPEAKING: An Ethnographic Grid

Hymes's (1972) classificatory acronym known as SPEAKING (see Fig. 3.1) proves a useful analytical tool that can serve as the etic basis for discovering emic communicative units, that is, units that are "in some way bounded or integral" (p. 56) to the speech event. The acronym can be used to examine instances of communicative competence, noting patterns of language use that reflect not only the internalized knowledge of language of the person with dementia but also communicative skills that are still functional within her or his everyday interactions.

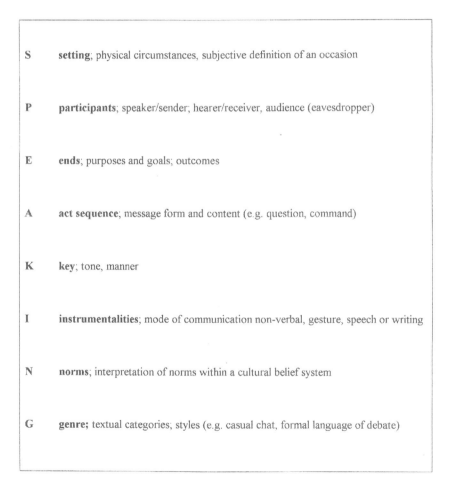

S   **setting**; physical circumstances, subjective definition of an occasion

P   **participants**; speaker/sender; hearer/receiver, audience (eavesdropper)

E   **ends**; purposes and goals; outcomes

A   **act sequence**; message form and content (e.g. question, command)

K   **key**; tone, manner

I   **instrumentalities**; mode of communication non-verbal, gesture, speech or writing

N   **norms**; interpretation of norms within a cultural belief system

G   **genre;** textual categories; styles (e.g. casual chat, formal language of debate)

FIG. 3.1. SPEAKING GRID.

We can summarize the grid as follows. Speech situations embed speech events, which in turn embed speech acts. To illustrate, a speech situation might consist of a social occasion (e.g., visit at a nursing home or mealtime) in which speech (a conversation) may occur. Therefore, the speech situation provides the setting in which the speech event takes place but is not in itself governed by a single set of rules. Speech events are seen as "activities, or aspects of activities, that are directly governed by pragmatic rules or norms of the use of speech" (Hymes, 1972a, p. 56), for example, conversations, sermons, or report writing. Speech events can then be further broken down into speech acts (e.g., commands). Following Hymes (1972a, 1972b, 1981), we use a broad definition of speech acts to include those easily defined by their illocutionary force (e.g., requests) and those that are less easily defined by illocutionary force (e.g., jokes, sarcastic remarks) and also nonverbal communication acts (see chap. 6, this volume, for further discussion of speech acts). We use capitals within the text when referring to elements taken from Fig. 3.1 (e.g. PARTICIPANTS). A summary (see Fig. 3.2) of the main dimensions used in EC research to investigate social interactions both within cultures and across cultures may further illuminate the EC methodological approach.

1. Speech community, or the group itself and its boundaries e.g., who is included.
2. Setting-where the interaction takes place (e.g., nursing home, university).
3. Speech situation, times when communication is considered appropriate or likely in the community (e.g., one assumes that in a social visit, a conversation will occur).
4. Speech event, or those episodes that can be recognized as constituting specific communicative frames (e.g., an interview) for the speech community.
5. Speech act, specific utterance identifiable as an instance of (intentional) communication within the speech event (e.g., a question).
6. The ideal speaker, someone who is communicatively competent within his or her own speech community.
7. The speaker's status-who the speakers are (e.g., doctor or patient), what their relationship is, and their functional role within the interaction.
8. The speaker's goals-the interactional goals of each participant.
9. The rules of speaking in the speech community (e.g., pragmatic norms).
10. Ways of speaking-patterns of communication familiar to members of the group (e.g., complaining about "bosses" in a workplace).
11. The functions of speech in the community, what communication is believed to accomplish (e.g., the general assumption that communication involves an exchange of information).

FIG. 3.2. Communicative Units.

EC gives analytical and theoretical priority to categories of language use. Thus, EC is

> Reluctant to assume a closed set of language functions that apply equally to all languages and all speech communities.... rather diversity is assumed and the limits of diversity are explored.... it is categories of language use e.g. acts, events not language structure, that have theoretical priority: language use itself is patterned.... structures and functions are relative adaptations to different cultural systems.... a single speech community is itself an "organization of diversity." (Schiffrin, 1994, p. 143)

While EC attempts to explore the nature of this diversity, it also recognizes the problematic nature of its most fundamental concepts (i.e., the systematic categorization of interactions into analytical units such as speech acts, speech events, and speech communities) and seeks to investigate the data before "any generalizations can be made" (Schiffrin, 1994, p. 143). EC forces researchers to consider not only all aspects of the interaction itself but also to reflect on the analytical categories we impose on the data and the ways in which both the interaction and the analysis are embedded within particular cultures. This is particularly important in dementia interactions.

Speech Communities in AD and Dementia

One of the goals of our research is to highlight the fact that bringing assumptions of what is normal to an interaction with a person with AD, and dementia, may result in either communicative dissatisfaction or complete communication breakdown. We intend to investigate whether, given the unpredictable nature of interactions involving people with dementia, it is possible to make predictions about the intentions of the person with dementia or whether the problem actually arises from a listener's need to make predictions about the illocutionary force (intention) of a speaker's utterance. Acknowledging the difficulties of making predictions in interactions involving people with dementia should not, however, deter researchers from seeking to discover features that may, to some extent, be predictable. When we interact with a person with dementia, we do so from the basis of a normal speech community in which the rules and norms of interactional behavior are generally understood or at least implicitly known. However, in the presence of dementia, we find ourselves in a context in which the norms may no longer apply, and this often leads to a breakdown in communication. Examining interactions between speakers with a normally functioning communication system and speakers with a communication system that is both variable and deteriorating can thus provide valuable insights into the dynamics of conversational management at a local level in populations with cognitive impairment.

We propose, then, to view people who have dementia (most of them with a diagnosis of probably AD) as belonging to a particular speech community, albeit a speech community in which participant abilities are highly variable and the interactions often unpredictable. We see the person with dementia as a member of a subgroup embedded within the larger speech community of dementia. This larger speech community includes individuals with dementia, their families, their primary caregivers, and professionals (e.g., physicians, nurses, occupational therapists, speech therapists) who regularly interact with them. The media would also be included within this speech community. It acts as an interface between the AD and the non-AD communities by providing a powerful voice that both reports on and recreates the culture in which dementia is embedded. We also suggest a further division of the AD speech community to include a second subgroup of persons with early onset AD. Although there is some expectation of cognitive dysfunction and memory loss in later life, and images of the "confused elderly" are common in our society, one does not typically include, for example, people in their early 50s within this category. Information gathered in interviews with caregivers of individuals in this subgroup suggests they experience many additional life span problems, for example, they may be actively involved in bringing up children, working to support a family, or have no long-term health coverage. LB, a caregiver who took part in our study, commented on the added stigma and social avoidance that has resulted from her partner's diagnosis of early onset AD.

Speech Situations and Speech Events in Dementia

The speech event itself represents "a non-linguistic unit" that "becomes the frame of reference for interpreting speech" (Duranti & Goodwin, 1992, p. 25). Duranti and Goodwin (1992) further noted that EC attempts to describe the most important dimensions of the speech event "on the basis of culturally defined categories" (p. 25); therefore, it is important to consider the speech event as a contextually situated "holistic" event before engaging in more detailed linguistic analysis. There is always the potential for an infinite variety of speech events in any individual's life; however, our typical daily interactions consist of recognizable routines that tap into the cognitive schemas (stored mental representations) associated with those particular speech events. For example, a visit to the doctor may include (a) assumptions about the actual environment (e.g., the image of a clean, white office with a waiting area), (b) routine behaviors during the visit (checking in with a receptionist, waiting, etc.), and (c) expectations about the communicative routines (scripts) of conversations associated with that particular speech event.

A general cognitive schema of our expectations for interactions in and with dementia is harder to define, although we hypothesize that it is likely to include some assumptions about disordered and confused communication. We might suggest some interactions that are likely to be routine daily events in the life of the mid to late stage person with dementia in a nursing home. These include being given help with daily care tasks (bathing, dressing, etc.), taking part in medical consultations or nursing routines (tests, medications, etc.), the social visit that might involve family and/or close friends or less easily recognized visitors (e.g., volunteers from the individual's church, synagogue, etc.), and often overlooked are interactions with other nursing home residents. With the exception of the final example, the preceding are all speech situations that we try to map onto our preexisting schemas of such events. Therefore, people bring "prefabricated" attitudes and assumptions based on the NORMS of prior experiences. Interlocutors anticipate a recognized script within the ACTS SEQUENCES of a particular speech event. This script reflects similar speech events stored in cognitive schemas of such events (e.g., the asking of questions about health in a medical interview or the use of phatic routines in a brief encounter with a neighbor). Of course, it is precisely because people have such well rehearsed cognitive schemas for these frequently encountered speech events that one often fails to allow for the changes in the "script" that may arise in interactions with persons with dementia.

Our discussion here, reflecting the nature of our data, focuses on the ethnography of interactions with persons with dementia within an interview format. However, as our short-term goals (to interview people with dementia) diachronically shifted to long-term goals (to carry out longitudinal case studies), so the research interview evolved into a social visit as the participants became better acquainted. The interactions collected in interviews recorded in the early stages of this project can be situated into a framework of the generic research interview; however, the interactions recorded at later stages of the research, although still constrained by the ENDS of the research agenda, often reflect communicative features associated with a social visit. We also suggest that as the person without dementia becomes more experienced in interacting with a person with dementia, there is a shift in the asymmetry of the PARTICIPANT ROLES. The person without dementia may also perceive the exchange within an ACTS SEQUENCE to be more fluid once a relationship has been established, that is, they become a more experienced communicator. Therefore, as the person without dementia becomes more familiar with the NORMS of the other's conversational routines, she or he is better able to keep the conversation flowing.

Sociolinguistic (SLX) Research Interviews

The interviews examined here were a data-gathering exercise (i.e., our purpose was to collect language/conversation samples regardless of the content), and therefore, the structure of the interviews was not formalized.

Form is not a reliable indicator of meaning, and depending on contextual variables such as situation and participants, the same set of words may be a request, compliment [or] insult (Hymes, 1972a). Therefore, in any analysis of interactions, we need to establish the contextual constraints and norms of communication before attributing any social meanings to our data. In this section, we use EC to examine the interviews as speech events. We examine data from two different interview contexts: (a) a university speech pathology clinic and (b) two different nursing homes.

Schiffrin (1994) notes that in modern society, interviews are a familiar speech event that "share some common features" (e.g., the use of questions to seek information) but also "differ amongst themselves" (p. 146). For example, a televised media interview is a speech event where the ENDS are to seek information and also entertain an audience. In televised interviews, PARTICIPANT roles are more symmetrical; indeed, the interviewee may have more celebrity status than the interviewer, and therefore, role reversal is more likely. PARTICIPANTS may use multiple speech acts (e.g., requests, jokes, narratives). The KEY has a wide range, and speech styles may shift rapidly. A media interview is typically "enacted" as a private dialogue between two individuals but in reality also includes both a studio audience and the public viewing audience. There is also a trade-off between the private dialogue and explicit involvement of the audience. In contrast, the ENDS of a police interview are to gain information. One participant, the police officer, attempts to elicit very specific information from another participant, the suspect or witness, to solve a crime. In a police interview, PARTICIPANT roles are well defined, asymmetrical, and not likely to be reversed. The KEY is narrow; tone and manner are likely to be serious and restrained. The ACTS SEQUENCE will be more rigid in terms of turn taking; the police officer is typically the only participant who can ask questions. Questions may have a specific formulation (e.g., "Can you tell us your movements on the night of the fourth?"). Furthermore, while the two examples cited above belong to a superordinate category of speech event, namely, the interview, they also reflect very different cultures-the culture of media entertainment and the culture of police investigations.

The research interview, as with the police interview, has some very obvious ENDS-the researcher hopes to gain information about the interviewee's life and beliefs-but in linguistic studies, the researcher may also have covert ENDS that involve collecting a detailed and varied speech sample. These covert ENDS may have an effect on the KEY and ACTS SEQUENCE of the linguistic research interview. For example, to elicit a "representative" sample, the researcher may need to vary her or his style, and therefore, the KEY may be less restricted than in other forms of research interviews (e.g., health care interview). In interviewing persons with dementia, there is also a greater awareness of politeness issues. For example, the researcher may be concerned to ensure that she or he acts both appropriately and ethically by not saying anything that will threaten the self-esteem or "positive face" of the person with dementia (Brown & Levinson, 1987; see also chap. 4, this volume). Thus, research interviews involving persons with dementia are subject to a wider range of interactional constraints than research interviews involving populations who are not cognitively impaired.

In Western society, nursing homes are institutions that often evoke negative associations of dependence and deterioration (Golander & Raz, 1996; Williams & Guendouzi, 2000; Williams & Nussbaum, 2001). Indeed, we suggest that the negativity associated with these institutions is one of the NORMS that affect speech events occurring in this SETTING. The speech clinic also has associations with communication disorders but in some ways can be seen as a more positive SETTING. It is a place where people come for therapy and therefore may get better. However, a feature both SETTINGS share is the fact they are constrained by institutional ENDS. For example, in both SETTINGS, there are legal and ethical considerations involved in interacting with the residents or clients. The relationship of the PARTICIPANTS is asymmetrical. The resident or client is dependent on the professional's expertise and help. Collecting data in the previously mentioned SETTINGS also requires the researcher to adhere to another set of NORMS based on an institutional protocol of behavior. For example, clinicians and therapists undertake to guarantee confidentiality. In the nursing home, residents and visitors may need to remain in certain areas and schedule visits within the hours the institution sets aside.

A further factor in research involving participants with cognitive impairment is the institutional requirement of obtaining ethics approval; institutional review boards (IRB; see chap. 2) require that researchers' ENDS be overt. Before collecting the data, a researcher may be obliged, for example, to submit exact formulations of the questions that will be asked during the interview. The researcher is thus constrained by both a preset research agenda (as submitted to an IRB) and by monitoring her or his own behaviors for appropriateness. However, to avoid respondent bias, the researcher's overt ENDS (although explicit to peers via the IRB) may remain covert to the respondent. We should also note that the ENDS of secondary researchers (e.g., graduate students/assistants) may be tied to academic requirements or other benefits, and therefore, they may not necessarily reflect the same goals as the primary researcher.

The ENDS of the respondents in a research interview are a more complex issue. For example, individuals with certain health conditions may take part for material reasons (e.g., health care cost reductions or free medications). Alternately, a person may simply want to help further knowledge of the behavior or condition under study. In the case of the persons with dementia and their caregivers, respondent ENDS become even more difficult to define. Caregivers may initially view an interview as an opportunity to contribute to the knowledge of living with AD, but the interaction may also be a cathartic experience in which someone listens to their individual difficulties in coping with AD and dementia. The ENDS of the person with dementia are even less clear, although our experiences in collecting this data suggest the following: (a) that individuals in the early stages of AD may see the interview as a chance to express their fears of future trauma (see chap. 7); (b) that the interview is a means to assert themselves as individuals who have identities, concerns, and indeed, lives beyond AD; and maybe (c) that they themselves can make an active contribution to the knowledge about people with dementia, tell, as it were, "the inside story." There is no initial goal on the part of individuals in the advanced stages of AD. The family or caregiver agrees to include them in a research interview, and we have noted in our observations that persons with dementia often prove very "compliant" to a caregiver's suggestions. Although we cannot claim any "validated" conclusions about the ENDS of this group, we have noted that for some persons with dementia, one interactionally situated goal appears to be the attempt, through both verbal and nonverbal channels, to continue the conversation. Contrary to common belief, individuals with dementia prove to be very willing and responsive, and indeed, are often very competent conversational partners. Once dementia has advanced to a stage in which a respondent does not recognize the interviewer (or visitor) from one visit to the next, we may still minimally assume that the interactional goal for this participant is to interact, namely, to enjoy a friendly conversation with an unfamiliar but attentive interlocutor (see also chap. 8, and the discussion of repetitive patterns in conversations).

Schiffrin (1994) suggests there is "fluidity" (p. 162) within the ACTS SEQUENCE of certain interviews (e.g., reference library queries) because both PARTICIPANTS have congruent ENDS as they work toward a shared joint outcome. In research interviews, there is an asymmetrical distribution of knowledge, and the PARTICIPANTS may have noncongruent ENDS. As Schiffrin (1994) notes, the information that "researchers seek to gain … depends largely on the theories, hypotheses, issues and current problems in their field" (p. 161). The information gathered may be used to inform the public, although it is not always given to the individuals who take part in the interviews. However, the final product (e.g., in this case, a book intended for an academic audience, other researchers, or students of this field) is typically only available to a limited audience of "experts." Therefore, the ENDS of the researcher and interviewee are not congruent, that is, the PARTICIPANTS are not moving toward a mutually satisfactory outcome (e.g., dealing with a query). This further adds to the asymmetry of PARTICIPANT roles within the research interview. The researcher has an agenda and is working toward a future product (a paper, book, thesis, etc.), whereas the interviewee is following the locally situated interactional ENDS of responding to the questions asked in the interview. The researcher thus controls the interview through an ACTS SEQUENCE that involves asking specific questions to guide the interaction. In SLX interviews, the researcher's aim may be to gather a representative sample of the interviewee's conversational skills. Thus, one of the researcher's ENDS is to keep her or his interlocutor engaged in conversation, a strategy that results in an ACTS SEQUENCE that may be less structured than in other interviews (e.g., a service interview). Furthermore, in any interview involving people with dementia, the ACTS SEQUENCE of the interview may be crucially influenced by the (perceived) abilities of the partner with dementia.

The verbal channel, by default, is the most common mode of communication used in research interviews. However, individuals who have limited or failing language systems are more likely to use other INSTRUMENTAL-ITIES. In our data, we have noted that some participants rely heavily on nonverbal channels (e.g., facial expressions, gesture, and body posture) to signal active participation in the interview (see chap. 4).

The KEY (tone or manner) adopted in the research interview can vary more than in service-oriented interviews. However, for researchers, there may, initially at least, be restrictions on the tone in which they conduct the interview. In contexts of dementia, there is always the potential for the interviewer's utterances to be interpreted as "face threats" (see chap. 4). The person without dementia must maintain a balance between two interactional positions. On one hand, she or he may not wish to appear to be taking the person with dementia's problems too lightly, but she or he also needs to avoid appearing too serious or patronizing. In the typical SLX interview, the KEY is less restricted, and both interactants may freely alternate between moments of seriousness and humor. Although this shift in KEY may also occur in dementia interactions, researchers enter the conversation with the understanding that they should monitor their own contributions to facilitate communication with the person with dementia. Therefore, the constraints on KEY may influence and restrict the range of speech styles the researcher uses within the interview.

The term genre is associated with the "formal" characteristics of texts rather than "situational understandings supplementing text types" (Schiffrin, 1994, p. 63). Schiffrin (1994) sees sociolinguistic interviews "as very 'mixed' or 'hybrid' genres" (p. 63), and for that reason prefers to refer to them as speech events. Schiffrin's discussion of GENRE highlights an aspect of Hymes's (1972b) SPEAKING grid that may cause some confusion. What is the difference between genre and a speech event? Genres are textual categories, and therefore, form and structure are important. In literature, for instance, the term genre refers to specific categories of literature (e.g., the gothic novel) in which features of form and style are conventionalized, and adhering to the accepted format is a requirement for classification within a particular genre. It is a little more complicated when it comes to interactional patterns. Categorizing experiences into recognizable speech events such as the media interview or the medical exam gives the individual an economic way of cognitively storing what would otherwise be a large mass of continuing sensory input. Cognitive schemas allow individuals to store and process their experiences more efficiently. Thus, when they encounter similar events, they can utilize that information within the new interaction. This does not mean that a speaker rigidly follows a ready-made script; rather, this means that she or he may use communicative strategies used in similar speech events in the past. Furthermore, a speaker is likely to expect her or his interlocutor to react in similar ways to previous conversational partners. It is important, however, to remember that speech events are not bounded entities; even in a business meeting with a fixed agenda, there is the potential for the PARTICIPANTS to change the "footing" (see chap. 4) and redefine the genre of talk. PARTICIPANT goals may shift from instrumental (deciding new work schedules) to interpersonal (casual chat). Thus, talk itself can contextualize an interaction. For example, when people take time out (Guendouzi, 2001) to gossip with colleagues in a departmental meeting, the ENDS of the participants are momentarily suspended; the global ENDS of getting through the business agenda are giving way to the localized ENDS of relieving boredom or tension by talking about personal, mundane matters.

   Therefore, any speech event has the potential to incorporate embedded speech events that belong to different genres of conversational style, for example, business talk versus gossip. GENRE refers to the styles and modes of talk typically associated with a particular speech event; therefore, we see GENRE as an embedded element of the speech event rather than a term that is interchangeable within a speech event. The GENRES that are likely to be used within the SLX research interview are: (a) the GENRE of the structured interview, which involves an exchange of questions and answers between PARTICIPANTS who have well-specified roles (e.g., researcher and respondent); (b) the GENRE of personal storytelling (narratives) that form the main body of the interview (this is a GENRE in which the PARTICIPANT roles may shift and the respondent's contribution is leading the interaction); and (c) a GENRE of casual conversation that may emerge as the PARTICIPANTS become more comfortable and begin to interact on an interpersonal level (during these exchanges, the PARTICIPANT roles are more symmetrical).

Exploring the SLX Interview in Interactions With and About Dementia

Our main analytical aim in this chapter is to explore the research interview as a speech event within interactions that involve people with dementia and a diagnosis of AD. We examine two different SLX interviews: the first involving a person with dementia, E, who lives at home, and the second involving F, a nursing home resident. For comparative purposes, we also refer to an interview with E's primary caregiver, LB. LB was interviewed by the same graduate student who interviewed E. Drawing on the SPEAKING grid (Hymes, 1972a), we analyze the interviews to both illustrate the application of EC to conversational data and to better understand the dynamics of the interactions presented throughout this book.

The SETTING for E and LB's interviews was a university speech-language pathology clinic, an environment that is subject to institutional constraints (both medical and educational) that normally result in asymmetrical PARTICIPANT roles. In the university clinic, the clinician or academic professor may be perceived as having expert status; therefore, the client is likely to be led by the professional's agenda. However, on the occasions we described here, rather than being a health consultation, the interview is being conducted for research purposes, and the interviewee has something the interviewer needs: information. This factor reverses the expected PARTICIPANT roles. In a normal health care consultation, the expert would be expected to ask questions and eventually provide the client with information, whereas in the research interview, the expert plays a more supportive conversational role, and typically it is the interviewee who takes longer turns and provides the expert with information (for a discussion of the SLX research interview, see Schiffrin, 1994).

The additional factor of dementia results in changes to the structure and dynamics of the SLX research interview. Thus, if research interviews are occasions in which the researcher seeks to gain information from the interviewee, we would expect the role of the interviewer to be that of a facilitator supporting and guiding the interviewee throughout the interaction. Therefore, we might expect the interviewee's turn lengths to be greater than those of the interviewer. This was the case in the interview (see below) with the caregiver LB. In contrast, this pattern is reversed in the interview with E. It is M, the graduate student, who takes lengthier conversational turns and provides more detailed information. The following below are typical of the turn-taking patterns exhibited by M in interaction with the caregiver (Example 3.1) and with E (Example 3.2):

Example 3.1

123 LB: yeah mhm (.) you know I first got (.) the (.) the memories thing started (.) eight or nine years ago

124 M: wow that long?

125 LB: yeah (.) and so we took him to a neurologist and he did all these tests (.) depression vitamin B mhm (.) mini strokes (.) which is what they worry about with diabetics cause of blood pressure (.) low blood pressure can make that Alzheimer's none of it (.)

125 M: oh okay (.) okay (.) uh huh

126 LB: showed up so they said it might be just be the diabetes cause there has been some studies showing that long term diabetes can affect you

Example 3.2 (see Appendix D)

36 M: how long were you in H?

37 E: {piano oh man.} (2.5) fifteen?

38 M: fifteen (.)how d- how d' you like it? (3.0) it's too big for me (.) but then if you're from N maybe- maybe it's little.
        (2)

39 E: I liked it. (2.0) but (.) it's, (.) to me it- it was like, (2.0) well you get off your block (2.0) you're lost.

40 M: ((laughs)) yeah you're right that's how I see it too (.) I've never been able to drive to H to see somebody. (.) and find it without ending up (.) way:: over there somewhere. ((laughs))

Prior knowledge of E's AD and dementia can be seen to affect M's interactional style from the early stages of the interview. M is quick to respond to E's inability to find the relevant information by giving him her own views about the city being discussed. In the interview with LB (Example 3.1), M is simply offering minimal support, and LB is providing the information sought by the researcher. PARTICIPANT roles in the interaction with E are less symmetrical, and M dominates the conversation with her partner with AD. Thus, M's PARTICIPANT role and instrumental ENDS are influenced by her prior knowledge of E's condition. M's research agenda was to obtain information and a representative sample of E's communicative ability, but M's interpersonal ENDS relate to protecting E's positive self esteem (chap. 4) and override both her primary PARTICIPANT role of research facilitator. In contrast, when interacting with LB, M's conversational contributions reflect her instrumental ENDS of collecting data from the interviewee, and her PARTICIPANT role is that of facilitator. It appears, as might be expected, that M's overt instrumental ENDS (collecting a language sample of LB) are restricted by the interpersonal ENDS associated with face threats (Brown & Levinson, 1987) to E's self-esteem (see chap. 4). In the initial interviews with E, M is very conscious of pauses and appears uncomfortable with moments of silence.

Individuals with dementia may need to be given longer time to process information, and time is a factor of the SLX interview NORMS that differs in the context of dementia. In other SLX interviews, giving the interviewee prompts or further elaborations may help the researcher gain the information she or he needs, but in cases of dementia, this can be counterproductive to the interaction. LB's ENDS were both instrumental, helping to further the knowledge of AD, and interpersonal, helping with a friend's (J. Guendouzi) research project. We cannot presume to know E's ENDs, but we suggest that they may have been compliance with a caregiver request (E was extremely affable in complying with the wishes of others), being occupied by a novel occurrence in his daily routine, or wishing to be helpful. We should note here that E was in denial about his dementia and chose to view his cognitive handicaps as related to other health issues (see chap. 2, participant information); therefore, although he was informed he was taking part in research examining how people with health problems cope with everyday communication, we did not mention the word dementia or AD.

The ACTS SEQUENCE of the research interview can be seen as having a four-part structure:

1. A greeting stage: This sequence is typically unrecorded and often takes place away from the interview room.
2. An initiatory stage: The researcher explains procedures (e.g., taping, filling in of permission slips, etc.) and then asks specific questions to focus the interviewee. This section of the interview is typically dominated by the interviewer.
3. The main body of the interview: The interviewee is likely to be the main speaker, and the interviewer plays a more supportive role.
4. The Coda: The interviewer concludes the interaction (although in the context of dementia, it may be the person with dementia who terminates the interview).

In the interview with LB, the ACTS SEQUENCE proceeded through all four stages: M greeted LB (1) and initiated questions relating to her experiences with dementia (2); LB then produced short personal narratives about her life with E (3), and M closed the interview down approximately 40 minutes later (4). Given their structured ACTS SEQUENCE, one might question whether research interviews are speech events that can be seen as representative of normal conversational contexts. However, the research interview is not an "anomalous form of communication ... misleading as to the nature of reality"; the research interview also "instantiates normal communications" (Cameron, Frazer, Harvey, Rampton, & Richardson, 1992, p. 13). Indeed, in the interview with LB, M responded in ways that have been noted in the literature on the talk of female friends (e.g., Coates, 1996) by mirroring (matching) one of LB's stories with a similar account from her own life experience and by helping to coconstruct some of LB's responses. Furthermore, as we show below, in some SETTINGS, the research interview can be seen as sharing the features of another common speech event: the social visit.

In her discussion of EC, Schiffrin (1994) suggests that there are three main types of questions used in research interviews: information-seeking questions (I–SQs), information–checking questions (I–CQs), and clarification-seeking questions (C–SQs). In research interviews involving participants with dementia, the researcher may not be seeking specific informational content; rather, the object of study may be communicative or metacommunicative ability. Therefore, it is less likely that the researcher might feel obligated to check information, and indeed there are issues of face and self-esteem that might preclude the use of I–CQs. The research objective in these particular interviews is to establish how conversations with persons with dementia occur, are managed, and proceed (or do not proceed), and therefore, the researcher focuses on keeping the conversation flowing rather than checking the validity of the information obtained. Although informational content is very important, we are interested in evidence that illustrates the person with dementia's communicative ability in conversational contexts. A further concern is the ability of the interlocutor without dementia to communicate. In contexts of cognitive impairment, the SLX interview varies from other research interviews in that it is not just an information-seeking measure, it is also a linguistic and communicative data-gathering exercise that may contribute to the assessment of the interviewee's communicative functioning.

The Use of Questions.   In research interviews, the use of questions is often defined by PARTICIPANT roles. The researcher typically controls the conversational floor and asks the majority of I–SQ and I–CQ, although both PARTICIPANTS use C–SQs to establish if they have understood their interlocutor's intentions. As noted, checking speaker intentions can be a sensitive issue for both PARTCIPANTS. A person with dementia may avoid C–SQs for risk of appearing confused, and conversely, the person without dementia may avoid C–SQs to save the person with dementia's positive face (self-esteem). We noted that other than self-directed rhetorical questions, which appeared to function as memory prompts, E did not, apart from directions for the restroom, ask any direct questions in his interviews. In contrast, FM, a nursing home resident we interviewed, appeared to use questions, or more specifically use the same question, to maintain a conversation (see chap. 8). We review the use of questions below, first in the interview with LB, and then consider how it differs in the interview with E.

Example 3.3

4   LB: I could start let's see (.) what's the most problematic as a caregiver? (.) well, that's hard to say (X) as far as communication I guess the main thing is that you go from being an equal partner in a marriage to being like a parent (X) and that's probably the hardest thing to adjust to (.) um (.) I think it's harder in my case we have no children no family nearby (X) so I think it is harder in my case we have no children no family nearby so

5   M: you are it?
           C-SQ

6   LB: I am it

7   M: yeah

8   LB: and E was my best friend so

9   M: aw

10 LB: someone I could confide in (.) still can do that but how much he actually understands depends on the day

11 M: or hour even?
           I-CQ

12 LB: oh yeah

13 M: yeah (.) yeah

14 LB: he used to be extremely outgoing

15 M: really?
           I-CQ

16 LB: yes

17 M: wow

In this interaction, M's conversational role is supportive. She formulates direct I–SQs and then allows LB to develop the topic. M then offers supportive remarks that both show solidarity with LB and help coconstruct her responses. M frequently uses I–CQs to ascertain the extent of E's cognitive deficits and to encourage him to elaborate. Although this is a strategy that does not interfere with speaker selection, LB continues to hold the floor after responding to M's queries. There is, however, some evidence of constraint on the use of I–SQs if they occur when M is pursuing potentially sensitive information, for example, when M is attempting to get LB to recall the occasion that she and E received E's diagnosis of AD. M asks a direct I–SQ about the occasion but marks awareness of the sensitivity of the topic by qualifying her question with a "hedged" (chap. 5) or incomplete comment:

Example 3.4

121 M: so (.) what was that like? and that must be kind of (.)
         I-SQ

When interacting with E, M asks more I–SQs than with LB, but they are typically formulated with additional qualifying statements that serve to provide further information or rephrase the question. As noted, when interacting with individuals with dementia, restrictions on the use of I–CQs and I–CQ come into play (i.e., the researcher may attempt to avoid questions that imply the interviewee has not understood the question as a result of dementia):

Example 3.5
. = indicates omitted utterances

1   M: tell me about stock car driving? (.) cause I don't know a thing about it I did find a Magazine and it's got one cool picture in it you'll probably like it

          I- SQ + further information

2   E: well

3   M: it's got a crash (.) you made me think of Louis Lamour only stock car racing style (.) let's see where is it? a friend of mine helped me pick this out cause I didn't know what I was looking for now I can't find that picture there (.) there (pretty) impressive what do you think of that?

          Information + I-SQ

4   E: ((looks confused))

5   M: can you see? do you need your glasses?

          C-SQ

6   E: no right here (.) this page

                              .
                              .
                              .

13   M: so do you know like all the stars and everything in stock car racing? Are you familiar with all the different players (.) drivers

          I-SQ + further information

14   E: well I guess so (.) guy (.) I just know there's ((looks confused))

15   M: (3.0) pass it back

                              .
                              .
                              .

33   M: do you still watch TV? Like Nascar and that kind of thing

          I-SQ + prompt

34   E: yes I do

35   M: you do? (.) Daytona? (.) that's another one huh? **(C-SQ)**

36   E: yes that's another one (.) that's right

In Example 3.5, M's use of C–SQs or I–CQs is not as frequent as with LB, and M's strategy of adding further information to prompt E generally misfires. E becomes confused when trying to process all the added information. Overall, M's strategy of adding further information or attempting to reformulate her I–SQs interferes with E's ability to respond and take his turn effectively in the interview. Thus, in this interaction, the use of I–SQs is negatively affected by M's attempt, through the inclusion "helpful" extra information, to facilitate E's contribution to the interaction. However, E is able to incorporate M's use of the clarification-seeking tag "that's another one huh" into his own next response, "yes that's another one that's right," thus using M's remark to form his next response and maintain his turn in the conversation.

When interacting with LB, M asked questions that were more direct and contained less information, and it is probably the case that this type of construction might have been a better strategy when interviewing E. This can be seen in a second interview (Example 3.6) in which M allows E more time to process his responses to I–SQs that consisted of single-clause constructions with no added information or reformulations:

Example 3.6 (see Appendix D)

10 M: what did <u>you</u> do.
         I-SQ
11 E: I was- (4.0) man. I gotta <u>think</u> <u>now</u> (1.0) uh I guess I was responsible for (.) getting out the work, (.) getting out- (.) I was in industry.=
12 M: =o::h.=
13 E: =before I came [<u>here</u>.*
14 M: [okay,*
15 E: =and,=
16 M: =like an expeditor?
         C-SQ
         (2.0)
17 E: n:ot really.
18 M: oh okay,
19 E: uh:, (6.0) man. that- that's a good question (.) I was in industrial
         management.=
20 M: =okay, okay,
21 E: and (4.0) they gave me (.) at one place in H (while xxxx) company=
22 M: =oh okay,=
23 E: =in H. (.) I was responsible for all the production they put out

Although E takes five turns to formulate a complete response to M's question, it is notable that when M restricts her contributions to minimal responses such as "okay" E is better able to answer the question "what did you do?" There is one example of a C–SQ, and E responds appropriately to M's comment by pointing out he was not an "expeditor." We might suggest that M's C–SQ distracts E from his attempt to access the information about his former job. E abandons his attempt to answer M's question and twice repeats the utterance "no not really." However, we might also suggest that rather than acting as a distractor, M's C–SQ provides E with a means of retaining his turn while gaining extra processing time to find the correct response, "I was in industrial management." Certainly, M's less intrusive style of restricting her own contributions to minimal responses and strategically using C–SQs gives E more time to process her questions.

The Nursing Home Interview

The research interview in the nursing home SETTING is subject to different constraints than the interviews that took place in the university pathology clinic. First, there are more environmental distractions. The interviews in our data typically took place either in the resident's own room or a public recreation area where recording conditions are less than optimal. For example, there may be interference from other residents, janitorial staff (noise of vacuuming, etc.) and interruptions for routine events (e.g., coffee break or taking medications). The background noises may affect the clarity of the recordings, and on many occasions, recording is not possible. For example, during some visits to F, J took her (in her wheelchair) for a walk in the grounds of the nursing home. It is also the case that residents in nursing homes are usually in the later stages of dementia and may also have more severe comorbid health issues, for example, hearing loss, visual impairment, or loss of mobility. Furthermore, in this SETTING, the person with dementia is the PARTICIPANT on "home ground," whereas the researcher is the "visitor."

It has been our experience that research interviews that take place in the nursing home SETTING are typically experienced by the person with dementia as a "social visit." This is not unexpected inasmuch as the ACTS SEQUENCE of both speech events is similar. The SLX research interview can be easily mapped onto the person with dementia's cognitive schema of the social visit (a speech event that may be a frequent occurrence in this SETTING). As suggested above, the SLX research interview goes through a greeting stage, initiatory stage (the researcher asking questions about the interviewee), main body (with the interviewee telling personal stories or opinions), and then a leave-taking sequence. The nursing home visit follows a similar ACTS SEQUENCE, greetings are exchanged, the visitor typically asks the person with dementia about their health (e.g., how they have been getting on, etc.), and then the person with dementia may respond with stories of their past (and at times recent events), and eventually there is a leave taking. We would suggest, therefore, that in the context of the nursing home, the resident is accustomed to people arriving (both visitors and health professionals) who greet them and then ask them questions. Even when they are informed that the visitor is a university researcher or student, they may simply slot that person into a general schema of "visitor who comes to chat."

Even in the initial interviews in nursing homes, people with dementia typically assimilate the researcher into their cognitive schema of a social visit and therefore respond to the researcher as a potential friend or acquaintance rather than an expert or medic. This process is further facilitated by the researcher's desire to maintain a friendly, "naturalistic" relationship and avoid any face-threatening behaviors such as reality orientation (i.e., continually reminding the person with dementia of their institutional identity or their instrumental goal-data gathering). Thus, the PARTICIPANT roles assume a less asymmetrical dimension, and the ENDS of both PARTICIPANTS may appear to be (and arguably are) orienting primarily to interpersonal ENDS. Research has shown that speakers converge to their conversational partner's style or dialect (e.g., Giles & Coupland, 1991). Rather than "correct" the person with dementia's interpretation of the speech event, the researcher will converge to her or his reality and orient to interpersonal ENDS rather than the instrumental goals of her research agenda, and this may best achieved through the interaction of a social visit. Certainly, for the primary researchers, these visits changed from research interviews to social visits, and J continued to visit F after the data collection was complete.

Given these factors, the dynamics of the nursing home interviews share similarities with the dynamics of a social visit. The PARTICIPANT roles were less asymmetrical than in the clinic context where the interviewer is in her professional environment. In the nursing home, the resident is in their home environment, and this factor may impact the dynamic of the interviews; and therefore, the GENRES that emerged from these interactions may have less in common with the interviews recorded in the university speech clinic. Typically, in the nursing home interview, the talk could be classified within the GENRE of casual conversation; for example, topic choices were likely to relate to family details, health, and general small talk about the weather and holidays. In the university SETTING, the ACTS SEQUENCE included I–SQs relating to the person with dementia's past life history, personal interests, and in some cases, how they were coping with their AD and dementia. Thus, in the university SETTING, the types of questions asked and topics covered were consistent with the NORMS of the standard research interview (i.e., the interviewer seeks background information, personal beliefs, or preferences from the interviewee). In contrast, as we show below, the questions asked in the nursing home SETTING are more likely to relate to current events and the person with dementia's immediate physiological needs. We also note that F's general health, cognitive and communicative function, and mobility were, at the time of the interviews, more impaired than that of E.

In the following example, J has just arrived to visit F. It is the first week in
January, and J has not been to visit for a month.

Example 3.7 (see Appendix C)
Key to discourse line in transcript:

SDrQ = self-directed/rhetorical question
R-AQ = request for object or action
I–SQp = I–SQ (phatic)
I–SQr = I–SQ (repeat)
C–SQ
C–SQh = C–SQ (humorous remark)

69 J: have you been <u>well</u> over Christmas (.) have you been well.
        I-SQp
70 F: eh?
        C-SQ
71 J: have you been okay over Christmas.
        I-SQr
72 F: ((sniffs)) yes I seem to keep well and (2.0) (Xxx)
73 J: mhm,
74 F: can you make me some er (1.5) (in wa:ter), (.) me orange juice.
        R-AQ
75 J: do you want some orange. okay. hang on,
76 F: (if you can) fi::nd it ((4 s, sound of rummaging))
77 F: ((brief utterance; too quiet to make out; turned away from microphone?))
78 J: there's no uhh cup.
79 F: (x) (anything that x 'll hold it.)
80 J: uhm, (.) no. (3.0) no cup. m:. (5.0) let me go and ask. (3.0) ((to nurse:))
        um she wants a glass of squash but there's no cup or anything

                        .
                        .
                        .

85 J: ((light laugh)) mhm (.) did sh- did they come from Aus<u>tra</u>lia at all.
        I-SQ
86 F: [ə]::
87 J: not yet,
        C-SQ
88 F: well the first one's arrived,
89 J: the <u>first</u> one. **(C-SQ)**
90 F: m:: (arrived) last week, (.) ↓ooh (1.5) ([wa:ɪ] I haven't got em x)=
        SDrQ
91 J: =you haven't got your <u>teeth.</u>
        C-SQ

92 F: mm?
93 J: your <u>teeth</u>.
        C-SQ
94 F: yeah (.) will you call for them (.) (Xx xx) (1.0)
                (R-AQ
        (oh he's tickled to be Xx if you ask a fellow)?
95 J: mhm? (5.0) so was it S came or P.
        C-SQ
96 F: P that's come from Australia, she should be here this week, (.) now
        she's [ə] (3.0) she (.) is [ə] (3.0) she should be here sometime this week.
                        .
                        .
                        .
108 F: ((3 s; sounds of F drinking)) that's lovely. oh-?
109 J: do you want me to put it down? (1.0) okay.=
        C-SQ
110 F: =no I'd like some more,
        R-AQ
111 J: oh you want some more. okay,
        C-SQ
112 F: ((35 s; sounds of F drinking)) {W a:h that's beautiful. }
113 J: okay. I'll put it on there. ((to nurse:)) she wants some more (xX)? (12.0)
        ((sounds of R returning to chair, sitting down)) ((to F:)) you get uh (.)
        quite thirsty 'cause of the heating probably, [central* heating makes you
        dry,
114 F: [yea,*
115 F: yeah it makes you dry and (.) me lips dry (2.0) but [ə] (.) we never go out
        of this ↓room.
116 J: m:,
117 F: not even for half an hour or hop or skip about [ə],
118 J: ((laughs)) {LV can you hop or skip about? }
        C-SQh
119 F: well I would try if I (ever felt like it.)

The first I–SQ that J asks (turn 69) can be seen as fulfilling the phatic
function of initiating the conversation with an enquiry about F's health.
Typically, within the NORMS of everyday conversation, a speaker does
not expect a lengthy reply to this type of question (Coupland, Coupland,
& Robinson, 1992). Within the SETTING of a nursing home or hospital,
however, this phatic token serves both as a greeting and an I–SQ (i.e., the
speaker on this occasion does require the addressee to give details about
her current health status). Unlike E, F does ask questions, but they are all
R–AQs that relate to immediate needs (e.g., thirst or obtaining her false
teeth). Like E, F often asks SDrQs when confused about something, for example, when she notices her teeth have not been put in that morning. J's

questions, in these extracts, are mostly clarification-seeking formulations (see chap. 6) to check that she has understood F's requests or intentions. J's use of C–SQs allows her to check F's intentions without disrupting the conversational flow or claiming the conversational floor. F responds appropriately to J's C–SQs and it appears that they help J and F negotiate those moments of the conversation when there is a potential for communication breakdown. Because the research interview is enacted as a social visit, there may be less constraints (relating to issues of self-esteem) when using C–SQs in the nursing home SETTING. Overall, throughout the conversation, it is J who uses more I–SQs, either as clarification-seeking devices necessary for intelligibility or to encourage F to elaborate. At times, F's speech is hardly intelligible, and J, through the use of questions, needs to maintain a balance between potential face threats and understanding (see also chap. 9, on intelligibility). The social visit is a speech event in which PARTICIPANT roles are perceived as being more symmetrical. In this case, the researcher's ENDS have converged to those of F, which we might suggest were to engage in a pleasant conversation and enjoy human contact and attention.

A problematic issue arising from F's blurring of the boundaries between the two speech events was that F came to view J as a fixed part of her social life, and ending the interview or visit became increasingly difficult as F's perception of J focused more on her PARTICIPANT role as welcome visitor than as researcher. Institutionalized interviews are governed by fixed time slots, and it is possible, within the NORMS of that speech event, to suggest that the interview must end at a specific point in time. In this case, F became emotionally dependent on J's visits and often behaved as she did when family members came to visit by crying or begging J to stay longer. Interviews with the staff suggest that she did not behave this way with professional visitors (doctors, clerics, etc.) or the nursing home staff. Thus, in carrying out ethnographic research, we need to be aware of the risks and responsibilities attached to the role of participant observer and remember that research ENDS may conflict with those of the individuals they are observing. PARTICIPANT roles and ENDS may change over time, and the ethnographer needs to continually reassess the parameters of the analytical units they apply to their data.

A further aspect of the research interview that differs between SETTINGs is the use of the narrative GENRE. As noted above, the ACTS SEQUENCES of the interactions that took place in the university SETTING were more reflective of the NORMS of traditional research interviews (see Schiffrin, 1994). As the interview proceeds, the interviewee takes longer turns and provides short narratives within a turn to explain, or elaborate on, aspects of her or his life. Labov and Waletsky (1966) suggest the following stages (see below) in the construction of personal narratives, although we should note that not all categories will always apply.

[A]bstract: brief summary of the story to come.
[O]rientation: sets the scene and characters, why something is happening, and so forth.
[C]omplication: something happens, a problem or crisis arises, and so forth.
[E]valuation: justifies the story; gives the point of the narrative (so what?).
[R]esolution: brings the story to a conclusion, resolving the problem.
[Co]da: wraps up the story, and so forth.

The following extract illustrates this pattern. LB, E's caregiver, is telling M about E's attitude toward dogs

Example 3.8

94 LB: … he's very intolerant of the dog (.) [A]
95 M: really
96 LB: yeah (.) [O] which he used to when I had a dog and he loved dogs and when our former dog died he was the one who wanted another one (.) and [C] now the dog is in his way (.) or making a noise (.) [E] on the other hand he's always checking the gate to make sure the dog didn't get out =
97 M: =that's what I remember when I came over he was kind of doting on her
98 LB: yeah [Co]

In this example, M's interruption disrupts LB's story, and there is no resolution or comment about how she actually deals with E's unpredictable treatment of their dog.

As regards E's use of the narrative GENRE, our data suggest that although he is not able to produce a narrative within a turn, he can construct a narrative over several turns as is illustrated in Example 3.9.

Example 3.9 (see Appendix D)

102 E: well, (2.0) we grew up, (3.0) some of us grew up, [A]
103 M: ((laughs)) (2.0)
104 E: we get older. (1.5) and I'm trying to- I'm- I grew up- I (.) was in a small town. [O]
105 M: =oh okay,=
106 E: =I was living with my grandmother.= [O]
107 M: =oh really.=
108 E: =and my two aunts. (3.0) who are very religious. [C]
109 M: oh really?=
110 E: =born-again Christians.= [E]
111 M: =oh my goodness.=
112 E: so [Co]

In contrast to the examples collected in the university SETTING, the interviews with F in the nursing home contained fewer successful examples of the GENRE of personal narrative, and the PARTICIPANTS were more likely to abandon stories due to breakdown; therefore, the interactions involving F reflect the GENRE of casual conversation in a social visit. For example, F requested objects (e.g., a tissue) or requested actions (e.g., going outside for a walk):

Example 3.10 (see Appendix C)

128 J: =well there you are. *((handing F a tissue))*
129 F: they have mixed uh (tissups).
130 J: m:.
            (6.0)
131 F: *((belches softly))* excuse me,
132 J: m:.
133 F: I would just to come for a walk with you.
134 J: it's <u>rain</u>ing today though, (.) that's the only problem, maybe- maybe next week when its not raining, (.) <u>if</u> it's not raining, (.) there's gonna be a bit of a storm today,
135 F: oh yeah=
136 J: =it's getting win[dier*
137 F: [(xxXx*xxxx <u>nice</u> xxx,)
138 J: the weather forecast said there's gonna be a big storm I think,
139 F: I like to get out when its sunny. (.) and the- (2.0) e- when its (xx) sunny like that. (2.5) eh- (6.0) *((coughs))* ……

J and F frequently talked about the weather, family visits, F's grandchildren, and nursing-home activities. Thus, the conversations between J and F (by default) focused on F's immediate physical needs and the daily events in her life, reflecting the diachronic shift in the ENDS and PARTICIPANT roles of the interactants.

CONCLUSION

EC, as Schiffrin (1994) showed, is a useful methodology when investigating the characteristics of specific speech events such as the SLX interview. EC forces researchers to consider aspects of context that influence both the interaction and their interpretation of that interaction. Examining features of interactions that are beyond analytical units, such as words, turns, or behaviors can better explain the ways in which similar speech events may differ within different SETTINGS. The expectations or NORMS associated with specific speech communities or speech events may, as was shown above, both help and hinder the communicative process in interactions involving persons with dementia.

Through EC, one can explore how in the context of dementia one speech event, the interview, maps onto another speech event, the social visit. By examining the patterns within the ACTS SEQUENCES of both these speech events, we suggest that social visits to a nursing home and sociolinguistic interviews have similar formats and contain similar speech acts sequences (e.g., I–SQs). Thus, the researcher needs to remain vigilant to the fact that a person with dementia may not recognize speech events in the same way as the person with whom they are interacting. This raises an important issue for the clinician or caregiver in the case of conversations (speech events) associated with daily routines such as health care checks, bathing, or medication. Persons with dementia may not recognize the END in an assessment task and may not respond if they do not perceive the whole speech event as a relevant communication context.

The data we examined here suggests that when conducting SLX interviews with populations who have cognitive impairment there are greater constraints on the researcher's use of C–SQs and I–CQs. The constraints on the use of I–CQs arise from an inferred interactional threat to the positive face or self-esteem of a listener with dementia (see chap. 4, this issue). EC thus helps to reveal (a) the constraints on use of specific speech acts within interactions in the context of dementia, (b) the types and formulations of speech acts used within the ACTS SEQUENCE of a speech event, (c) the effects that PARTICIPANT roles may have on the interaction, and (d) how a speaker's ENDS may influence their choice of acts. For example, one of an interviewer's ENDS may be to avoid upsetting the person with dementia and therefore her interpersonal ENDS may place constraints on her use of I–CQs. However, the person without dementia may also find that on some occasions, using I–SQs can better aid the flow of conversation and assist the interlocutor in processing a response. On the other hand, I–CQs are precisely the type of speech act that are considered an integral part of the ACTS SEQUENCE in a standard SLX interview (Schiffrin, 1994). EC, by focusing on the dimensions of context, also reveals the impact of different SETTINGS on the NORMS (expectations) of the speech event as in the case of the research interview in a nursing home context, a speech event that shares many features with the social visit.

Finally, EC's biggest contribution to the field of discourse studies is that it brought information previously seen as background information to the focus of analysis in language and communication research. In EC analysis, language samples are situated within the culture of the speech community in which they occur. Interactions are compared with similar speech events both within and across SETTINGS. EC research pursues an agenda that is very important when analyzing interactions with dementia; it is an agenda that seeks a detailed analysis of not only the language sample but also the contextual features that accompany and therefore effect the interaction. The speaker with dementia has to negotiate an unpredictable world of mismatched expectations that may include inappropriately mapping speech events to their daily experiences, choosing the wrong speech acts within an ACTS SEQUENCE, mistaking their own and others' PARTICIPANT roles, and mismatching their own and others' ENDS when interacting. Communication researchers should address this issue by systematically incorporating these elements into their investigations. However, language and communications specialists should also be aware that while they seek to find patterns in their research, that may help them to communicate with persons with dementia; they are not a homogenous group whom one can neatly classify into categories or grids. We are wary of suggesting that working and communicating with populations with dementia is an easy task. Nor do we suggest that a methodology like EC can help to produce a set of bullet points, instructing a caregiver or professional how to ask a question or suggest what forms of questions work or don't work in interactions with dementia. Rather, EC is an approach that gives greater insight into (a) the potential contextual factors (e.g., the NORMS one brings to specific speech events) that might be causing problems and (b) reveal some of the strategies that work or conversely don't work in individual interactions involving speakers with dementia.

4

Interactional Approaches

INTERACTIONAL SOCIOLINGUISTICS

In chapter 3, we examined conversations, specifically interviews, from the perspective of the EC. We showed how contextual factors can be seen as analytical units that when systematically incorporated into research investigations, reveal many of the differences between the SLX research interview and the research interview in dementia. Although EC is a useful starting point when undertaking DA, it does not seek to examine context from the microlevel dynamics of the interactional moves. To further examine our data and explore the "meanings" that interlocutors exchange, understand, or do not understand within their interactions, we intend to refocus the "lens" of our analytical "camera" and look at speaker roles and ends from the perspective of interactional sociolinguistics (IS).

IS is an approach that has "diverse disciplinary origins ... based in anthropology, sociology, and linguistics" (Schiffrin, 1994, p. 97). Since its early inception, IS has grown to encompass a wide range of approaches, and it would prove impossible to include examples from all the applications of IS to communication studies. Therefore, we use analytical categories taken primarily from the work of John Gumperz (1982a) and Erving Goffman (1981). We consider the interactive construction of identities in conversation in light of socially and mutually assigned roles and speaker alignments to shifting age or health-related identities. We also consider the relation of politeness (Brown & Levinson, 1987) strategies to shifts in speaker realignments.

Contextualization Cues

A basic assumption underpinning the work of Gumperz is the notion that the "meaning structure and use of language is socially and culturally grounded" (Schiffrin, 1994, p. 98). Although Gumperz stresses the importance of social knowledge in understanding how language structures become part of the verbal repertoires of a speech community, he also notes the importance of the analysis of linguistic structure in the understanding of culture and cognition: "Structural analysis furnished empirical evidence for the contention that human cognition is significantly affected by historical forces.... What we perceive and retain in our mind is a function of our culturally determined predisposition to perceive and discriminate" (Gumperz, 1982a, p. 12).

Gumperz (1982a, 1982b) calls for a theory of verbal communication that integrates structural knowledge of language with the conventions of how we use language in a social context. He suggests a listener's interpretation of an utterance depends on his or her pragmatic knowledge of a speaker's inferred intentions and his or her ability to read the nonverbal and paralinguistic cues that accompany the actual utterance. Thus, speakers and listeners need to be able to identify not only "lexical, phonetic and syntactic options" of an utterance but also to be aware of the significance of specific "signaling mechanisms such as intonation, [and] speech rhythm" (Gumperz, 1982a, p. 16) that accompany an utterance. It is often these "marginal" features of language that lead to misunderstandings, which, as Schiffrin (1994) points out, can lead to "the formation of racial and ethnic stereotypes and contribute to inequalities in power and status" (p. 99). Gumperz (1982a) refers to these signaling mechanisms (both verbal and nonverbal) as contextualization cues that help to relate a speaker's utterance to (a) specific activity types (speech events) and (b) the implicature (chap. 6) or "intended" meaning (e.g., a speaker may utter the words "nice dress," but their intonation may signify they actually intend the opposite meaning, i.e., it is not a nice dress at all). Thus, contextualization cues are not conventionalized meanings overtly assigned to language; they are learned through continual exposure to face-to-face interactions over a period on time. Contextualization cues may not always be evident until we examine interactional data, particularly in cases in which communication breaks down or is not established (as may be the case in autism). In the case of dementia, the misreading of contextualization cues on the part of either the person with dementia or the person without dementia may result in exacerbating communicative misunderstandings already compromised by the language and memory deficits of the person with dementia. Gumperz (1982a) saw contextualization cues as crucial to the understanding of speaker inferences. In dementia, inferred meaning is highly problematic (see chaps. 6 and 7), not only for the interlocutors but also for the researcher analyzing the data. Although a speech community may have tacit agreement on the meaning attached to specific contextualization cues (e.g., a raised eyebrow may signal disbelief), the conventionalized use of these cues may not be obvious or consistent across speech communities, particularly clinical populations. We have noted in our data that some individuals with dementia use hand gestures to signal that they intend to maintain their turn at moments when confusion may prompt the interlocutor to interject and take the conversational floor. Alternately, a person with dementia may use hand gestures or other paralinguistic devices to signal an interlocutor to take over a turn. For example, F used a slight laugh to signal her inability to continue with an utterance. The laugh functioned both as a face-saving device to mask her confusion and as a turn transition point (see chap. 5, this volume). It is not easy, therefore, to assign meaning to contextualization cues away from the context of specific interactions and individual participants. "While some aspects of Gumperz's work seems 'rooted in the individual' it is also: 'grounded in a view of the self and what it does (e.g. make inferences, become involved) as a member of a social and cultural group and as a participant in the social construction of meaning'" (Schiffrin, 1994, p. 101).

It is this aspect of Gumperz's interpretation that differentiates from and expands on Hymes's work in EC. Gumperz (1982a) reinterprets Hymes' (1972a, 1972b) notion of communicative competence to include "the knowledge of linguistic and related communicative conventions that speakers must have to create and sustain conversational cooperation" (p. 209). Although similar to Hymes's notion of the competent speaker, Gumperz's description differs by suggesting that speakers create and sustain their conversational roles within their interactions. Thus, PARTICIPANT ROLES and speaker ENDS may emerge not only from socially sanctioned positions and predetermined aspects of an individual's identity (e.g., doctor vs. patient) but also from the dynamics of the interaction itself. Examining our data from an IS approach allows us to extend our definition of context and explore its role. Like EC, interactional research incorporates context into the analytical framework by suggesting that one cannot interpret talk without reference to cultural setting, speech situation, and shared cultural knowledge. IS focuses the observer's eye on both the macrolevel features of context in which, for example, a speaker could be said to hold a more powerful interactional position based on their institutional role of clinician and microlevel features (e.g., a shift in speaker alignment based on what is uttered at the time) that emerge within the interaction. As Goodwin and Duranti (1992) note "talk is hierarchically organized and different notions of context may be appropriate to different levels of talk" (p. 3).

Goodwin and Duranti (1992) further suggest that "context thus involves a fundamental juxtaposition of two entities: (1) a focal event; and (2) a field of action within which that event is embedded" (p. 3). In interactions, the focal event is the "main attentional track" of the participants, whereas the field of action is the context in which the focal event is embedded; in the case of research, the focal event is the behavior or speech event one is examining. These two elements, the focal event and the field of action (context), are mutually informing and exist within a dynamic relation; focal events form the context for further focal events. Thus, if we collect data from a specific focal event we wish to examine (e.g., the research interview) and we then select a smaller sequence of talk from within that speech event (e.g., questions and answers), those question–answer sequences then become the focal event for our analysis, and the research interview itself becomes the context or field of action. As noted in chapter 3, the "dynamic mutability" of context is such that "participants rapidly within talk invoke contextual frames" (Goodwin & Duranti, 1992, p. 3); talk itself contextualizes other talk. Thus, we can say contexts and focal events are multiply embedded, and therefore, it is not always easy to define explicit boundaries between context and behavior or focal event and field of action.

IS takes "as its point of departure the perspective of participants" and how "the subject organizes his perception of the events and situations" (Schiffrin, 1994, p. 105). With respect to our own data, we cannot be certain how the person with dementia organizes his or her perceptions of the event.[1]

Discursive psychologists (e.g., Edwards & Potter, 2001; Potter & Wetherell, 1987) have suggested discourse should be seen not as an underlying cognitive process but as a social practice of the participants. Analysis should involve uncovering the participants' understanding of what is being said (see chaps. 5 and 7). With clinical populations however, this is not always possible, but one of our goals in undertaking qualitative research is to attempt, at least, to better understand how people who have dementia cope with interactional features such as contextualization cues or inferred meaning. Ethnographic research examines communication within a specific cultural group and draws conclusions about what norms might function for that group. The researcher's observations can then be checked with those who are members of that particular speech community, but in the

---

[1]We are aware that no one can be certain of their conversational partner's perceptions. Speakers/listeners organize their understanding of an interlocutor's perceptions based on their own beliefs. Therefore, the more similar they view their interlocutor's understanding of a situation the easier it is to incorporate that person within their own schema of that event.

context of dementia, we may not be able to reliably check our observations with the participants, and therefore, it is difficult to approach data from the perspective of the participants themselves. McDermott (1977) notes that people become environments for themselves, and thus, individual conversational moves can reshape factors within an interaction, for example, speaker ENDS may change; therefore, IS attempts to approach interaction from the perspective of the individual. However, IS approaches do not suggest that reality is relative or that cultural and social factors can be ignored, rather that speakers by their strategic orientation to context (within an interaction) are influenced by "large social and cultural patterns" (Goodwin & Duranti, 1992, p. 4). Furthermore, it is not always the case that a speaker's interactional stance will be ratified by his or her interlocutor; therefore, prior knowledge of a speaker's intention cannot predict the outcome of an utterance. This is particularly true in the case of dementia, in which communicative breakdown may result from either partner's (mis)reading of the contextualization cues that accompany an utterance. Thus, in such interactions, the relationship between field of action (context) and focal event is potentially unpredictable.

Participation Frames and Footing

The work of Goffman (1967, 1976, 1981) had a major influence on IS and although differing, complemented Gumperz's (1982a) work on contextualization cues. Goffman (1967) focused on the issue of self in face-to-face interactions and suggested that self is a socially constructed phenomenon that emerges from our interactions. He claimed that a speaker's interactional stance is influenced by issues of self-identity or face. Face, Goffman (1967) suggested, is "the positive social value a person effectively claims for himself by the line others assume he has taken during a particular contact" (as cited in Schiffrin, 1994, p. 102). Goffman (1967) noted the "maintenance of both self and face is a condition of interaction, not its objective" (p. 12). Thus, the individual is a social actor whose performance (interactions) are shaped by both the environment and his or her audience. Face-to-face interaction thus becomes a matter of impression management, and for people who are seen as belonging to stigmatized groups (as in dementia), there is the added pressure of managing the tension that their stigma invokes within an interaction (Goffman, 1964).

Face becomes "significant in interaction as people work jointly to present and preserve one another's public image" (Trees & Manusov, 1998, p. 564). Brown and Levinson (1987) have extended Goffman's work to include two aspects of face; "negative face," which refers to an individual's desire to neither impose upon, or be imposed upon by another person, and positive face, which refers to an individual's desire to be approved of and liked by others. Brown and Levinson suggest a speaker's choice of speech act is influenced by the degree to which it may pose a threat to their interlocutor's negative or positive face. Thus, contextual factors, such as social distance, may affect whether a speaker uses direct speech acts (see chap. 6) when, for example, requesting a favor or commenting on another's performance or appearance. As Trees and Manusov note, "positive face is threatened by acts that overlook the hearer's feelings or wants" (p. 566), and speakers therefore are likely to adopt discursive strategies that will minimize or alleviate face threats within their interactions. In interactions that involve individuals who have dementia, the issue of negotiating potential face threats becomes highly salient for the partner without dementia. For example, a simple request for clarification (see chap. 3) of an unclear remark could be viewed as an imposition on self-esteem of the person with dementia, and (as was the case with one of the researchers) the person without dementia may therefore feign understanding to avoid the potential face-threatening act (FTA) of pursuing explanations or disrupting the conversational flow. Likewise, the partner with dementia may feign comprehension rather than admit to being confused by requesting clarification. Face, therefore, can be seen as a crucial aspect in interactions involving individuals with disabilities and particularly in adults who have neurological disorders.

Goffman (1974) further developed his work on self-presentation to include the methodological concepts of frames, participation frames, and footing to account for the ways in which individuals "organize their experience" (Schiffrin, 1994, p. 104). Goffman suggested the individual approaches a situation with the internalized question, "what is going on here?" They then attempt to answer this by supplying a definition of the situation or by framing the event in light of both prior and current knowledge. As Levinson (1983) notes "the notion of inferential schemas or frames" grew out of work in cognitive psychology and artificial intelligence (e.g., Minsky, 1977): "A frame in this sense, is a body of knowledge that is evoked in order to provide an inferential base for the understanding of an utterance (see e.g. Charniak, 1972) ... reference is made ... to frames for teaching, shopping, participating in committee meetings, lecturing and other speech events" (p. 281). Thus, frames are the "organizational and interactional principles by which situations are defined and sustained as experiences" (Schiffrin, 1994, p. 104). We could posit, therefore, that an inferential frame for a visit to a nursing home or a conversation with a person who has dementia may include specific types of communicative behaviors (e.g., the repeating questions or utterances) and the expectation of misunderstanding. An inferential frame, we suggest, is the knowledge a participant relies on to play out the scene, whereas participation frameworks are the configuration of the participants. The term *participation frameworks* refers to positions that individuals within perceptual range of an utterance may take in relation to that utterance, for example, an "animator" produces talk, an "author" creates talk, a "figure" is portrayed in talk, and a "principal" is responsible for talk (Goffman, 1974). Each position within a participation framework "is associated with a codified and normatively specified conduct such that our recognition of shifts among animators, figures, authors and principals is facilitated by our normative expectations about the conduct appropriate for each position" (Schiffrin 1994, p. 104). Goffman's (1974) participation framework highlights the issue of individual versus social "voices"; by physically producing an utterance, a speaker is the animator of the utterance, but the illocutionary force or meaning contained in their words may be authored by others (e.g., a newsreader recounting the day's events or a nursing assistant reading a birthday card, sent by family, to a nursing home resident). In a participatory framework, we might argue that clinical workers and clinicians represent (and are therefore perceived) as the voice of authority.

INTERACTION BETWEEN SELF AND SOCIETY

The work of both Goffman and Gumperz presents a study of 'self' grounded not in psychology but in the "study of the traffic rules of social interaction" (Goffman, 1981, p. 128). Goffman noted that shifts in speaker alignments require structural means to signal changes in footing; thus, contextualization cues signal shifts in speaker alignments, and as such, the analyst should be able to identify the means by which both speakers and listeners use linguistic, paralinguistic, and nonverbal cues to both manage and adjust their presentation of self within an interaction. Gaik (1992), for example, has shown how a participant's interpretation of what is happening in therapeutic situations is cued by alternative speech styles.

The availability of multiple interpretations of speaker intention (see chap. 6) makes conversation a complex and multilayered phenomenon, and indeed, it is this aspect of language that has often limited DA as an analytical tool. As Schiffrin (1994, p. 129) notes, speakers have available a range of responses that retain sequential coherence within an interaction. Both speakers and analysts rely on inference to interpret meanings or project their feelings, and this may lead to highly subjective interpretations of data. Thus, DA needs to adopt both a macrolevel and a microlevel approach. In chapter 3 we focused our analysis on some of the macrolevel factors that may have affected the interactions examined here. We noted that PARTICPANT ROLES and speaker ENDS may be influenced by social and institutional norms; for example, the institutional role of academic researcher could be said to convey more power to that participant. However, we should be careful of generalizations that base their validity on socially imposed PARTICIPANT ROLES because each utterance is situated not only within the global context of the particular speech event, for example, the research interview, but also within the dynamics of the conversation itself. As we show below, a more microlevel IS approach suggests that interactional power is not only conferred by institutional roles; it can be claimed through the strategic management of speaker's contributions to the interaction.

Work in IS (Gumperz, 1982b; Goffman, 1964) has often focused on institutional settings and the language used by speakers from different sociocultural backgrounds, but sociolinguists also draw upon naturally occurring conversations among friends (e.g., Coates, 1996; Schiffrin, 1994; Tannen, 1984). As discussed in chapter 3, the data we examine here falls into both of these categories. An interaction involving interpersonal goals, that is, talking with a friend, becomes a speech event embedded within an interaction that has specific transactional goals (e.g., a researcher collecting data within a nursing home). Furthermore, these goals may be negotiated via the tape-recording, adding yet another layer of meaning to the interaction. IS relies on examining utterances both within situated social contexts (e.g., the research interview, the nursing home visit) and within their interactional contexts, that is, the conversation itself. Thus, IS focuses on an emergent construction of negotiated meaning and is functional in its approach.

Signaling Participation

The work of Charles Goodwin and Majorie Harness-Goodwin (see, e.g., 1999, 2000) has extended the notion of participatory frameworks to include any embodied practices (linguistic, prosodic, and nonverbal) that individuals use to signal their participation within an interaction.[2] Although Goodwin & Harness-Goodwin's (1992, 2000) work is often situated within the field of CA (see chap. 5), a method that seeks to understand the orderliness of human interaction through microlevel analysis of conversational exchanges, it also includes extensive ethnographic research (Harness-Goodwin & Goodwin, 1992) and for that reason, often features in discussions of both IS and CA. The Goodwins' analytical focus on the situated practices that are involved in human interaction includes any interactional device-for example, a nod, wink, laugh, or body posture-that allows an individual to participate or signal intention within an interaction. Harness-Goodwin (1994) suggests that both utterance structure and embodied

---

[2]Goodwin and Harness-Goodwin's (1992, 2000) work on participatory frameworks appears to conflate the notion of inferential frame and participation framework. It is understandable that the use of these two terms may confuse students (and researchers), but it is wise in reading the literature to be aware of the differences in the way researchers may be using these terms.

actions such as gestures can be seen as markers of participation, for example, the silent audience in a storytelling context can signal through laughter or applause their response to the speaker's monologue; their responses act as contextualization cues reflecting the footings or alignments, which indicate whether they are taking up oppositional or supportive positions within the interaction.

Goodwin and Harness-Goodwin's work on participation is particularly relevant in contexts of impairment and disability (e.g., Goodwin, 2003) in which paralinguistic and nonverbal contributions may be an individual's sole means of communicating changes in meaning. They cite the case of "Rob," a man with nonfluent aphasia who has a vocabulary of four words: *yes, no, and,* and *oh.* Rob uses intonation and the sequential organization of these tokens to "construct a diverse range of meanings" (Harness-Goodwin & Goodwin, 1994, p. 13). In our own data, we have examples of individuals with dementia who use nonverbal tokens as structural devices to both maintain conversational turn taking and to signal meaning that may not be evident in the propositions of the utterance itself. Nonverbal and paralinguistic tokens are also used by all participants to mitigate potential FTAs. For example, one of us often produced a light laugh in response to moments when F made negative references about being confined in a nursing home or made comments about her inability to function since the onset of her dementia. In contrast, F used laughter as a response to potential face threats and as a turn-yielding signal at moments when her responses broke down. Thus, for F, the use of laughter functioned both as a structural turn-taking device and as a means to mitigate the potential face threat to F herself in that it masked her inability to respond fully to J and also to mitigate the FTA to her interlocutor, that is, a potential imposition on J to take over the turn (for a more detailed discussion of F's use of laughter, see Müller & Guendouzi, 2002). An alternative conversational move for F would have been to continue attempting to process the incoming information, an action that may have resulted in dysfluency, incorrect word substitutions, or overly long pauses, features typically associated with disability and a negative identity. Based on our observations and data, we suggest that retaining an active stake within a social activity that becomes increasingly confusing and effortful allows a person with dementia to retain a greater sense of competency and therefore self-esteem-the participants of our research showed a high sense of communicative responsibility and appeared to use whatever strategies they could to maintain the flow of conversation.

The Data

Example 4.1 (see Appendix D)
Key to gaze and gesture lines (only E's gaze and gestures are included):

Gaze line:	Gesture line:
„ changes gaze direction	(( )) indicates gesture
--- gaze direction is maintained	fh folds hands
bec briefly breaks eye contact	hn head nod(s)
ghl gaze half left	hs head shake(s)
ghr gaze half right	lf leans forward
ghd gaze half down	htf head tilt forward
gm gaze toward M	

```
      -----------------------
10  M: what did you do.
```

```
               ---------------„ghr----------------------------------„gm------------------------------------------------
11  E:  I was- (1 2 3 4) man. I gotta think now (1.0) uh I guess I was responsible for
```

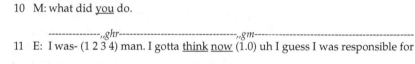

```
               ------------------------------------------------------------------------------------------
                        ((frown))
        (.) for getting out the work, (.) getting out- (.) I was in industry.=
```

```
      ----------
12  M: = o::h.=
```

```
      -------------------------------
              ((points right index finger))
13  E:  =before I came [here.*
```

```
                         ---------
14  M:                   [okay,*
```

```
      „ghr--
      ((fh))
15  E:  =and,=
```

```
      ---------------------------
16  M: =like an expeditor?
```

```
        (2.0)
```

```
      „gm--------
             ((hn))
17  E:  n:ot really
```

```
         ----------
18   M: oh okay,

      „ghd--------------„gm-----------------------------------------------------------------------
                ((hands half open))                    ((hm))
19   E: uh:, (6.0) man. that- that's a good question (.) I was in industrial

         -------------------
      management.=
```

In the preceding extract, M is asking E questions about his past life; at this particular moment, M asks E what he did before taking disability retirement. E has problems recalling details of his former profession, and M finally prompts him with the suggestion "like an expeditor?" (turn 16). E responds with a negative reply (turn 17), and he gazes away from P, an action that typically coincides with moments when he appears to find it difficult to process a request for information or has problems recalling a word. Like many of the people with dementia we have recorded, E is a very cooperative conversational partner and often relies on nonverbal devices to both maintain his conversational role and to mask any inability to recall words or process information. E's 6-s pause (turn 19) suggests that the processing load, in attempting to respond to M's request for information, may be using up much of his cognitive resources. When E's word-finding difficulties become too great, he produces the token "man" (turn 19), which he often uses emphatically at moments when he is frustrated by his own inadequacy to remember words.[3] E's use of this token may mitigate the potential FTA to his own positive face (self-esteem), which is threatened by the fact that (a) he cannot remember the information required to answer M's query and (b) that he also has ceased to adequately contribute to the conversation (see chap. 6). There is also a negative face threat to M at this point; cultural norms dictate that in most English speaking societies, a speaker would typically seek to fill a pause of this length. However, as a speech pathology student, M is aware that because E has dementia, she should give him time to formulate his response, and on this occasion, she does not attempt to repair or prompt E. E, who had directed his gaze away from M during the pause, then formulates his response "that's a good question" while looking directly at M with a smile and a gesture that involves half opening his hands outwards. This interactional move diverts attention from the preferred response, that is, a description of his former employment, and allows him to continue contributing to the conversation. Both the utterance and the gesture signal a change in footing, realigning E's presentation of self from a confused, powerless person with dementia to someone who is responding

---

[3]This information was confirmed both through E's use of "man" in subsequent interviews and by his wife who noted he often said this when he was struggling to remember information.

to his interlocutor's request for information by making what appears to be a meaningful comment. This strategy not only allows E to mitigate the potential face threat to his self-esteem by allowing him to remain an active conversational partner but also may act as a memory prompt because after a momentary pause (turn 19), E does manage to retrieve the correct information.

This example raises interesting questions about the role of affective mood on memory (Kazui, Mori, Hashimoto, & Hirono, 2003). Although we concede this is a speculative claim, in our data, we have noted that for some people with dementia, at moments when there is a threat to either the conversational flow and/or the presentation of self by the partner with dementia, the positive effects of actively contributing through self-prompting (preferential organization of self-repair; see chap. 5) to a conversation may to some extent improve the communicative performance of some people with dementia.

THE PRESENTATION OF SELF WITHIN
THE NURSING HOME

There is a dialectical tension inherent in any speaker's projection of self in relation to (a) who a speaker wants to be and (b) who a speaker is taken to be. In populations with communication impairments, this may be further confounded by a lack of access to the normal range of communicative devices that individuals use to project self within social interactions. Institutionally conferred identity roles often dictate that contributions to a conversation by the person with dementia are received and interpreted through the frame of dementia. The diagnosis of dementia, particularly for those individuals in institutional settings, is typically associated with negative aging and expectations of helplessness (Williams & Guendouzi, 2000). In analyzing interactions involving people with dementia, two questions arise in relation to participatory frameworks (Harness-Goodwin, 2000): What is the participants' relationship to each other, and what are they engaged in doing together? The relationship between the two participants in the preceding example is that of researcher and interviewee, and the task they are sharing involves collecting and providing information. In relation to the SLX interview, we might say that initially, the focal event for the researcher is collecting the data itself and although the researcher's goals might not be overtly foregrounded, they do covertly influence the researcher's contribution to the conversations. However, as noted in chapter 3, unlike the researcher, the person with dementia may have no predetermined goals, or they may be quite different from, or go beyond, contributing to research.

The extract in Example 4.2 is taken from a conversation between B and MA, with occasional contributions from C, MA's wife. B visited MA first as a part of his assignment as a graduate assistant, then as a friendly visitor. B's goals were well defined prior to his visits; he was to interact with MA and record their conversations. Although MA was made aware of B's status and goals as a student visitor, this was not a role that B made salient within their conversations. For the nursing home resident, a normal day may include a number of different encounters with, for example, professional caregivers, medical staff, and social visitors, for example, family members. Many of these encounters happen unannounced and involve people asking "how are you?" or "what have you been doing?" B's official status and role were revealed to MA, but owing to MA's dementia, we cannot be sure that he ever internalized this information. It may also be the case that because MA did not receive many visitors, he particularly welcomed B's visits, foregrounding B's role as a young inexperienced student by taking on the role of mentor. The routine visits of medical and care staff are likely to be brief and to the point, whereas B's visits to MA are different in that they last for a length of time, and it may be B's attentiveness that leads MA to take on the role of mentor (i.e., MA may feel validated by the attention of a younger man). MA's reactions to B suggest that he takes B to be a social visitor rather than an official visitor or researcher (with a specified research agenda). We make this assumption based on both MA's conversational style when interacting with B and the mentor role MA appears to adopt when talking to B (see below). In the following two extracts taken from the same conversation, one can see a pattern within both the structure of the conversation and the way in which MA uses both the pronoun *you* and the discourse marker "let me tell you" as footing devices to help discursively shift his projected identity from dependent nursing home resident to that of an elder mentor, a "man of experience" who can pass on useful tips to his younger and "naïve" interlocutor.

Example 4.2. (see Appendix E)

24 B: so what do you normally do l- here.
25 MA: huh?
26 B: what do you normally do here in- in a day.
27 MA: huh?
28 B: what do you here in a day.
29 MA: who.
30 B: you.
31 MA: what I used to do?
32 B: yea.
33 MA: for my livin?
34 B: yea.

35 MA: I run a dairy.

36 B: you run a dairy?

37 MA: eh: sell the milk, (xxxx) creamery. (3.0) hello cher.

38 C: how are you doin.

((2:28 to 4:00 untranscribed))

39 B: how long were you a dairy farmer.

40 MA: huh?

41 B: how long were you a dairy farmer.
          (2.0)

42 MA: how long I- I run a dairy,

43 B: yea. how long did you run the dairy.

44 MA: sixteen years.

45 B: sixteen?

46 MA: sixteen years. (send) the milk (xxxx) creamery.
          (2.0)

47 B: wow.

48 MA: oh ya. I don't work for nobody. I work for <u>my</u>self.

49 B: that's right.

50 MA: (x) you make a dollar for you I make a dollar for me. eh: make a dollar
          for you, that not good for me, is for you, *((chuckles; B joins in))* oh ya.
          (4.0) anybody can do that, (2.0) when started (x) I didn't have nothing. (x)
          people give me credit, 's I'm goina pay. (1.5) and if I (x) got ten dollar go
          pay. after a while, everything is for me. but uh- I want to run the business
          straight. crooked business you know what is, (.) goin to jail.

51 B: yea, *((chuckles))* {LV you gotta keep it a straight business. }

52 MA: oh ya.

((9 s pause; untranscribed until 5:58; other speakers))

53 M: if you see, come whatever. two three week, (1.5) let me tell you. if you
          not (crazy), you be smart.

54 B: yea?

55 MA: you understand?

56 B: I understand.

57 MA: if you come over there. and you- you got you not crazy, 'bout three week
          in (there) {LV you won't be crazy. }

58 B: really *((M laughs; B joins in))*

59 MA: mais ya, (3.0) oh well. (3.0) the best thing you do. take all you save.

60 B: yes.

              .
              .
              .

74 B: you get your morning coffee in here?

75 MA: huh?

76 B: you get some coffee. today.

((intercom announcement in background))

77 MA: oh, don't worry. (xx gon' miss that.) (1.5) you don't drink coffee?

78 B: oh no. not much.

((7:46; intercom announcement continues until 9:09.0))

79 B: is your coffee good?

80 MA: yes, you- you don't drink coffee?

81 B: no. I try not to.

82 C: you don't drink coffee?

83 B: no. not normally.

84 C: (xxx you used to.)

85 B: yea I used to a little bit.

((shouting in background))

86 MA: well, y- you better start drink, (1.5) because (1.5) you (lo- lose all that) if
          you don't (xxx) no drink no coffee, y: you (x), you lose that. *((shouting
          stops)) ((B chuckles))* let me tell you, (1.0) take (everything) you got a
          chance. *((B chuckles, M joins in))*

The ACTS SEQUENCES in Example 4.2 involve B requesting information from MA. If, as in chapter 3, we took an EC approach, we might predict
that B would hold a more dominant position within the interaction because
he is young, healthy, and not a dependent resident in an institution that MA
acknowledges is full of "poor people" who B should "pray for" (turn 528;
see Appendix E). Our preconceptions of who is in control of the conversation might appear to be well founded, because at the outset, B produces the
tape recorder and microphone, asks very explicitly whether he can he turn
it on, and then places it between him and MA on the table in front of them. B
then proceeds to initiate questions, selecting the topic and guiding the
conversation. However, although MA appears to have trouble either
hearing or comprehending B's questions, if we closely examine the
interactional patterns of conversational moves (see chap. 5) within the acts
sequences emerging from B's requests for information, it appears that MA
is actually negotiating a more powerful discursive identity than his early
confusion might suggest.

B's queries typically involve requests for information that is current; for
example, B asks MA what he normally does during the day and then later
asks whether MA got coffee that morning. These are requests that put a
greater processing load on M's memory. However, although we cannot claim
to know MA's actual intentions, it does appear that his strategy to deal with
B's enquiries involving current information is to reformulate the question to
suit his own conversational needs. For example, in response to MA's query
about daily activities, B reformulates the question to a request for information about his former work. The length of MA's turn 50 suggests that running
a straight business is a topic he is keen to talk about; furthermore, talking
about this topic (e.g., "I run a dairy," turn 35) allows him to present a more active and powerful identity based on his prior achievements in the dairy business; it is also an identity without ill health and dementia. Thus, in the first

example of footing, he uses a reformulation of B's request to shift alignment from the potentially negative identity associated with being elderly, disabled, and dependent to a more positive identity that might be associated with an active, independent, business man contributing to society. A second change in footing is marked through the use of personal pronouns that create a participatory framework based on an egalitarian relationship between MA and B: "you make a dollar for you I make a dollar for me." He then marks yet another change in footing when he uses the phrase "let me tell you" (e.g., turns 53 and turn 86), a discourse marker that allows him to now take a more powerful conversational position in which he appears to portray himself as B's mentor passing on sage advice. This conversation also shows that MA is able to negotiate Goffman's (1974) speaker positions within a participation framework (Schiffrin, 1994, p. 104). In producing the talk, he is obviously an animator, but he is the spokesperson for the voice of moral society (the principal) when giving B (the recipient) the following advice: "crooked business you know what is, (.) goin to jail" (turn 50).

Through the creation of a participation framework in which he is animator but not principal, MA is also able to mitigate some of the potential face threat inherent in (a) changing the topic by reformulating B's requests and (b) in attempting to offer information that as a result of his increasing dementia, may be imparted in a nonfluent way (e.g., through word-finding problems). As Schiffrin points out (1994) "offering unsolicited advice" (p. 109) is a violation of negative face (Brown & Levinson, 1987), but on this occasion for M, it seems to be a successful strategy in negotiating a competent identity in this particular interaction. We should also note that this is a jointly constructed relationship in which B casts himself in the role of the young man who accepts advice, taking MA's lead in the way their partcipant roles are negotiated.

Previously we noted that the projection of self in conversations is an interactive process that is dependent on two factors: (a) who a speaker wants to be and (b) who a speaker is taken to be. We have argued that MA presents himself in a way that projects his identity as an able, experienced person who is capable of advising B on various aspects of life. However, we have not yet fully considered how B receives the identity that MA is presenting. B has been primed prior to this interaction about how to interact appropriately with people with dementia. He is aware that he should not engage in reality orientation and try to force the conversation back on track, and he should allow MA enough time to formulate or process responses. B thus was coached in how to be a cooperative interlocutor, and therefore, in considering B's role in this conversation, we need to remember that unlike MA, he was more likely to be influenced by predetermined goals-those of a student carrying out a professor's instructions-and secondly, as a researcher collecting data. It should be noted that B, along with the other graduate students who participated in collecting this data, had expressed an interest in getting to know people with dementia, to find out what they had to say and more particularly how they managed to say it. Thus, although interested in the content of MA's stories, B was also interested in getting a lengthy conversational sample from someone with dementia. The interest in both content and length of sample may have contributed to B's acceptance of how MA redefines or refocuses his role. By foregrounding his "learner" self, he coconstructs a constellation of speakers that is more symmetrical and more conducive to the development of a positive emotional bond between MA and himself. We may assume that this developing bond (and a feeling of responsibility for having encouraged it) was at least part of the motivation for B's continued visits to MA:

Example 4.2 (see Appendix E)

454 MA: but a long time ago, (.) I used to be a good cowboy.
455 B: you used to be a good cowboy?
456 MA: oh ya, I can rope any cow, (.) I got a good horse, I got two (whole) but I
             got one. I can rope 'em, I- I called it [te:p], I said (tip) hold it. (.) don't
             hold it, I'm go ho- go over there and I (tie it). I said (x) come
             on you come with me, (1.0) I said (tip) hep me, ((two clicks)) you (know an' tie
             yourself). ((B laughs)) I- I don't want, I can't make you jump (on it), eh if
             you can't get down, (xx goin) take you back. (it goin) bite you.
457 B: really.

MA is able to realign the footing by changing the topic to subjects he wishes to talk about, and B accepts this realignment and redefinition. This strategy allows him to define the speaker roles for both himself and B. Indeed, the exchange above leads to a later sequence in which B reveals details about his own family, and MA goes on to offer personal advice relating to girlfriends and marriage. Despite being the "disabled" partner, M is very skillful in controlling the topics of discussion, managing his presentation of self in conversation, and in backgrounding his impairment.

CONCLUSIONS

In this chapter, we looked at speaker interactions as examples of situated meaning, that is, meaning that is embedded not only within the macrolevel of social contexts, for example, the nursing home or the SLX interview, but also within the context of the conversation itself. Drawing on the work of Goffman (1967, 1974, 1981) and Gumperz (1982a, 1982b, 1992), we considered how speakers use linguistic tokens and nonverbal behaviors to mark footings, points in the interaction when there is an identifiable shift in speaker alignment, particularly in relation to the presentation of self. By considering the utterances through the context of the conversation itself, for example, speaker turn length and topic management, we showed that speaker roles emerge not only from institutionally designated roles but also from the ways in which people interact.

By using IS to examine the changes in footing that occur within an interaction we can see that speaker roles and ends are not imposed on an interaction through referencing the macrolevel social context alone. Indeed, if we had approached this data from an EC perspective, we might have been tempted to allocate speaker roles on the basis of institutional identity. For MA, a person with dementia living in a nursing home, that might have equated with a negative or powerless identity, whereas B would have been seen as the interviewer and therefore the person who was controlling the conversation. However, as was shown above, this was not in fact the case that emerged from the interaction between B and MA. B could not foresee MA's contributions and therefore, it was the context of the talk itself that reproduced the speaker roles. While EC defines and identifies the macrolevel social context within which the interactions are embedded, it is the microlevel interactional moves that contextualize the ongoing talk and allow interlocutors to negotiate and project identities that suit their own individual needs. In all his interactions with B, MA seems to be the dominant partner who not only controls the flow of the conversation but manages to create a discursive identity in which B is the dependent partner, that is, the naïve young man who requires M's experienced advice.

The data examined here shows that although they may have communicative impairments, people with dementia preserve until quite late in the progression of the disease the skills to actively utilize both verbal and nonverbal strategies to "reorient the participation framework" (Schiffrin, 1994, p. 133). In the example discussed above, MA situated his contributions within a participation framework that enabled him to distance himself from the dependent role of the nursing home resident and project a competent and socially powerful identity of the wise mentor. Thus, rather than imposing institutional identities on the participants, an IS approach allows the researcher or clinician to examine the ways in which speakers themselves project and index identities in their everyday interactions. Furthermore, IS shows that meaning exists at multiple levels, and conversations are multilayered; both speakers and listeners rely on information taken from both their preexisting knowledge of social and cultural contexts and the cues that emerge from the dynamics of the interaction itself.

These are important issues for clinicians who are professionally obligated to approach clients through the interpretive frame of their knowledge of a particular disorder and therefore expect certain communicative behaviors or weaknesses. However, as is evident from MA's ability to control the way in which the above conversation developed, an individual with a diagnosed communication disorder is not necessarily the "powerless" participant in an interaction. IS is "basically a functional approach" (Schiffrin, 1994, p. 134) to examining examples of discourse, and its importance is that, like EC, it focuses our attention on both social and cultural contexts. IS refines the ethnographic approach by examining of the patterns of communication that emerge from the dynamics of the interaction itself.

5

Conversation Analysis

INTRODUCTION

CA attempts to "discover the methods by which members of a society produce a sense of social order" and "how language both creates and is created by social context" (Schiffrin, 1994, p. 232). As with IS and EC, CA is concerned with human knowledge (i.e., communicative competence) and focuses on the detailed analysis of particular sequences taken from the transcripts of recorded conversations. CA, however, has very specific theoretical assumptions and provides its own methodology for looking at the sequential organization of talk (see Goodwin & Heritage, 1990; Heritage, 1989; Schiffrin, 1994; Wootton, 1989; Zimmerman, 1988).

CA, unlike DA, which has its roots firmly in the field of linguistics (e.g., Labov & Fanshel, 1977; Sinclair & Coultard, 1975; van Dijk, 1985a, 1985b) and pragmatics (see chap. 6), evolved from the field of sociology and particularly the work of ethnomethodologist Harvey Garfinkel (see Button, 1991; Garfinkel, 1967; Heritage, 1984; Turner, 1974). Within the field of communication studies, there has been a longstanding debate about the validity of methods used in both CA and DA. As Levinson (1983) comments:

> Both approaches are centrally concerned with giving an account of how coherence and sequential organization in discourse is produced and understood. But the two approaches have distinctive and largely incompatible styles of analysis, which we may characterize as follows. Discourse analysis (DA) employs both the methodology and kinds of theoretical principles and primitive concepts (e.g. well-formed formula) typical of linguistics ... in contrast, conversation analysis (CA) ... is a rigorously empirical approach that

avoids premature theory construction. The methods are essentially inductive; search is made for recurring patterns across many records of naturally
occurring conversations ... again in contrast to DA, there is as little appeal as
possible to intuitive judgments. (p. 187)

This debate is important to language researchers working with clinical
populations because we may be tempted to use the analytical tools that best
illuminate the data with little thought to their philosophical or academic
roots. However, a clear understanding of the traditions of CA, DA, and
pragmatics (chap. 6) is essential to avoid subjective interpretations based on
individual intuition rather than theoretically grounded analysis. Some clinical language studies using a DA or CA methodology have misunderstood
the principles behind pragmatic theory, and the resulting analyses (or assessment protocols) may seek to identify "rules" (e.g., Bliss, 2002, p. 27) that are
presented as if they control human behaviors in the way the laws of gravity
control an object's descent to earth. Pragmatic frameworks (e.g., Grice's maxims; see chap. 6) were designed to exemplify the discussion of the theory
rather than provide a set of rules that control communicative behaviors.
Thus, DA allows the researcher to apply intuitive linguistic judgments to the
data, whereas CA, in contrast, insists the researcher should not bring any
preassumptions to their analysis (e.g., participant roles should be allocated
in relation to subject positions that emerge from the interaction rather that
from predetermined social roles such as doctor–patient). Being aware of
these differences will alert researchers (and students) to the potential limitations (and strengths) of qualitative research. It can be problematic for someone in clinical research to undertake "pure" CA analysis because
professional responsibility in diagnosis and intervention relies on a thorough knowledge of patterns of behaviors in pathologies, and therefore, the
clinicians will always have prior expectations of what they might encounter
in clinical populations. This is also true of our own analysis; at times, the nature of the data and the context in which it was collected make it neither possible nor practical to do pure CA.

ETHNOMETHODOLOGY AND CA

CA developed from the research of sociologists working within the field of
ethnomethodology, a movement that "arose in reaction to the quantitative
techniques, and the arbitrary imposition on the data of supposedly objective categories (upon which such techniques generally rely) that were typical of mainstream American sociology" (Levinson, 1983, p. 295).

Sociologists argued for the "study of 'ethnic' (i.e. the participant's own)
methods" of "interpretation of social interaction" (Levinson, 1983, p. 295).
Like Hymes (1972a, 1971) and the EC movement, ethnomethodologists
sought to establish the analytical units from the participants' perspective of

the interaction. Ethnomethodologists saw "language and (action through language)" as "no less a situated product of rules and systems than other typifications" (Schiffrin, 1994, p. 234). Schiffrin (1994) notes that CA "analyses do not always acknowledge their ethnomethodological heritage" (p. 234), but the distrust of linguistic categorization of words or expressions, typical of CA approaches, evolved from the ethnomethodological suspicion of "idealizations as a basis for either social science or ordinary human action" (p. 234). CA researchers drawing on these ideas suggested that analysis should seek to avoid "premature theorizing and ad hoc analytical categories: as far as possible the categories of analysis should be those that participants themselves can be shown to utilize" (Schiffrin, 1994, p. 243). As Levinson (1983) points out, this has led to a strict "theoretical ascetism" (p. 295) that has fueled debate among researchers who work in the DA approach. CA also shares with IS a belief that every utterance is both shaped by context and is also context renewing (i.e., an utterance is influenced and shaped by the preceding utterance). However, as noted previously, CA "pays little attention to social relations and ... social context" (Schiffrin, 1994, p. 235). By ignoring what other approaches assume to be "static features," such as participants' occupations or social status (e.g., nursing home resident), CA is able to avoid "premature generalizations and idealizations" (Schiffrin, 1994, p. 235). For CA, a participant's social identity, rather than being conferred through prior social status, emerges within the interaction itself. "The fact that they (the social interactants) are 'in fact' respectively a doctor and a patient does not make those characterizations *ipso facto* relevant ... (for example 'the one who tipped over the glass of water on the table') may be what is relevant at any point in the talk" (Schegloff, 1987, p. 219). When using a CA approach, the researcher should not assume that because a person has dementia (and therefore occupies a less socially powerful role) that the dynamics of the interaction will be any less symmetrical, rather, whether the shaping presence of the dementia will emerge (as one of many factors) over the course of the interaction. Thus, CA analysis seeks to ground its claims in the text; "it is only within organizations of sayings and doings that assignably 'personal' attributes are made manifest" (Coulter, 1989, p. 103).

CA METHODOLOGY

Much of the seminal work on the organization of talk was carried out by Harvey Sacks, Emmanuel Schegloff, and Gail Jefferson. Their research noted that talk, by and large, proceeds in an orderly fashion with an even distribution of turns betweens participants (Sacks et al., 1974). Furthermore, the transition from speaker to speaker often appears seamless with the "gaps between one person speaking and another starting" often being "measurable in just a few micro-seconds" (Levinson, 1983, p. 297). Sacks and colleagues suggested that conversation is like an economy with a "local management system" in which the mechanism governing turn taking is a "set of rules with ordered options" (Levinson, 1983, p. 297). One way to view these rules is to see them as a means to manage a "scarce resource i.e. the speaker turn" (Levinson, 1983, p. 297). Analytical units such as the transition relevance point (TRP) (i.e., those points in the conversation when a second speaker can enter the conversation) are important tools for CA analysis. Conversation is seen as a social action in which participants are continually involved in trying to (a) negotiate a potential TRP and gain a turn or (b) hold onto their current turn; conversation is a systematic process governed by organizational patterns that emerge at a local turn-by-turn level. CA, through microlevel analysis, seeks to identify the conversational mechanisms that interlocutors use to negotiate their daily interactions. CA research typically examines naturally occurring interactions rather than talk taken from experimental tasks. However, ethical practice dictates that researchers should make their participants aware of the fact that their conversations are being recorded and gain informed consent before proceeding with data collection. It is also prudent to be aware that participants may be influenced by the fact their interactions are being recorded. Within our own data, there is the added issue of acknowledging that although we informed the person with dementia of our intentions, they may not keep research purposes in mind.

The Sequential Organization of Turn Taking

According to Sacks et al. (1974), talk is organized such that one and only one party talks at a given time, although typically speakers will yield the conversational floor quickly. If there are more than two people involved in the interaction, the current speaker selects the next speaker through (a) utterance type (e.g., question directed at the selected interlocutor) or (b) through paralinguistic or nonverbal signals (e.g., intonation, gaze, or gesture). Speaker selections in everyday conversations typically occur utterance by utterance, for example, we do not normally select the next but one speaker (although in formal contexts, such as at debates, courtrooms, or the classroom, both current and subsequent speakers can be decided in advance). In multiparty conversations, if the current speaker doesn't self-select, another speaker may self-select, and if no other speaker "jumps in," by default, the turn goes back to the original speaker. The question then arises how other interactants know when a current speaker is completely finished or ready to yield his or her turn. This is particularly relevant in the context of dementia because we can not always guarantee that a person with dementia has the attention span to monitor the evolving turn. Sacks et al. suggested that a next speaker can never really know when a current speaker is completely finished. Next speakers, therefore, are always concerned with potential points of turn completion and with identifying possible TRPs. One TRP where a speaker is always vulnerable to loss of turn is at the end of sentences; therefore, speakers must seek to justify or gain their audience's permission for taking overly long turns. This does not mean literally asking for permission; rather, it means that speakers need to negotiate their turn in a manner that justifies their holding on to the conversational floor. Therefore, speakers may avoid lengthy pauses at the end of a sentence to avoid another speaker jumping in. According to Sacks et al., this is the reason for the low incidence of overlapping and silence in normal conversations. Overlapping is dealt with by one speaker yielding or ending their turn: Turn taking is typically smooth, successive, and without noticeable gaps or overlaps. Thus, for CA, conversation is a highly skilled (and at times competitive) social action.

Longer turns, however, are not uncommon in conversations, and CA suggests the notion of "conditional relevance" (Levinson, 1983, p. 293), which like Grice's maxim of "relevance" (see chap. 6), suggests a speaker's length of turn is sufficient for the context. For example, a speaker who is describing a road accident would be expected to give all the relevant details, and therefore, their turn is likely to be lengthy. Thus, turn length is conditional to the task at hand and may vary according to the needs of a particular speech event or, as in the case of dementia, to the needs of an individual interlocutor. As noted, in the case of dementia, the issue of turn length and speaker selection can be more problematic due to issues of politeness (Brown & Levinson, 1987). An interlocutor may feel that jumping in will be perceived as an FTA to the positive face of the person with dementia; furthermore, it may not always be evident when the person with dementia has ended their contribution. Within the interactions examined here, we have noted that the interlocutor is likely to allow the person with dementia a longer time per turn than would normally be expected. To maintain the self-esteem (or positive face) of the person with dementia, their interlocutor may seek opportunities to select them as next speaker. Also, in the interactions examined here, prior expectations regarding the cognitive processing needs of a person with dementia often result in longer periods of silence and more unfilled pauses than might normally be expected.

Adjacency Pairs and Preference Organization.   For CA, the smallest sequence of talk that can be analyzed is the adjacency pair, a basic unit that comprises a first pair part and a second pair part. An example of an adjacency pair would be a greeting that normally elicits a response and/or similar greeting:

Example 5.1

speaker A: how are you? (1st pair part)
speaker B: fine and you? (2nd pair part)

Common adjacency pairs include the following:

First pair part	Second pair part
questions	answers
offers	accept–refuse
requests	comply–not comply
complaints	apologies–justifications
invitations	accept–refuse

Initial sequences of adjacency pairs can be separated by inserted or embedded sequences of adjacency pairs whose function is to help clarify or give further information needed to respond to a speaker's initial request or utterance: In the following example, Q refers to question, QI to inserted question, A to answer, and AI to answer to inserted question.

Example 5.2
Phone call:

T:	I don't know where your place is?	Q	1st pair part
J:	where are you now?	Qi	1st pair part
T:	by the Amoco garage	Ai	2nd pair part
J:	well you're just around the corner	A	2nd pair part

Adjacency pairs are also considered to have a "preferred" second part; for example, the preferred response to an invitation to a party (given that the speaker's intentions are genuine) would be an acceptance. CA refers to this interactional pattern as "preference organization" (Atkinson & Drew, 1979; Pomerantz, 1978, 1984) and suggests that it is an important factor in a speaker's choice of utterance. Preference organization helps to explain conversational phenomena such as the use of politeness strategies that protect both the speaker and listener's positive or negative face. Dispreferred second part responses are more also more likely to contain hedges such as minimal interjections ("um" or "er"), unfinished words, or other dysfluencies.

Example 5.3

A: um I was (.) well I thought er perhaps you would like to come out with me?

To avoid a potential FTA, speakers are more likely to use prerequests or preinvitations:

Example 5.4

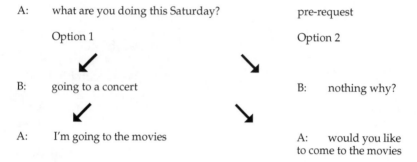

A: what are you doing this Saturday?   pre-request

        Option 1   Option 2

B: going to a concert   B: nothing why?

A: I'm going to the movies   A: would you like
                                                                      to come to the movies

Thus, preference organization gives a speaker options that protect him or her from potential FTAs. In the scenario above, the use of a preinvitation (a) reduces the risk to A's positive face if her invitation were to be refused outright and (b) reduces the risk to B's negative face by not imposing on him to comply or refuse. Thus, preinvitations and preoffers allow speakers to negotiate a position in which they are at less risk of losing face. Preference organization therefore appears to be an important element of normal conversations, an interactional mechanism that allows interlocutors to avoid direct speech acts that may disrupt the conversational equilibrium. Preference organization appears to require an awareness of the needs of other speakers, and therefore, it is important to examine contexts of dementia to see whether interlocutors use this conversational mechanism when negotiating conversations that involve people with dementia.

Repair Sequences and Trouble Spots.   Interlocutors need to monitor both their own and others' understanding (chap. 9) of the intentional meaning and content of an utterance. Conversations routinely include instances (troubles) in which insufficient or unclear information results in misunderstandings or even communicative breakdown. Even highly competent speakers can make phonological slips, ambiguous statements, and leave utterances unfinished. When such misunderstandings occur, both speaker and listener have the opportunity to repair the utterance, but as conversation analysts have noted, repair sequences are an area of conversation "where preference organization routinely operates within and across turns" (Levinson, 1983, p. 339).

What makes CA such an attractive area for clinical contexts is that it assumes all conversation is potentially troubled and in need of repair, and therefore, the focus is on how an interaction unfolds rather than the disorder situated in the person. Trouble (see chap. 8) is essentially any instance in which the conversation needs to be realigned, and a repair sequence is what is done to repair the trouble. CA sees repair as a conversational device that has specific properties. Four types of repair are suggested: self-repair (carried out by the speaker of the problem), other repair (carried out by the another party), self-initiated repair (repaired by speaker with no prompting), and other-initiated repair (repaired by speaker after prompting from another party). Drawing on Sacks et al. (1974), Levinson (1983) suggests that the preference organization of repair "provides a number of systematic slots across (at least) a three-turn sequence in which repair, or at least its prompting, can be done, as follows:

"T_1 (includes repairable item) = first opportunity: here for self-initiated self-repair

Transition space between T_1 and T_2 = second opportunity: here again for self-initiated self-repair

T_2 = third opportunity: either for other repair or for other-initiation of self-repair in T_3.

T_3 = fourth opportunity: given other-initiation in T_2, for other-initiated self-Repair" (1983, p. 340)

The conversational phenomena that give rise to repair might include word-finding difficulties, phonological slips, lengthy pauses, and self-correction where no noticeable trouble occurred. Although there are many ways to initiate repair of troubles (e.g., echo questions, repetitions, or other-initiated remarks like "excuse me?" or "what?"), CA suggests the "same system handles the repair of all these problems" (Levinson, 1983, p. 341), particularly in relation to preference ranking based on the most commonly used (self-repair in own turn) to the least used resource (other repair).

"Preference ranking for repair

Preference 1 is for self-initiated self-repair in opportunity 1 (own turn)

Preference 2 is for self-initiated self-repair inopportunity 2 (transition space)

Preference 3 is for other-initiated, by NTRI (next turn repair initiator) in opportunity 3 (next turn) of self-repair (in the turn after that)

Preference 4 is for other-initiated other-repair in opportunity 3 (next turn)" (Levinson, 1983, p. 341)

Preference organization suggests that an interlocutor's choice of repair mechanism is influenced by factors relating to positive face (i.e., being corrected by another is a greater FTA to a speaker's self-esteem). This is even more salient within the context of dementia in which interlocutors

may either be too quick to repair the "errors" of the person with dementia or, in contrast, reluctant to repair errors for fear of imposing on the
other's positive face. Thus, handling repair sequences is an area of
communication management that requires a great deal of skill to maintain a balance between (a) avoiding offending the person with dementia and (b) giving them the assistance they may require when engaging
in a conversation.

Topic Management

It has been claimed that people with dementia have poor topic management skills within their conversations (Garcia & Joanette, 1997; Glosser
& Deser, 1990). The monitoring of prior topics and the introduction of
new topics puts a strain on memory that may be beyond the person with
dementia's cognitive capabilities; however, as we noted elsewhere
(Guendouzi & Müller, 2002), the conversational abilities of many people
with dementia is often surprisingly good in relation to "appropriate" responses to their interlocutor's conversational moves. By appropriate,
we mean that in terms of adjacency pairs, people with dementia often
provide the appropriate type of response (e.g., offers are met with re-
fusal or acceptance), although it may be the case that the semantic content of a response appears to be off target. In Example 5.5, J's question
requires a denial or agreement, and F provides a structurally appropriate response (denial) but is semantically off target because she does in
fact have a problem with her leg, which is giving her some discomfort at
this moment (hence J's question) and also makes a tense error in her response:

Example 5.5 (Appendix C)

120 J: m:. (.) have you got a <u>problem</u> with your legs.   Question
                                                                              ] adjacency pair
121 F: no? I I didn't have,   Response

Many people with dementia also appear to cope well with phatic remarks (greetings, compliments, etc.) and formulaic utterances (e.g., "it's
a lovely day today"), suggesting that many communicative tasks may
operate as "automatic" response systems that require less cognitive effort. Given that memory impairment is a major effect of AD (Buchan et
al., 1997; DeLacoste & White, 1993), it is not surprising that topic management should be problematic. In our own data we have noticed that
people with dementia show a bias for topics (see chap. 8) that they (a) remember well (often events in their early past) or (b) feel they can "cope"

with through the use of circumlocutions or semantically empty words that allow the topic to continue despite either partner's lack of semantic understanding. Caregivers (Guendouzi, 2003) have reported that this type of communicative behavior can lead to communicative conflict particularly when a person with dementia continually reintroduces a specific topic (although as is shown in chap. 8, this can also be a useful strategy for keeping a conversation going). We have also noted in our own data that some people with dementia (even in the more advanced stages) do initiate new topics:

Example 5.6 (Appendix C)
(F and J have been discussing the changes in the city in which F lives when F makes the following topic shift)

219 F: and what about my poem. has it come to a stop or (xx soon xx).
220 J: ↓o:h it's still going,

F's question about the poem is an enquiry about J's research, and although she cannot always remember the correct formulations, F has constructed a mental schema for J's work that includes references to objects and activities related to education and writing. For example, on another occasion (off tape), F greeted J's arrival with "oh the typewriter."

Introducing a new topic that necessitates a narrative sequence requires speakers to alert their audience to the fact that they are about to hold the floor for a longer than usual turn. Typically, preference organization in the form of preannouncements or introductory cues allows speakers to signal to their audience that they are about to tell a story or impart something of importance. For example, instances of gossip may be heralded by a comment or preannouncement such as "have you heard." The other participants are then aware that they are being given a signal to pay attention and give the floor to the speaker. Similarly, when people tell a story about their past (e.g., incidents from childhood, working life, or other such life events), they typically use some form of discourse marker to preannounce what is to follow. Therefore, story cues and preannouncements are an important part of contributing to and negotiating everyday conversations.

THE DATA

CA's attention to detail at the local level has resulted in it becoming a popular methodology when analyzing data collected in clinical contexts (see, e.g., Guendouzi & Müller, 2002; Lindsay & Wilkinson, 1999; Perkins et al., 1998; Watson, Chenery, & Carter, 1999), although as noted previously, it is often an adapted form of CA.[1] Perkins et al. (1998) note that it is important to examine:

> pragmatic ability within the social context of the person with dementia, including an examination of the role of the conversational partner in interaction. In doing so, the discussion focuses on the analysis of the conversational data between people with dementia and their caregivers. The merits of Conversation Analysis (CA) for characterizing the pragmatic abilities and impairments of people with dementia are highlighted. (p. 34)

Perkins et al. (1998) argue for the greater use of CA when examining the context of therapy, which happens in face-to-face interactions rather than in experimental conditions that describe and quantify the surface manifestations of language in dementia. Experimental studies often involve narrative or descriptive tasks that do not involve "a key conversational partner" and are "topic directed" (Perkins et al., 1998, p. 34).While CA also identifies patterns within talk, those patterns include not just the contributions of the person with dementia but also the input of their interlocutors. CA examines how the partner's responses contribute to the overall conversation and how the impairment is as much a product of the interaction as it is an underlying cognitive deficit that resides in the person with the dementia. As Perkins (Perkins, 2006, 2000, 2002, 2003) has argued, pragmatic impairment is an "emergent phenomenon." CA focuses on conversations as collaborative efforts of joint action and joint responsibility (Perkins et al., 1998, p. 38; see also Clark, 1996; Perkins, in press). The interactive and narrative ability of people with dementia differs greatly across partners and is therefore not just dictated by underlying cognitive deficits but also interactional contexts (see, e.g., Ramanathan-Abbot, 1994).

Although it would be possible to exemplify all the conversational moves associated with CA through a lengthy and detailed analysis of our data set, constrictions of space do not allow for this type of exercise. We therefore limit our analysis to some specific areas of CA, but we are aware there are many more layers of meaning to be obtained from the transcripts, and we encourage the reader to carry out their own analyses of the data (see Appendices A through F). In this chapter, we focus our analysis on the organization of topic management, turn taking, repair sequences, and the use of pauses within the context of dementia. For the purposes of analysis, we draw on terminology derived from the work of Sacks et al. (1974).

---

[1]As noted earlier, clinical researchers adapt CA methodologies to their own purposes, and unlike pure CA, methodologists do not avoid assuming behaviors based on prior knowledge of a person's background. When dealing with people with communication disorders, a clinician or researcher has to be prepared for potential behaviors (e.g., circumlocution or word-finding problems) that are likely to arise from an underlying pathology.

Transcription key of conversational moves

I–SQ   = information-seeking question

C–SQ   = clarification-seeking question or clarification-seeking utterance

R–AQ   = request for object or action

TI   = topic initiation

TS   = topic shift (new topic introduced)

TIB   = trouble indicating behavior

R accept = acceptable response

Rs   = self-repair within utterance

Rs*   = self-repair in next utterance/transition space

Ro   = repair by other

Adj.P   = adjacency pair

P–A   = pre-announcement

P–R   = pre-request

Turn-Taking Routines

Example 5.7

```
1   B:    so what d'you feel like talking about today.
          TI I-SQ
2   MA:   huh?
          TIB C-SQ
3   B:    what do you feel like talking about.
          Ro I-SQ (repeat utterance)
4   MA:   huh?
          TIB C-SQ
-----------------------------------------------------------------------------------4 turns-----
5   B:    how's your week been.
          Ro TS I-SQ (reformulate)
```

        (3.0)

6   MA: (x x?)

           TIB (C-SQ?)

7   B: how was your week.

           Ro I-SQ (repeat utterance)

                               ] Adj.P

8   MA: oh it's alright,

           R accept

9   B: it was alright?

           C-SQ

10 MA: oh ya.

           R accept

11 B: yea?

           TIB C-SQ

12 MA: oh ya.

           TC R accept

---8 turns----

13 B: where is your wife today,

           TS C-S

                              ] Adj.P

14 MA: ([ɪ i:dɛ], y-) over there.

           R accept

15 B: she's over there?

           TIB C-SQ

16 MA: he goin take his bath.

           R accept (pronoun error)

17 B: ah, take a bath. (18.0) so's she goin- be coming out soon,

           Ro

18 MA: huh?

           TIB C-SQ

19 B: is she going- be coming out soon?

           TIB C-SQ (repeat utterance)

20 MA: who,

           TIB C-SQ

21 B: your wife?

           Ro C-SQ

22 MA: ya, pretty good. thank god.

           off-target response

23 B: thank god,

           topic closes

---12 turns---

((1 min untranscribed; conversation with third person))

24 B: so what do you normally do l- here.
         TS I-SQ
25 MA: huh?
         TIB C-SQ
26 B: what do you normally do here in- in a day.
         Ro I-SQ (repeat utterance)
27 MA: huh?
         TIB C-SQ
28 B: what do you here in a day.
         Ro I-SQ (repeat utterance)
29 MA: who.
         TIB C-SQ
30 B: you.
         Ro
31 MA: what I used to do?
         TIB C-SQ (off-target)
                          ]Adj.P
32 B: yea.
         R accept.
33 MA: for my livin?
         TIB C-SQ
34 B: yea.
35 MA: I run a dairy.
         R accept.   12 turns

In Example 5.7, taken from the opening sequence of a conversation between B and MA (see Appendix E), it is evident that "getting a conversation
going" in the context of dementia often takes a great deal of work. B attempts to engage MA in conversation through an I–SQ (turn 1), but MA appears not to have understood B's question and responds with a
clarification-seeking response "huh?" (turn 2). B then repeats his I–SQ and
receives another C–SQ from MA. MA's conversational moves indicate that
at this point, the conversation is potentially in trouble, and B attempts to repair this through a topic shift and by asking another I–SQ enquiring how
MA has spent the past week. MA's response to the new topic appears to be
another C–SQ (the intonation suggests a questioning utterance). B stays
with the topic and again repeats his I–SQ, and on this occasion, MA responds with an appropriate answer. Turns 7 and 8, in contrast, are an example of the typical organization of adjacency pairs, that is, a question is asked
and the interlocutor immediately responds with an appropriate response.
Following this successful move, B then attempts (turn 9) to get MA to elaborate on his week by asking MA to clarify his remark "oh it's alright" (turn 8).
B's aim was to engage MA in a conversation about the week's activities, but

MA's minimal response "oh ya" (turn 10) does not lead to an expansion on the topic. His conversational stance at this point appears to be very uncooperative, and B again attempts to repair the conversation through a topic shift to enquire about MA's wife (turn 13). The new topic seems to interest MA, and on this occasion, he responds immediately with an appropriate reply, although he does make a pronoun error that B corrects in his next contribution (turn 16). Despite the acceptability of MA's response, B again seeks clarification, an act that may have resulted from the lack of mutual understanding in the previous two ACTS SEQUENCES (turns 1–12). MA at this point begins to take a more active role in the conversation by elaborating on his wife's activities (turn 16). MA appears to view B's comment "ah take a bath" (turn 17) as a closing remark, and there is an 18-s pause before B tries to restart the conversation by enquiring when MA's wife is "coming out" (turn 19). MA at this point appears to have lost his place in the sequence of the topic flow, and B attempts to reorient MA by answering "your wife?." MA responds to B's C–SQ as if this is a new topic and therefore a general enquiry about his wife's health (turn 22). B deals with this potential trouble spot by closing the topic down and echoing MA's "thank god."

The 18-s pause (turn 17) suggests that B had selected MA as next speaker at this point, but when MA does not respond, B initiates a new topic and asks MA what he does during the day. MA does not immediately understand B's pronoun reference and seeks to clarify who B is talking about (turn 29). B's repair move pointing out it is MA he is referring to is greeted with an slightly off-target reply in which MA shifts the topic from his normal routine to the more specific question of what he use to do for his living (turn 33). B accepts MA's topic shift, and MA goes on to elaborate about his experiences in running a dairy. Within a dyadic SLX interview format, researchers obviously select next speaker when asking the interviewee questions. However, other speakers cannot always be sure what it is that an interviewer may wish them to talk about; therefore, there are likely to be a many examples of C–SQ's checking whether they are keeping their contributions relevant to the task at hand (see chap. 6). However, we would not expect to see the extended question sequences and multiple C–SQ's moves that are seen in Example 5.7. Questions such as "how are you feeling" are typically organized in a simple adjacency pair structure, which may include an embedded sequence, for instance, in the following example:

Example 5.8

A: how are you feeling? A: how are you feeling?
C: fine and you   C: who me?
                       A: mhm
                       C: okay I guess

In Example 5.7, the first topic involves 4 turns before being abandoned, the second involves 8 turns, and the final two topics involve 12 turns each. This extended turn taking with potential trouble spots and multiple CS–Qs is a regular pattern in this particular conversation (see Appendix E). However, although the talk is troubled due to the extended C–SQs sequences, it is not a deviant pattern as it follows the typical pattern of topic-initiating adjacency sequences. The data we examine here shows that the interlocutor without dementia has to do a great deal of interactional work when initiating and elaborating on topics in conversations. B, as a graduate student who has been exposed to communication disorders in his studies, responds with a great deal of patience to MA's repetitive C–SQs. Caregivers, on the other hand, have reported this type of conversational behavior as highly frustrating and "difficult to cope with" (Guendouzi, 2003).

Our analysis suggests that in relation to turn-taking patterns, some of the features a conversation partner might encounter when talking to someone with dementia are extended turn-taking sequences, particularly when dealing with topics that would normally be handled as short phatic routines, no uptake of turn when the person with dementia is selected as next speaker in a question sequence, potential trouble spots following the asking of questions, and frequent requests for clarification on the part of both interlocutors. In Example 5.7, B generates all the I–SQs and appears to control the flow of topics; therefore, initially, it might appear he has the more active participant role. We might, however, suggest an alternative explanation for MA's communicative behaviors in that MA is reluctant to join in B's choices of topic and is manipulating the topic selection to one he prefers (i.e., his former role as a dairy manager).

It should be noted that generalizing behaviors to a group of people based on the performance of one individual is always a questionable assumption; however, we did find similar patterns with other participants. For example, F showed similar difficulties in initially engaging with her interlocutors:

Example 5.9 (Appendix C)

10 J: =did you have a good Christmas?
         I-SQ
11 F: pardon?
         TIB C-SQ
12 J: did you have a good Christmas?
         Ro-repeat I-SQ
13 F: ((sniffs)) ([wi.aʊtʃɑd])
               TIB (unintelligible)
14 J: m?
         C-SQ

15 F: (what we- what were [(xx)*
                              TIB (unintelligible)
16 J: {lento [did you* have a good <u>Christ</u>mas.}
        Ro repeat I-SQ
17 F: well. (.) alright,=
        R accept.
18 J: =it was alright.=
        C-SQ
19 F: = m:, (.) didn't (x) do {LV anything, (xx)}=
        R accept. (TIB)
20 J: =did you get any presents?
        Ro TS I-SQ
        (4.0)   ] Adj.P
21 F: ↓no::. (we've- we're just left here dead,)=
        R accept.
22 J: =mhm.=
        closes topic
23 F: =↓oh:: wha- what I want is to (4.5) I don't know, (.) what you call it. (2.0)
        I call it when (something changes or) your own brain.
        TI
24 J: [o:h*.
        minimal response (sensitive topic)
25 F: [{LV (xxx*xxX, xx)}=
        TIB (unintelligible)
26 J: =your brain. ((light laugh)) {LV <u>my</u> brain. <u>my</u> brain is going, }
        face reduction move
        (3.5)

In Example 5.9, one sees a similar pattern emerging in the exchange sequences as in MA and B's conversation. J initiates a topic by asking F about her Christmas activities, and F, like MA, responds with a clarification-seeking move; J, like B, is forced to repeat the question on two other occasions before F finally answers it was "well. (.) alright" (turn 17). There is a further similarity here between F and J's exchange and the exchange involving MA and B (Example 5.7, turns 8–9) in that both MA and F's replies imply that things were perhaps not alright. J uses a similar strategy to B and repeats F's response with a rising intonation, suggesting she is seeking clarification of whether F's Christmas had in fact been enjoyable. As was the case in Example 5.7, there are several instances when potential trouble spots arise, and J is forced to attempt to repair the conversation through repetitions and C–SQ moves.

Speaker selection on this occasion seems to present no problems, and F responds immediately to J's questions; there are fewer between-turn pauses (although several within-turn pauses for F). Contrary to claims in the literature that topic initiation is problematic for people with dementia, F does initiate new topics within her interactions. When the topic about Christmas is closed down (turn 13), F asks J a question about dementia (turn 23), and on this occasion, it is J who avoids a direct response and merely offers the minimal response "o:h" (turn 24). This is due to the sensitive nature of F's question, a potential FTA that imposes on J the obligation to offer F both reassurance and information about F's dementia. J tries to reduce the face threat by making a humorous remark that claims her own "brain is going" (turn 26), and it is evident from the light laugh at the beginning of her remark that J treats F's question as a sensitive topic that may lead to conversational trouble.

While the turn-taking sequences in Examples 5.7 and 5.9 are extended due to multiple requests for clarification, the following example shows a different exchange structure both as regards the responses of the partner with dementia and the strategies of the interviewer. It should be noted that E lives at home and that (a) his dementia is less advanced than either MA's or F's, and (b) he is much younger than the other two participants. E is able to manage activities of daily living without aid but has quite severe memory problems when recalling information needed to respond to his interlocutor's questions:

Example 5.10 (Appendix D)

----
36 M: how long were you in H?
       TI +I-SQ

----------------------,,ghr--,,gm---
37 E: {pian. oh man.} (2.5) fifteen?
       R. accept + TIB (face threat)

---,,ghd---------------------------------------
38 M: fifteen, (.) how d- how d' you like it? (3.0) It's too big for me. (.)

----
       but then if you're from N maybe- maybe it's little.

       I-SQ + topic elaboration
       (2)

----------------------,,gm----------------------------,ghd---------------gm----------------------
                                                              ((points))
39 E: I liked it. (2.0) but (.) it's, (.) to me it- it was like, (2.0) well you get off your block (2.0)

       ((unfolds hands))

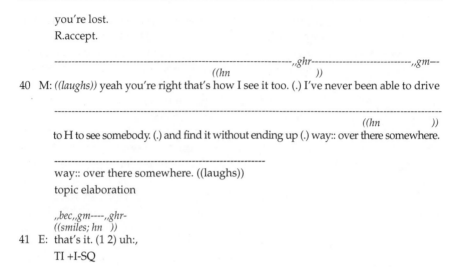

you're lost.

R.accept.

```
--------------------------------------------------------------------,,ghr---------------------------,,gm--
                                         ((hn                                    ))
```
40 M: *((laughs))* yeah you're right that's how I see it too. (.) I've never been able to drive

```
----------------------------------------------------------------------------------------------------
                                                                    ((hn            ))
```
to H to see somebody. (.) and find it without ending up (.) way:: over there somewhere.

```
----------------------------------------------------------
```
way:: over there somewhere. ((laughs))

topic elaboration

```
,,bec,,gm----,,ghr-
((smiles; hn  ))
```
41 E: that's it. (1 2) uh:,

TI +I-SQ

M opens this particular exchange with an I–SQ asking how long E had spent living in H, a city in a different state. Unlike the previous two examples, there is no extended exchange involving C–SQ's. E attempts to provide the correct answer, but he is unable to access the correct information immediately and responds with the phrase "oh man" (turn 37), a discourse marker that, as noted in chapter 3, he uses frequently when he is having problems processing information. There is a 2.5-s pause before he gives a tentative answer of 15 years (turn 37). His intonation and nonverbal signals suggest he is not confident of his reply, and he appears to be looking for M to confirm this information. M's strategies are very different from those of B and J; rather than asking C–SQs, she takes longer turns[2] and gives further information elaborating on the topic of her questions. It is difficult to say whether this strategy helps or hinders E in formulating his own responses. On one hand, M's lengthy turns give E no time to process information and respond appropriately, but on the other hand, they may be prompting him with further information and therefore helping cue his memory. Certainly the organization of M's responses helps produce a seemingly coherent conversation, but whether this is because M's elaborations prompt E's memory or whether they simply give him a proposition to agree with is arguable. After M's lengthy turn (40), E is able to reply with what appears to be an appropriate response by simply confirming the content of M's remarks. Turn taking between M and E is more orderly and appears less problematic than in the previous two examples. M often uses laughter to signal her turn is over and to select E as next speaker. This is a strategy that is effective with E who appears to respond well to paralinguistic cues (see also chap. 3).

---

[2]She had been given instructions to allow E time to process information.

Although there are less visible organizational problems within this conversation, we can see that within E's own turns, there are many pauses and restarts (turn 39), suggesting he is struggling to access the information he needs to reply to M's questions. The face threat of not being able to respond with the appropriate information results in several potential trouble spots and may account for M's lengthy turns, particularly as she was instructed to allow E time to respond and to avoid jumping in. This suggests that face threats are a dynamic of interactions that are likely to override other participant goals. This was M's first encounter with E, and thus, she is an unfamiliar (and inexperienced) conversational partner, a fact that might also have contributed to her lengthy turns; she has yet to come to a point where she is comfortable with the longer pauses that frequently occur in dementia discourse. Thus, in this example, the turn taking is orderly, with M initiating topics and E attempting to respond on the next-turn position; however, E, unlike F, does not initiate any topics of his own and appears to allow M to dictate the flow of the conversation. As noted in chapter 3, he was a very compliant interlocutor and would attempt to answer all of M's questions rather than ask C–SQs or initiate a topic shift.

In relation to topic management and turn taking, there are two different patterns illustrated in the data examined here: (a) Interactions with extended turn-taking sequences in which the trouble spots are indicated by the use of numerous C-SQ's and topic shifts, and (b) An interaction in which the turns follow a normal adjacency pair organization; that ism M asks a question and E attempts to answer. The trouble spots in this interaction are indicated through hesitations and pauses reflecting E's information-finding difficulties.

Preference Organization in Repairs

All of the examples above involve repair moves on the part of the partner without dementia: both repair of word errors (e.g., B corrects MA's pronoun error in Example 5.7, turn 19) and repair of the conversation itself by the use of C–SQ repetitions and topic shifts to avoid trouble. In contrast to the literature on preference organization in normal conversation, the participants who took part in this research project did not typically attempt to self-repair linguistic errors within their own utterances. F, on one occasion, self-repairs a pronoun error: "what did I say my er your son my son" (Guendouzi & Müller, 2002, p. 18). E does show some concern about his information-finding difficulties but his frustration is self-directed and marked by the use of formulaic (see chap. 8) discourse markers (e.g., "oh man"). This strategy might also be a way of retaining his hold on the turn, thereby buying himself more processing time and avoiding the face threat inherent in not being able to respond accurately.

Pauses

The preference organization of repair sequences is based on norms of politeness and the degree to which the error (and indeed repair move) may pose a face threat to either conversational partner. As we noted elsewhere (Guendouzi & Müller, 2002), the conversational skill of people with dementia is often more intact than has been previously acknowledged. F, for example, showed an ability to use small talk and compliments to negotiate potential trouble spots in the conversation. People with dementia are, as we have shown, able to respond appropriately to their partner's conversational moves (e.g., respond to questions with answers). Thus, in terms of the structural development of conversations, the people we interviewed were able to maintain the conversational flow, and as we show later in chapter 8 often use resourceful compensatory strategies in attempting to remain an active partner within an interaction. We might assume that the global face goal for the participants in a conversation is to actively participate and jointly work toward keeping the talk flowing. Certainly the participants with dementia in our data did in various ways (and to varying degrees) attempt to keep the conversations going. However, more interesting for the CA researcher investigating communication in dementia is the question of how instances of trouble and repair are managed at a local level and what effect those moments have on the conversation as a whole.

As noted earlier in this chapter, speaker turns are valued, and for this reason, lengthy gaps or silences are not tolerated within the norms of most conversations. Pauses may indicate a TRP and therefore allow a next speaker to jump into the conversation. Pauses, therefore, are likely to be seen as marker of speaker selection, that is, if a speaker finishes a clause or intonation unit and leaves a pause, the other speakers will interpret this as a TRP and assume they are supposed to respond at this point. In most Western cultures, interlocutors are typically uncomfortable with unfilled silences, as they are potential trouble spots that may pose a face threat to both participants. In the conversations examined in Example 5.7 and 5.9, the face threat of both repair moves and unfilled pauses are an interesting phenomenon in that overall, the participants with dementia did not show any overt signs of being uncomfortable when trouble spots occurred. In the extended questions sequences between MA and B, MA seemed comfortable with B's repeated C–SQs, and as was shown earlier (Example 5.7, turn 18), MA did not attempt to fill the 18-s pause that occurred when B asked about his wife. Indeed, it is B who responds to the potential face threat of the prolonged pause and takes a next turn. In this data set, we have noticed that people with dementia are extremely tolerant of their partners' attempts to repair both the structure and content of misfired utterances and of their attempts to realign conversational topics. Although on occasion, the person with dementia may opt for the preferred self-repair, it is typically the partner who tries to repair misfired or semantically off-target remarks.

This raises a question we have asked elsewhere in this book: Is trouble a product of the person with the disorder, or is it an emergent property (Perkins, 2002, 2005) of the interaction itself? In the examples involving MA and E, we argue that the disorder that arises within these interactions emerges from the non-AD interlocutor's reaction to, and management of, trouble spots at a local level. In the interaction with E, M appears uncomfortable to allow E to struggle for any length of time and often jumps in with lengthy elaborations on the topics under discussion rather than sit back and allow E to answer in his own time. Although B and J appear more willing to give their conversational partner more time, both still use the default response of embedded sequences of C–SQs to realign participant goals when their interlocutor does not respond to their questions or shows little interest in the topic. It may be that the turn-taking structure of a conversation is, like formulaic language (see chap. 8), a highly automatic behavior. Thus, even "trained" conversational partners may fall into the trap of jumping in with repair moves before allowing the person with dementia a reasonable amount of processing time, for example, in some cases, people with dementia may take several minutes to accurately respond to a question. Thus, as noted earlier, it appears that for the interlocutor without dementia, face threat is a highly salient factor influencing their choice of conversational moves in contexts of dementia.

A further question arising from analysis of face threats in interactions involving dementia concerns the "ownership" of pauses. Pauses have multiple roles in conversations; for example, as a TRP, to give emphasis to a new piece of information or as a trouble indicating behavior (TIB). It is the pause as an example of a TIB that we are concerned with here (see also chap. 8) and more specifically, who actually owns the pause. It may seem odd to speak of owning a pause, but given that it is a time period within a conversation during which neither of the interactants is speaking, we might ask who has decided to allow that time to be unfilled? Typically, we might assume that the prior speaker owns the pause because they have decided to stop their contribution, but we might also consider that it is the next speaker who assumes ownership by deciding to delay their contribution, that is, that when the first speaker pauses and selects the next speaker she or he has relinquished the conversational floor, and now the next speaker owns the pause. Pauses in dementia typically indicate two types of trouble: (a) the need for more processing time (things are working but the person just needs greater time to respond) or (b) the inability (typically in mid-to-late-stage dementia) to comprehend an interlocutors's intentional meaning (Perkins et al., 1998).

Example 5.11 (Appendix F)

35 R: *{pian.* mhm*}* you have been to O before?
                  I-SQ
                                          ] Adj.P

36 FM: yes I did go to O.
             R accept

37 R: How do you like that city.
             I-SQ
                                          ] Adj.P

38 FM: I like it. I think O is fine. *((M and R laugh))*
             R.accept
             (2.0) pause 1

39 M: what school did you teach (.) at.
             I-SQ
             (2.0) pause 2
                                          ] Adj.P

40 FM: u:h (3.0) well it was HR most of the time and that's where they wanted me you know, (1.0) so that's where I was at HR.
             R.accept

41 R: *{pian.* mhm,*}* (5.0) pause 3 what kind of students do you teach.
                                    I-SQ

42 FM: huh?
             C-SQ+ TIB

43 R: what kinds of students to you teach. (2.0) the primary school or the middle school.
             I-SQ + Ro + repeat

44 FM: what.
             C-SQ + TIB

45 MH: what grades [do y- you* teach.
             Ro + repeat

46 R: [what grades* yea.
             Ro + repeat

47 FM: oh. that was uh uh. at school?
             Rs + C-SQ

48 MH/R: mhm,
             minimal response
             (2.5) pause 4

49 FM: m:: first (1.0) until (5.0) the seventh I believe.
             R. accept

50 R: from first grade to [seventh*?
             C-SQ

51 FM: [ye-* yes::.
             R.accept

The first two instances of turn-taking sequences in Example 5.11 are relatively ordered, with R asking I–SQs and FM responding appropriately. We noted above that pauses may indicate two types of potential trouble: the need for more time and the inability to formulate a response. The first example of a pause that we discuss here occurs at the end of turn 38 where there is a 2-s pause following FM's response to MH's I–SQ. In this case, FM has answered MH's question and given enough information (see chap. 6) to warrant relinquishing her turn, and therefore, she has selected one of the researchers as next speaker. This particular pause can be seen as being within R and MH's "conversational space," that is, it is reasonable to assume that as FM has fulfilled her conversational obligation, they are to be next speakers and therefore should select the next topic. In the case of the second pause following MH's next question (turn 39), which relates to FM's former position as a school teacher, the pause has shifted into FM's conversational space; it is she who should respond, and therefore, her delay could be seen as potential trouble spot where her interlocutors might feel obligated to fill the pause with a further I–SQ or elaboration of the question. On this occasion, however, the students allow FM time to respond, and given that there are two within-turn pauses in FM's response, it appears that Pause 2 is not indicative of communication breakdown but rather that FM needs more processing time to access the information to produce an acceptable response, which indeed she does on this occasion.

Pause 3 at the beginning of R's next I–SQ is similar to Pause 1; FM's response (turn 40) to MH's question asking at which school FM taught is adequate both in terms of quantity and relevance (see chap. 6). It may be that on these two occasions, the students felt they should allow FM time to elaborate if she wishes, but the pause itself again could be said to be in the turn space of the next speaker (either MH or R). The sequence starting from R's I–SQ (turn 41) is more problematic than the two exchanges discussed so far. First, we see an extended exchange sequence with potential trouble spots (turns 42 and 44) where FM does not appear to have understood R's questions. Both R and MH attempt to repair the conversation (turn 43, 45, and 46) and get the conversation back on topic. FM's further C–SQ (turn 47) appears to be a self-repair and suggests that although she has stayed on topic, she has either not fully comprehended the intended meaning of her interlocutors' questions or requires confirmation. Both F and MH use minimal responses to support FM's interpretation of the question, and again there is a long pause before FM responds with an appropriate response (turn 49). F and MH's minimal responses reflect that they have carried out their obligation in this turn-taking sequence and have handed the turn and conversational space over to FM. Again, we see two within-turn pauses (turn 49) in FM's on-target response, suggesting that many of the pauses in this conversation occur as a result of FM's need for processing time rather than confusion, that is, not understanding her interlocutor's illocutionary force (see chap. 6). Furthermore, if she were confused, we might expect off-topic responses.

In the case of within-turn pauses when FM starts talking again after a long pause, we may assume she owns that pause in that it is still her turn, or, to put it another way, her interlocutors treat the pause as belonging to her because they do not fill it.[3] In other words, they do not typically treat the long pauses as TIBs, nor indeed as TRPs. This brings us back to the issue of identifying trouble sources. Is trouble only trouble when it is treated that way collaboratively? We might also say that repair is only repair when it happens collaboratively. In the interaction between FM and the students (see Appendix F), pauses can be looked at in conjunction with topics: At times, there are abrupt topic shifts as in FM's favorite questions (see chap. 8), and they often follow a long pause. However, at other times, as was shown in Example 5.11 (turns 41–50), a topic is maintained and extended across long pauses. Therefore, we suggest that there may be multiple indicators for trouble; that is, pause + topic shift tells the researchers in hindsight that there was trouble, but MH and R did not do anything to repair the trouble, hence the need for FM to self-repair (turn 47). Thus, TIBs may be products of the analyst's perspective as opposed to the interlocutor's perspective. FM in these examples appears to use the pauses to scaffold herself into a response, and as shown above these pauses are not acting as TRPs. Rather, they might be seen as belonging to FM; they are silent reflections that she is indeed processing her conversational partners' questions.

CONCLUSION

Unlike speech act theory (see chap. 6), an approach to language that was developed within the philosophy of language, CA is a more rigorous methodological approach that is underpinned by the theory and philosophy of ethnomethodology. CA analysis examines everyday conversations at the local turn-by-turn level, and it is this attention to detail that has led to its methodology (if not philosophy) being adopted by many other fields, particularly in the field of clinical interaction studies. However, one of the weaknesses of CA is that, in its purest form, it does not allow the analyst to draw on any preassumptions about their participants, a task most of us would find impossible and indeed unproductive. Clinical researchers and clinicians, by the very nature of their work, must draw on prior experience with similar disorders to treat their clients. However, the requirement inherent in all ethnographic approaches, in ethnomethodology, and CA, to

---

[3]To some extent, what is within a turn or across a turn depends on the transcript. We could have put all the long pauses that occur at the end of clauses in between turns and transcribed FM's talk as though she was self-selecting for another turn. However, the substance of what is happening is the same, that is, R and MH do not treat the pauses as TIBs or TRPs.

step back from one's preconceived ideas of how an interaction is supposed to work and to deal with the data at hand in an open-minded fashion is, we find, a salutary experience for both researchers and clinical practitioners.

One of the strengths of CA is that it reveals organizational patterns in conversations involving clinical populations and considers the preferential structure of conversational moves, thereby showing the multiple layers of meaning that can be attached to what are typically considered "insignificant" phenomena such as pauses. CA encourages researchers to systematically examine their data to identify the ways in which people typically organize their talk in order to (a) participate in social interactions and (b) impart specific meanings that are recognized by their interlocutors. It is the systematicity of CA's approach that allows the researcher or clinician to (a) better understand her or his participant or client and (b) help in developing appropriate therapies.

6

Speaker's Meaning and Listener's Understanding: Cooperation and Doing Things With Words

INTRODUCTION

The question of how listeners know or work out what speakers mean or intend to convey is of course central to any consideration of human interaction. In this chapter, we discuss the application of two approaches that originate in the philosophy of language, namely, Grice's pragmatics of conversational cooperation and speech act theory (e.g., Grice, 1957, 1975; Searle, 1969, 1975, 1979). In many textbooks on discourse or pragmatics, these two approaches are explored in separate chapters. However, we find it useful to integrate them into one chapter, because both deal with fundamental principles of conversation, albeit from a theoretical-philosophical rather than an applied-practical stance. Neither approach was, in its origins, particularly concerned with the application of its theoretical principles to authentic, contextualized data. Rather, the philosophy of language being geared more toward the general principles of the human ability to use language as a symbolic system and the relationship between language use and formal logic, the classic writings in Gricean pragmatics, and speech act theory tend to use constructed examples within constructed contexts to illustrate points of theory. Therein lies a potential problem in applying the constructs thus arrived at as a tool to analyze conversational interaction and particularly clinical data, and we return to this issue in our data analysis later in this chapter (see also Schiffrin, 1994, pp. 61 and following, 203–204).

GRICEAN PRAGMATICS AND THE PHILOSOPHY OF CONVERSATIONAL COOPERATION

The problematicity in defining the term *pragmatics* has been much discussed in the relevant literature (see, e.g., Grundy, 1995; Levinson, 1983; and Schiffrin, 1994, chap. 6 for summaries). We do not add to this literature here, but, for the purposes of this chapter, we maintain a distinction that is common to most definitions of pragmatics as opposed to semantics and syntax: Central to pragmatics, or pragmatic problems and their solutions, are a language user's intentions in using language as a tool to create meaning as opposed to the structural properties of conventional linguistic meaning (semantics) and the combinatory possibilities (syntax) afforded by the language system.

Grice's (1957) essay on "Meaning" divided the complex of meaning into two distinct categories: natural and nonnatural meaning, the former being the meaning inherent in naturally occurring events, whereas the latter pertains to deliberate human acts including the use of language. An example of natural meaning, the meaning inherent in an event that does not involve the human intention of expressing meaning is the sound of a ticking clock: The ticking sound I hear means that there is a clock and that it is working. Nonnatural meaning falls into two categories (discussed in more detail in Clark, 1996, p. 126ff): speaker's (or utterer's) meaning and what Clark (1996) calls signal meaning including, for example, the conventional meanings of words or gestures.[1] Crucial for speaker meaning is that a listener needs to recognize the particular meaning in the way in which it was intended by a speaker. Schiffrin (1994, p. 192), following Strawson (1964), lists three intentions that are necessary for a speaker to mean something by an utterance: (a) the speaker must intend to produce a certain response in a certain audience; (b) the audience needs to recognize the speaker's intention in (a); and (c) the audience needs to recognize the speaker's intention in (a) as functioning as at least part of the reason for their response to the speaker's utterance. Thus, in Example 6.1 below, N's intention in making her utterance was that M should respond with the infor-

---

[1]The term *conventional*, used in the context of word meaning, in itself encapsulates the fact that typically, there is no natural convention between the sound sequence that makes up a word in any given language and the meaning evoked by its utterance. Thus, the class of items labeled *chair* in English carries the labels *Stuhl, chaise,* and *cathair* in German, French, and Irish, respectively.

mation requested. M recognized this intention and did indeed treat N's utterance as a request for information, and his reason for offering his response was compliance with N's request to the best of his abilities at the time.

Having defined speaker meaning, we need to ask how speaker meaning relates to the conventional meaning of words, phrases, and sentences or indeed, to nonverbal means of communication. How do speakers work out what is meant from what is said, if that is indeed what we do?

The Cooperative Principle, and Conversational Maxims

In a paper entitled "Logic and Conversation," Grice (1975) states the following:

> Our talk exchanges do not normally consist of disconnected remarks, and would not be rational if they did. They are characteristically, to some degree at least, cooperative efforts; and each participant recognizes in them, to some extent, a common purpose or set of purposes, or at least a mutually accepted direction. The purpose or direction may be fixed from the start … or it may evolve during the exchange; it may be fairly definite, or it may be so indefinite as to leave very considerable latitude to the participants (as in a casual conversation). But at each stage, some possible conversational moves would be excluded as conversationally unsuitable. (p. 45)

Grice (1975) argued that participants in conversations act and expect each other to act according to a general cooperative principle and offered what Clark (1996, p. 142) calls "four rules of thumb" that allow the participants to work out what is meant by what is said and more specifically, to calculate implicatures, that is, meanings that are intended but not part of the conventional meanings of the words of the utterance and therefore are not expressed explicitly (more of which below). *"The cooperative principle:* Make your conversational contribution such as is required, at the stage at which it occurs, by the accepted purpose or direction of the talk exchange in which you are engaged" (Grice, 1975, p. 45). The four maxims are

Quantity:

1. Make your contribution as informative as required (for the current purposes of the exchange).
2. Do not make your contribution more informative than is required.

Quality:

1. Do not say what you believe to be false.
2. Do not say that for which you lack evidence.

Relation: Be relevant.

Manner: Be perspicuous.

1. Avoid obscurity of expression.
2. Avoid ambiguity.
3. Be brief (avoid unnecessary prolixity).
4. Be orderly.

Grice's formulation of his cooperative principle and maxims as exhortations may be confusing for students at times. It may be more helpful to think of these maxims as principles of behavior that people tacitly take for granted in conversations given their cooperative nature.

The cooperative principle and the maxims of conversation outlined by Grice, can serve as a basis for hearers to calculate conversational implicatures. Following Grice (1975, p. 50), Schiffrin (1994) summarized the information used by hearers to calculate implicatures as follows:

1. The conventional meanings of the words used, together with the identity of any references that may be involved.
2. The Cooperative Principle and its maxims.
3. The context, linguistic or otherwise, of the utterance.
4. Other items of background knowledge.
5. The fact (or supposed fact) that all relevant items falling under the previous headings are available to both participants and both participants know or assume this to be the case. (p. 195)

Implicature can be arrived at in several ways. The first is by interpreting an utterance in light of adherence to the maxims. Thus, an utterance involving the coordinating conjunction *and* to join two clauses typically gives rise to the implicature "in that order" as in, for example, "He made coffee and prepared sandwiches." The implicature "in that order" can be inferred by way of the maxim of manner (the order in which the two events are presented permits the inference that this is the order in which the events took place) and quantity (because the order of the events can be inferred from the order of their presentation, it is not necessary to explicitly state the sequence; see also Grundy, 1995, p. 37ff; Schiffrin, 1994, p. 195f). A second constellation giving rise to implicatures is one in which maxims are apparently at odds with each other (see Grice, 1975, p. 51f). Consider the following exchange, part of an early-morning conversation in N. Müller's household:

Example 6.1

N(shouting from the back of the house):   What's the time?

M (N's husband)
(coming back into the house via the back door):   The schoolbus just went by.

There is no reason to assume that M is being uncooperative. He knows that his contribution is less than maximally informative, but the information given is the best he can offer at the time of utterance. Background knowledge accessible to both M and N includes the regular pattern of the schoolbus driving past the house between 7:00 and 7:15 in the morning, thus offering an approximation of the time. Even though M's response is less than ideally informative, it conforms to the maxim of relevance (the regular appearance of the schoolbus giving a clue to the approximate time) and quality (hazarding a guess at the time would have been possible, but having seen the schoolbus is more solid, experiential evidence).

A further source of implicatures is provided by a speaker's deliberately flouting them. The following example, from a conversation with between F and J, can be read in this way:

Example 6.2 (see Appendix C)

115 F   yeah it makes you dry and (.) me lips dry (2.0) but ə (.) we never go out of this ↓room.
116 J   m:,
117 F   not even for half an hour or hop or skip about ə,
118 J   *((laughs))* {LV can you hop or skip about? }
119 F   well I would {LV try if I (ever felt like it.)}

F's contribution in turn 115, after the 2-s pause, can be interpreted in light of dementia, that is, as an instance of forgetting that she does indeed leave her room regularly, together with J or nursing home staff, or deliberately flouting the maxim of quality in a hyperbolic statement that underlines her desire to be out and about more and to be taken for walks (to which the conversation returns at a later stage). This interpretation can be carried into turn 117 where "not even for half an hour" continues the hyperbole of "never," and "hop or skip about" is clearly at odds with F's abilities, who is wheelchair bound. When J laughingly challenges this latter notion, F joins in the good humor. Thus, this seems to be an example of cooperatively flouting maxims, and this is of course an integral part of many normal conversations and has a variety of functions, for example, as face-saving devices (see chap. 4), to add humor, and so forth.

Problems in a hearer's interpretation of a speaker's meaning can at times be interpreted in light of a speaker unintentionally violating one or more maxims as in Example 6.3.

Example 6.3 (see Appendix D)

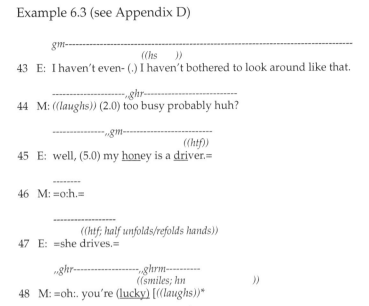

```
     gm----------------------------------------------------------------------------------
                       ((hs   ))
43  E:  I haven't even- (.) I haven't bothered to look around like that.


     ---------------------,,ghr--------------------------
44  M:  ((laughs)) (2.0) too busy probably huh?


     ----------------,,gm--------------------------
                         ((htf))
45  E:  well, (5.0) my honey is a driver.=


     --------
46  M:  =o:h.=


     ------------------
                  ((htf; half unfolds/refolds hands))
47  E:  =she drives.=


     ,,ghr-------------------,,ghrm----------
                    ((smiles; hn                         ))
48  M:  =oh:. you're (lucky) [((laughs))]*
```

In turn 45, E apparently shifts topics, away from discussing the city E used to work in, specifically, driving in it, and the difficulties of finding one's way to E's wife who has been the topic of conversation before. M's noncommittal "o:h" in turn 46 indicates that she has trouble constructing his meaning here, and E has to elaborate "she drives" before M understands E's intended meaning: His wife drives rather than E himself (and therefore, E has limited experience of getting lost while driving). E's turn 46 is intended as a further comment on the topic of driving rather than a topic shift. M's misinterpretation can be read as E unintentionally violating the maxim of manner: Both the prosody (marked stress on the initial syllable of both "honey" and "driver") and the grammatical structure (choice of "honey" as subject and use of the indefinite article with "driver") favor the treatment of "honey" as topic and "a driver" as new information and as a comment on the new topic. The long pause (5 s) following the discourse marker "well" does not help M with E's meaning because elsewhere in the conversation, both occur with new topics and with further elaborations on established topics. Similarly, E's nonverbal behaviors do not furnish an unambiguous clue either.

Potential Problems With the Cooperative Principle, Implicature, and Calculating What Is Meant From What Is Said

Clark (1996, p. 143f) views Grice's scheme for calculating implicature as problematic because of three underlying assumptions, namely, according to Clark

1. What is said is logically prior to what is implicated.
2. The way listeners determine what is said is different in principle from the way they "work out" what is implicated.
3. What is said is well defined for every type of utterance.

Assumption 1 encounters problems with homonyms or polysemous expressions for which hearers need to work out what is said, that is, which of several meanings was intended on the basis of what may have been implicated. Consider the following example as an illustration for a difficulty arising out of Assumption 2. When a student saw one of us make notes in mirror writing, using her left hand, he commented "That's very Da Vinci of you." Clark's argument here would be that the listener cannot work out what is meant from what is said because the literal meaning of "Da Vinci" (the name of a 15th- and 16th-century Italian painter, sculptor, architect, inventor, and scientist) does not fit the sentence, which would require some sort of an adjective or adjectival phrase in this position. Indeed, it is the violation of this requirement that allows the listener to work out what was meant, namely, that the student was alluding not to the person named but a quality of his: the fact that being left-handed, he used to make notes in mirror writing. Therefore, it would appear that a hearer needs to essentially use the same principles to work out what is actually said as in working out an implicature. Assumption 3 is problematic in terms of everyday communication because, as Clark (1996, p. 145f) points out, there are many commonly used words and expressions that do not have clearly defined meanings. This is especially true for expressions like "ah" (one of Clark's examples and defined in the *Oxford English Dictionary* (Brown, 1993) as an expression of "sorrow, regret, entreaty, remonstrance; surprise, pleasure, admiration; realization, discovery; dislike, boredom, contempt, mockery" (p. 43). Clearly, what is meant by a simple utterance of "ah!" depends in large measure on what is implicated rather than what is said, the latter being potentially wide open. We do not follow Clark's (1996) discussion of Grice and the cooperative principle any further at this stage. Suffice it to say that a close examination of the cooperative principle and the four maxims in light of real, authentic, conversational data will run into problems of definition and interpretation. Clark (1996, p. 146) describes the four maxims as rules of thumb, and this is a useful characterization to keep in mind. The origin of Gricean pragmatics being in philosophy, they were not developed as a ready-made tool for the analysis of authentic conversation. Such tools have been developed on the basis of Grice's writings, but a discussion would lead us too far afield here (see also Schiffrin, 1994, p. 203ff, on necessary methodological adjustments in using Grice's framework as applied to spoken discourse).

SPEECH ACTS: DOING THINGS WITH UTTERANCES

How to do things with words is the title of a collection of papers by John Austin (1962, 1967) originally delivered as a series of lectures in 1957 that forms the basis of a long discussion in the philosophy of language in pragmatics and in various subdisciplines of linguistics concerning what people do when they use utterances. The term speech act is commonly used for such an action. In this section, then, we discuss speech acts and how they have been defined and classified, which is yet another facet of the complex relationship between what is said (and how it is said) and what is meant or understood.

Speech act theory is thus concerned with the performative aspects of language use, the completing of actions accomplished through using language. Many utterances contain verbs that are easily recognized as completing actions by being uttered. Austin (1962) suggested a distinction between *performative* utterances and *constative* utterances. The former type contains a verb that names the act carried out by the utterance, whereas the latter type does not. A few examples are listed in Example 6.4; the performative verbs are underlined:

Example 6.4

I <u>promise</u> I'll cook dinner tonight I'll cook dinner tonight

I <u>order</u> you to wash the dishes. You have to wash the dishes.

I <u>apologize</u> for being late. I'm really sorry I'm late.

The distinction between constative and performative utterances is not unproblematic (see Searle, 1969, 1975) because the sentences in the right-hand column of Example 6.4 can be interpreted as performing the same acts as those in the left-hand column. Thus, a distinction on the basis of an utterance containing a performative verb does not help one work out how a listener arrives at the interpretation of a promise, an order, or an apology, respectively, for the utterances in the right-hand column of Example 6.4 as opposed to descriptions of states of affairs.

Describing and Analyzing Speech Acts

Austin (1962) proposed a three-way distinction for the discussion of speech acts between locutionary acts, illocutionary acts, and perlocutions. The *locutionary act* is a speaker's uttering words with determinate sense, that is, with unambiguous meaning, and reference.[2] The *illocution* or *illocutionary act* is the act carried out by the speaker uttering the locution. A crucial ele-

---

[2] This in itself is not unproblematic when applied to real language use. See the discussion in Clark (1996) on words without clearly defined meaning; also see our examples.

ment in this is the *illocutionary effect* (Searle, 1969), the listener's recognition of the speaker's meaning or intention. The effect that the utterance has on the listener or audience is called the *perlocution*. Thus, a sentence such as "The cat is in the kitchen" can describe a state of affairs. We can assign a truth value to the proposition expressed in this sentence; in this case, it will be true if and only if a previously identified or clearly identifiable domestic feline does indeed occupy the room typically used for preparing meals at the present time. Truth value of propositions is one source of meaning, which we distinguish from the effect, or force, of an utterance as a source of meaning. To illustrate, the utterance of the sentence "the cat's in the kitchen" can be intended as a warning not to leave the kitchen door open lest said feline escape. In this case, the illocutionary act would be that of a warning. The perlocution maps onto the illocutionary act if the addressee recognizes the speaker's intention and does indeed make sure that the cat remains where it is. This brings up another distinction, namely, between the truth and falsity of sentences and the felicity of utterances. Grundy (1995, p. 91) gives the example of John F. Kennedy's famous utterance "ich bin ein Berliner." While the sentence was not true,[3] it was felicitous as an expression of solidarity or a reassurance. The notion of felicity or *felicity conditions* for an illocutionary act is meant to account for the conditions under which an illocutionary act can be successful. As Austin (1962) noted, certain conditions have to be met for illocutionary acts to lead to the desired perlocution. For example, a bet can only work if the addressee accepts the bet: in Austin's (1962) words, if there is uptake (see Clark, 1996, for further discussion of the role of the addressee).[4]

Classifying Illocutionary Acts

Searle (1979) argues that illocutionary acts can be classified into five major categories most importantly distinguished by what he calls their illocutionary point, the purpose of the illocutionary act, which differs in part from the illocutionary force. Thus, the illocutionary point of a request is the same as that of a command because both are attempts to get the addressee to do something, but the illocutionary forces are different (Searle,

---

[3]Nor was it, strictly speaking, grammatical for the intended proposition equivalent to "I am a Berliner." However, truth value or grammatical structure were of secondary importance as sources of meaning here as compared to the intended effect of the utterance.

[4]Searle (1969, 1979) proposes a detailed classification of felicity conditions that we do not go into here. As Levinson (1983, p. 240ff) points out, its role in the classification of illocutionary acts is not as principled as Searle (1979) claims, and it is more plausible that "given Searle's essential condition [that locution X counts as illocutionary act Y], which generally states the relevant intention, the felicity conditions of each of the major illocutionary acts will be predictable from general considerations of rationality and cooperation of the sort represented by Grice's maxims" (Levinson, 1983, p. 241). A paragraph later, Levinson goes on to state, "However, it can be argued that the enthusiasm for this kind of classificatory exercise is in general misplaced" (p. 241).

1979, p. 3). To illustrate, whereas a command has an element of obligation or compulsion on the part of the addressee, a request does not. Searle's original classification has been variously modified and developed (see, e.g., Bach & Harnisch, 1979; Hancher, 1979; Levinson, 1983; Clark, 1996). The following classification is based on Clark (1996, p. 134).

Types of illocutionary acts:

1. Assertives
Illocutionary point: To get the hearer to form, or to attend to, the belief that the speaker is committed to a certain belief.
Thus, the point in a meteorologist's prediction that "there will be a 30% chance of rain tomorrow" is to get her audience to believe that she is committed to the belief that this is indeed the case.

2. Directives
Illocutionary point: To get the hearer to do something.
Subclasses: Requests for action and requests for information.
Thus, the point in N's utterance "what's the time" in Example 6.1 is to get M to provide the information requested.

3. Commissives
Illocutionary point: To commit the speaker to a future action.
Thus, "I'll cook dinner tonight" counts as a commitment by the speaker to prepare the evening meal.

4. Expressives
Illocutionary point: To express certain feelings toward the audience.
Thus, the point of "Thank you so much for a wonderful time," when uttered by a guest to a host after a particularly successful meal, expresses the guest's gratitude toward the host. We may note at this point that many expressions of thanking, apologizing, greeting, congratulating, and the like are of course highly conventionalized and may not express sincere feelings but rather the sentiment demanded by the communicative occasion.

5. Declarations: Effectives and Verdictives
Illocutionary point of effectives: To change an institutional state of affairs. A speaker, having certain specific, codified powers according to institutional conventions, may change a state of affairs within that institution by means of an effective. This also often involves fixed linguistic formulations. Thus, within the institution of a court of law, a judge may sentence someone; within the institution of a church, a priest or minister may baptize someone.

Illocutionary point of verdictives: To determine what is to be the case within the institution.
A cricket umpire's declaration determines whether a bowler is "out"; a jury's declaration determines that for the purposes of the institution, a person is guilty or innocent.

Although it is generally desirable in any approach to description or analysis of language use to have a classificatory scheme that limits the possible subcategories to a manageable number, the classification of illocutionary acts into these five major categories is not without problems. One objection that has been voiced is that this scheme does not account for all possible illocutionary acts. For our purposes, more important though is that Searle's classification and its various descendants imply that each illocutionary act belongs to only one category (see Clark, 1996; Levinson, 1983; and Schiffrin, 1994, for discussion). This brings our discussion back to a potential danger in applying speech act theory, with its original home in the abstractions of the philosophy of language, to contextualized human communication, a point raised by Schiffrin (1994). As we show below, the classification of an utterance as belonging to a particular class of illocutionary acts (and to only one) does not necessarily capture its force (or function) in the context of the conversation as a whole-which, as mentioned previously, is not the originally intended use of the taxonomies developed by Searle (and others). However, as Clark (1996, p. 136) noted, Searle's scheme is useful as a rough classification and also because its terminology and definitions (with minor variations) have wide currency in the relevant literature.

Direct and Indirect Speech Acts

Searle (1975) defines an indirect speech act as a case "in which one illocutionary act is performed indirectly by way of performing another" (p. 60). To illustrate, a request for information can be used and understood as a command: A speaker saying "Can you get the groceries from the car?" can perform the same action as in saying "Get the groceries from the car."[5] Although this seems quite straightforward from the point of view of day-to-day language use, there is the question how both speakers and listeners know when the indirect illocutionary act, as opposed to the direct one, is foregrounded. One way of approaching indirect speech acts is by way of implicature. Hearing an interrogative structure such as "can you get the groceries from the car?" used by a speaker, a hearer can calculate the implicature that what the speaker is doing is in fact giving an indirect command along the lines of:

---

[5]See Levinson (1983, p. 264f) for a discussion of direct versus indirect requests.

The speaker knows that I, the hearer, am capable of getting the groceries (hence, asking for that information violates the cooperative principle); I'm standing around the kitchen doing nothing while the speaker has two hands full; and so forth. Therefore, I calculate the implicature that the speaker's intended act is the command for me to fetch the groceries and act accordingly.

Another way to formulate the process of deciding which illocutionary act to foreground is by making reference to the felicity conditions for each act. "Can you get the groceries?" could be a request for information, but it violates a key felicity condition for such a request, namely, that the speaker does not already have the information requested. On the other hand, for the utterance to function as a command, relevant felicity conditions must be met, and one or more must be made explicit in the speaker's utterance. Among the felicity conditions for a request for action are that the speaker must be in a position to direct the hearer's action; that the speaker wants the hearer to carry out the action requested, and that the hearer believes the speaker can carry out the requested act. Thus, by way of questioning the latter condition, a speaker can indirectly perform the request for action.[6]

APPLICATIONS: GRICE'S COOPERATIVE PRINCIPLE AND MAXIMS AND SPEECH ACT THEORY IN DEMENTIA

Language users' intentions and goals are central concerns in pragmatics. As we saw above, speakers' intentions are clearly foregrounded in speech act theory and are the chief criterion in classifying them. The notion of speaker's intention or communicative intent is not unproblematic in the presence of dementia. Reconstructions of how a hearer calculates implicature or works out a speaker's communicative intent imply that first of all, there is communicative intent, and second, that such a reconstruction is in fact possible. Although we can (probably) take this for granted in a so-called normal interaction, the presence of a progressive brain pathology that gradually undermines and eventually destroys former cognitive and communicative skills means that from time to time, we need to question these implications. The question of whether there is always an identifiable communicative intention in the utterances of persons with AD, especially

---

[6]Peccei (1999) offers a summary of speech act theory (as well as of other issues in pragmatics) that is suitable for complete beginners. See Searle (1975) for a much more detailed treatment of indirect speech acts and Levinson (1983) and Grundy (1995) for a discussion of various theoretical approaches to direct and indirect speech acts.

at the later stages, cannot be answered satisfactorily at this stage, although it appears that in the earlier stages of the disease, accountable communicative intention is preserved (see Berrewaerts et al., 2003, for discussion of relevant research). It is also important to note that communicative intentions are not necessarily as one-dimensional as a categorization according to illocutionary act may tempt one to suppose, and even the identification of illocutionary acts can be less straightforward than our (constructed) examples may lead one to believe.

The classical formulation of the cooperative principle also greatly foregrounds the speaker as opposed to the listener, and it can be argued that Grice's (1975) formulation of the maxims as exhortations to the speaker in fact masks a large part of the principle he develops, that is, the actual cooperative nature of interaction.[7] The notion of speakers following, accidentally violating or deliberately flouting maxims again rests on the assumption of normal interaction. Further, it rests on the assumption that a common purpose of the interaction can be identified. Both these assumptions will meet with serious challenges in the presence of dementia. Equally important, we need to keep in mind that one person alone cannot be cooperative. What is cooperative or not always depends on the interlocutors' behaviors and states of mind. As we show, what may appear to be a face-value violation of the cooperative principle appears in a different light altogether given the right combination of background knowledge and awareness.

Grice's cooperative principle is used implicitly more often than explicitly in the analysis of dementia discourse.[8] As we discussed in chapter 1, there is ample work that discusses communicative effectiveness in terms of the amount of information conveyed relative to the amount of language used. The notions of verbosity on one hand and muteness or noncommunicativeness on the other have also already been discussed (see again chap. 1). In some studies, Grice's maxims are explicitly referred to in a way that seems to suggest (possibly unintentionally) a psychological reality for the maxims (see, e.g., Garcia & Joanette, 1994).[9] Illocutionary acts have been variously used as analytic parameters in the literature.

---

[7]See Clark (1996) for a critique of foregrounding the speaker's contribution to the near exclusion of the listener's actions, specifically, in Gricean pragmatics and speech act theory.

[8]However, see, for example, Linscott, Knight, and Godfrey (1996), and Hays, Niven, Godfrey, and Linscott (2004) for a "context-free" assessment of communicative interaction based on Grice's maxims and its application to AD. There are other assessments that have used Grice's maxims and/or speech act classifications as their starting point (see, e.g., Damico, 1985, 1992); however, because their purpose is a profile of behaviors according to a given set of criteria, we do not discuss them any further here.

[9]"Topic shading may signal that speakers are aware of the maxims of conversation and have chosen to simply notify their partners that they will violate the maxim of relevance" (Garcia & Joanette, 1994, p. 174).

Thus, Ripich, Vertes, Whitehouse, Fulton, and Ekelman (1991) found that persons with DAT use fewer assertives than normally aging controls but more requestives. The classifications used are from Dore (1979); *requestives* roughly correspond to directives; *assertives,* in Dore's terminology, roughly correspond to a subgroup of Searle's (1969) assertives. Hamilton (1994b) focuses on different subtypes of requests for clarification in a longitudinal study to map increasing comprehension difficulties. Causino Lamar, Obler, Knoefel and Albert (1994) include directives and responses to directives, comments and representatives, and expressives and commissives in a series of 13 pragmatic parameters in their investigation. The multiplicity of taxonomies of illocutionary acts available in the literature is on one hand not very satisfactory for a researcher looking for an analytic framework. On the other hand, it points to the fact that available taxonomies are not necessarily satisfactory in all respects, which in turn may indicate that imposing a categorization on the data may be less fruitful than letting a classification emerge.

This last point brings us back to a central concern of qualitative research, namely, the general reluctance in qualitative approaches to use prefabricated taxonomies or categorizations of behaviors and their underlying motivations. It is of course impossible to approach one's data without any expectations whatsoever-after all, any research question embeds in itself at least the assumption that there are patterns worth investigating in a given body of data. When we draw on speech act theory or the cooperative principle to analyze conversational data, we need to be aware that we are projecting a whole edifice of assumptions and categorizations onto our data, and it may be necessary from time to time to step back and reflect on this circumstance.

Illocutionary Acts and Grice's Maxims: Labeling Intentions and Efficiency of Their Expression

As mentioned earlier, the application of speech act theory and of Grice's maxims to continuous conversational data require some methodological adjustments (see also Schiffrin, 1994). The unit of description in speech act theory is, by implication and definition, a sentence used as an utterance: hence, the necessity to distinguish between sentence meaning and utterance meaning, for example. However, conversations contain many utterances that do not consist of sentences. A speaker's turn may consist of a word, a phrase, an incomplete sentence, several sentences, or indeed a vocalization that is not a word (consider for example someone giving vent to pain after stubbing a toe). In CA, typically the unit of analysis tends to be a speaker's turn. This, however, is not necessarily the best unit for an analysis of, for example, illocutionary acts, because extended turns may contain multiple illocutionary acts. Furthermore, a sentence is in itself an ambiguous label. Speech act theory appears to imply a definition of a sentence as that of a main clause (i.e., a verb, or predicate, with its necessary arguments). However, the implied notion of utterances as spoken sentences raises another question. Should units below the sentence level, for example, single-word utterances, be examined in terms of illocutionary acts (see, e.g., Clark 1996)? This is what we have done here, presupposing that speakers do things with utterances below sentence length. As we will show, however, it is not always straightforward to assign illocutionary acts to short utterances.

In essence, labeling illocutionary acts attempts to capture the speaker's intention in making an utterance. This intention can be quite different from the actual effect or perlocution of the utterance. How, then, can one capture the underlying intention, especially in cases in which there appears to be a miscommunication (i.e., a mismatch with a perlocution)? It is important to keep in mind that in labeling, one is at least in part imposing the analyst's perspective and perceptions onto the data; in other words, one is labeling what the analyst thinks the speaker's intention is. Similarly, labeling utterances for violations of Grice's maxims makes a judgment based on the analyst's reconstruction of a speaker's efficiency of expression as formulated according to the maxims and as reflected (at least in part) by the hearer's reaction.

The Data

Our data in this chapter are from a conversation between F and J; the setting is F's room in the nursing home. By the time this conversation was recorded, J had become a regular visitor of F's, typically seeing her once a week for several hours. We do not offer a turn-by-turn analysis here but restrict our discussion to some of the patterns that emerge from the data, specifically, with regard to J's use of questions.

Example 6.5 illustrates the use of a multitiered transcript layout incorporating two separate lines for discourse categories (see also chap. 2). The line labeled "CP" (for cooperative principle) contains information concerning violations of Grice's maxims abbreviated as follows: M = manner; R = relevance; Ql = quality; Qn = quantity; * = maxim violation; bold characters = flouting of a maxim. Illocutionary acts are marked on the line labeled "IA" abbreviated as follows: Q = Question (request for information); Q–Rp = a repeated question; R–Cl = request for clarification (only questions and other requests are included). Note also that both discourse lines include indications of analyst's doubt marked by "?":

Example 6.5 (see Appendix C)

9   F: (xxxxxx) (they don't-) they don't change their ([ʃoː]) for this (you know,)

    IA

    CP   *M   ?*M/*R

                (2.0) (xxx)=

    IA

    CP   *M

10   J: =did you have a good Christmas?

    IA   Q

    CP

11   F: pardon?

    IA   R-Cl

    CP

12   J: did you have a good Christmas?

    IA   Q-Rp

    CP

13   F: *((sniffs))* ([wi.aʊtʃɑd])

    IA

    CP   *M

14   J: m?

    IA   ?R-Cl

    CP

15   F: (what we- what were [(xx)*

    IA   ?R-Cl

    CP   *M

16   J: *{lento*[did you* have a good <u>Chris</u>tmas.*}*

    IA   Q-Rp

    CP

17   F: well. (.) alright,=

    IA

    CP   ?*Qn

18   J: =it was alright.=

    IA   ?R-Cf/El

    CP

19		F:	= m:, (.) didn't (x) do {LV anything, (xx)}=	
	IA			
	CP			*M

20		J:	=did you get any presents?	
	IA		Q	
			(4.0)	
21		F:	↓no::. (we've- we're just left here dead,)=	
	IA			
	CP		*M	**Ql**

"Who's Asking the Questions Here?"   Even a casual read through of the transcript throws up a distinctive distributional pattern: J asks the question in this conversation; that is, requests for information come from J rather than F. Consider Example 6.5: J asks the first question (turn 10) after an utterance of F's that is partly unintelligible and does not appear to relate to what has come before. In terms of the cooperative principle, we note that the maxims of manner and relevance have been violated here. F responds with a general request for clarification, whereupon J repeats her question and receives another unintelligible utterance in response. We have tentatively labeled J's "m?" in turn 14 and F's turn 15 as requests for clarification; note that F appears to be struggling to formulate her utterance, and J cuts the struggle short by another repetition of her question. F's response is clear and intelligible but could be described as a violation of the maxim of quantity because she only imparts minimal information. J's turn 18 appears to serve as a request, too, but for confirmation and indeed elaboration rather than clarification of an unintelligible utterance. F's attempt to elaborate is unsuccessful and in turn prompts another question from J, which in itself represents an elaboration of the original question "did you have a good Christmas." F's response contains a disfluency and can again be described as violating the principle of manner, but maybe more interestingly, we can also read "we're just left here dead" as a deliberate flout of the maxim of quality in the form of hyperbole (see also Example 6.2 above), permitting J to calculate the implicature on the basis of her knowledge that F has had several groups of visitors over the Christmas period (which is also made explicit later in the conversation) and did indeed receive presents; she appears to be less than happy with being in the nursing home (see also turns 27–39, 101–103, Appendix C).

We see a pattern in this conversation whereby J uses questions-that is, requests for information that has not been established previously in the conversation-when F runs into serious difficulty formulating an utterance, often an attempt to elaborate on a previous topic. Example 6.5 illustrates a scaffolding of a response by means of repeating the same question. In other instances, J uses questions as a means of topic shifting when F's difficulties in formulating an utterance appear to become unsurmountable. In terms of perlocutions mapping onto illocutions, it is interesting that a question representing a topic shift to a related topic is not necessary successful as in turn 40 (J requesting F's brother's name) or turn 42 (asking where he lives). In the latter case, even an attempted scaffolding process that moves from an open question ("where does your brother live") to two successive yes–no questions (turns 44–46) does not achieve the expected perlocution (but see turns 58–59 and 64–65 for examples in which such questions are successful in terms of achieving the intended perlocutions). On the other hand, questions that elicit information about unrelated topics can be successful as illustrated in turns 51 to 55. In this particular instance, J's question shifts the topic to the here and now, and once she elaborates on her question and a tangible anchor for the question "what've you done to your leg" is established (a bruise), F's response is fluent and clear, relevant, true (to the best of our knowledge), and sufficient.

A quantification of illocutionary acts on the part of J and F would reveal what would appear like a strong imbalance in that J asks the questions whereas F responds, often violating the cooperative principle in doing so-particularly the maxim of manner-and struggles to elaborate on responses, in other words, to make assertions. Many of these unsuccessful assertions are met with new questions, sometimes on unrelated topics. Thus, the picture that would emerge from a counting of illocutionary acts is one of a rather unsuccessful interaction in terms of perlocutions matching illocutions. However, we see that this conversation continues for almost 250 turns without either participant becoming audibly irritated or unresponsive. Therefore, we need to ask whether there is a mismatch between a first picture emerging from a classification of illocutionary acts and their success or lack thereof and the roles or functions they fulfill in the conversation as a whole beyond the relevant turn exchanges.

Face-Value Illocutionary Acts and "Structural" Acts.   Schiffrin (1994) discusses the multifunctionality of utterances in terms of illocutionary acts in some detail and illustrates how a question can simultaneously fulfill the functions of question, offer, and request. Our concern here is not so much with multiple illocutionary acts, nor are we going to discuss the (justifiable) question of whether all J's questions in her conversation with F fulfill the felicity conditions for questions (particularly the condition that the person asking does not already have the information requested). Rather, we are more interested in the differences and interactions between what we call face-value acts and structural acts. Speech act theory is, as we have explored already, concerned with what people do when they use utterances: They request information or action, they make assertions, and so forth. However, at the same time, they are having a conversation. One might object that the conversation is the vehicle for these illocutionary acts pure and simple, but this appears to be too simplistic and one-dimensional, especially in view of the fact that the conversation continues, even though a large proportion of illocutionary acts could be classified as unsuccessful as measured by matching illocutions and perlocutions. What, then, are the structural acts represented by successful and unsuccessful questions alike? J's requests for information and the frequent topic shifts they represent have an important structural function in this conversation (and in others with F), namely, that of conversation continuers that require (and generally receive) a response. This may seem too obvious to merit mention or analysis, but consider that we are dealing with a context in which dementia looms large but in which one-on-one interaction is desirable for its own sake. In such a context, structural acts can (and in this case do) gain the upper hand, and the success or otherwise of face value illocutionary acts can be seen in a different light such that F's generally intact turn-taking abilities (see also chap. 5) allows the conversation to continue, even if a response to a question is not sufficiently cooperative in the Gricean sense.[10]

There are other illocutionary acts that have a similar structural function as J's questions. For instance, example 6.5 contains several requests for clarification and what we have tentatively labeled a request for confirmation and elaboration (R–Cf/E; turn 18), which does indeed have the effect to scaffold a further relevant (if not entirely clear and somewhat vague) response. Furthermore, J uses many unspecific, minimal turns that can be interpreted as requests to continue; some of them also function as requests for clarification (see, e.g., turns 22, 24, 30, 34, etc., Appendix C).[11]

Very occasionally, F uses questions herself. The example in turn 219 (Example 6.6) looks, on the face of it, like a very abrupt, unflagged topic shift to an unrelated topic. However, coming after a 5-s pause, it can also be interpreted as an attempt, in this case successful, to keep the conversation afloat (see also chap. 5, on topic management from a CA perspective)

Example 6.6 (see Appendix C)

```
      (5.0)
219 F   and what about my poem. has it come to a stop or (xx soon xx).
220 R   ↓o:h it's still going,
      (2.5)
221 F   {LV am I in?}
222 R   yes, (3.0) do you like poetry.
```

[10]See also chapter 9 in which we discuss the repetitive use of questions by a participant with dementia. Her questions have a very similar function to J's.

[11]Rather than being "backchannel" behaviors that are typically defined as minimal utterances that do not interrupt the flow of an interlocutor's utterance, these minimal utterances attempt to establish a flow by inviting the conversation partner to continue to talk.

(2.0)

223 F   (there's some kind of) pieces I ↓li:ke but, *((coughs))* I don't seem to be
        interested in any(thing) lately.

Levels of Cooperativeness: Maxims and Beyond

F's question in turn 219 (see Example 6.6) looks, on the face of it, like a violation of the maxim of relevance: Thus far, neither participant has been talking
about poetry. However, J treats the term *poem* as a semantic paraphasia for
"book, a piece of writing," drawing on well-established joint background
knowledge that includes several previous discussions of and F's lively interest in J's writings about older people living in nursing homes and their life
stories. J's awareness not only of this joint knowledge but her alertness to
possible paraphasias and other communicative sequelae of AD means that
she can quite easily compensate in this case. This is also an illustration that
cooperation needs to be arrived at in a truly cooperative fashion in the context of dementia (and other impairments). What looks like an irrelevant contribution is in fact very relevant (albeit formulated with a paraphasia) in the
context of a casual conversation in which topic shifts to well-established,
shared knowledge are acceptable and, as here, are a productive way of keeping the conversation afloat. Thus, what we have here is not a problem with
the maxim of relation on the part of the speaker but a problem with word
finding, which puts additional demands on the listener.

   If we were to label F's contributions to the conversation according to violations of Grice's maxims (see Example 6.5), violations of the maxim of manner
would clearly dominate the picture: Many utterances are only partially intelligible; there are many disfluencies and false starts and many violations of
syntactic structure such as incomplete clauses. Thus, a large proportion of F's
utterances are less than clear. However, part of and maybe the most important part of F's and J's conversational context is that both partners desire to
have and to continue this conversation, and they do so for quite a long time.
This brings us to the question as to the established purpose of the conversation against which compliance or violations of the cooperative principle are
determined (see above). The overriding joint purpose of the conversation as
a whole is that of having a conversation. J has other (covert) goals in mind,
too, for example, gathering data and learning about conversations with persons with dementia. F may also have other goals, although these are not accessible to us. In light of this joint purpose, F's apparent violation of the
maxim of relevance in turn 219 or J's similarly abrupt topic shift in turn 10, a
similar face-value violation of the maxim of relevance, appear in a new light,
namely, as strategies to continue the conversation as discussed earlier. It
would appear that F's many manner violations may also have their source in
this joint purpose and that therefore, she attempts a contribution to fulfill her

conversational obligations, even though she has severe, although fluctuating, difficulties in utterance formulation.[12] In other words, F is cooperative vis-à-vis the overriding joint purpose even though an analysis that proceeds utterance by utterance detects many face-value violations of individual maxims. Thus, the purpose of a turn exchange may be subordinate to the purpose of a conversation, and this explains why this conversation can tolerate many unsuccessful requests for information (in terms of their perlocutions), many violations of the maxim of relevance (e.g., sudden topic shifts), and many violations of the maxim of manner (incomplete, unintelligible utterances) and still continue without a sign of either participant getting tired of it. This also means that cooperativeness needs to be evaluated both at the local (turn-exchange) level and at the level of the conversation as a whole.

PRAGMATICS AND BEYOND?

In this chapter, we did not set out to give our readers how to do Gricean pragmatics or an analysis (let alone an assessment) of illocutionary acts in the context of dementia. Rather, we wished to draw attention to some of the potential difficulties in applying approaches originating in philosophy unfiltered, as it were, to clinical data. This is not to say that we should never use a classification of illocutionary acts, nor consider Grice's maxims in the description of data. To the contrary, the taxonomies furnished by Grice, Searle, and others are a very useful starting point for description and analysis as long as we are willing to look further and question some of the underlying assumptions.

---

[12]For a more in-depth discussion of pragmatic or interactional difficulties as emergent phenomena, see the special issue of *Clinical Linguistics and Phonetics* (2005) edited by M. Perkins.

7

Critical Approaches
to Discourse

INTRODUCTION

Over the past decade, discourse analysis has developed beyond earlier descriptive frameworks (e.g., Sinclair & Coultard, 1975) to encompass work that takes a more critical approach to the examination of language use. In this chapter, we focus our discussion on critical approaches to discourse. In particular, we draw on critical discourse analysis (CDA), social construction theory (SCT), and discursive psychology (DP) to examine the issue of "selfhood" within the context of dementia. Critical approaches have become very influential in the area of dementia studies, particularly within the "caring professions" and social psychology (e.g., Golander & Raz, 1996; Kitwood, 1990, 1997; Sabat, 2001). CDA, for example, allows "practitioners of such disciplines whose professional practices are most obviously languaged, a means of describing, interpreting and explaining how their practices are discursively accomplished and thus offering a way of clarifying the ideological bases of the purposes, and methods of the professions themselves" (Candlin, 1995, p. xi).

Critical Discourse Approaches

CDA is a theory that has become highly influential within discourse studies over the past decade, but what is CDA? Van Dijk (2001) suggests the following definition:

> Critical discourse analysis (CDA) is a type of discourse analytical research that primarily studies the way social power abuse, dominance, and inequality are enacted, reproduced, and resisted by text and talk in the social and political context. With such dissident research, critical discourse analysts take explicit position, and thus want to understand, expose, and ultimately resist social inequality. (p. 352)

The key point in van Dijk's (2001) definition is the notion that CDA "analysts take" an "explicit position" when analyzing their data. CDA argues that discourses are the products of social and historical traditions, and as such, it is the analyst's job to situate current discourses within those traditions. CDA looks for discursive patterns in texts that reveal the hegemonic influence and dominance of powerful social groups. CDA therefore assumes from the outset that analysis of discourse will reveal the interests of particular groups within society. Although CDA emerged from both traditional DA and the field of critical linguistics (e.g., Fowler, Hodge, Kress, & Trew, 1979; Kress, 1988; Mey, 1985), it also "has counterparts in 'critical' developments in sociolinguistics, psychology, and the social sciences" (van Dijk, 2001, p. 352). The work in media studies of Hall, Hobson, Lowe, and Willis (1980), the Glasgow University Media Group (1976), and the work of Giddens (1976, 1991) in sociology are examples of work outside linguistics that have formed part of the tradition of CDA.

The central themes of CDA are language, power, and ideology (Fairclough, 1989; Hodge & Kress, 1992), an area of study that overlaps with many other social sciences, which may account for the wide range of disciplines that have been considered as working within CDA. The focus of CDA analysis is the text, and although texts are traditionally "understood to be a piece of written language-a whole work" (Fairclough, 1995, p. 4), CDA takes a broader perspective including written, spoken, and semiotic texts (Kress & van Leeuwen, 1996). For example, in cultural analysis, a text does not need to be "linguistic at all; any cultural artifact-a picture, a building, a piece of music can be seen as a text" (Fairclough, 1995, p. 4). This view is not without its "dangers; it can obscure the distinctions between different types of cultural artifact, and make the concept of a text rather nebulous" (Fairclough, 1995, p. 4). However, as CDA proponents stress, analysis should involve an examination of the "texture" of a text; that is, CDA is not just a commentary on the "content of texts" or description of artifact, it also includes systematic analysis of the "form and organization" of texts. There has been some debate amongst researchers doing CDA as to what should or should not be included within the field of CDA. For example, much of the research on gender difference in feminist sociolinguistics has taken a critical position (e.g., Cameron, 1992; Coates, 1996; Spender, 1980; Tannen, 1990), yet it has not been overtly labeled CDA. It is as well for the reader to be aware of the scope of work in CDA; a search in this area is likely to retrieve a confusingly wide range of topics and methodologies (see Fairclough, 1995; van Dijk, 2001).

CDA and Discursive Psychology

Fairclough (1995) claims that CDA views "texts as social spaces in which two fundamental social processes simultaneously occur: cognition and representation of the world, and social interaction" and he further suggests that a "multifunctional view of the text is therefore essential" (p. 6). Drawing on Halliday's (1978) work in systemic linguistics, Fairclough (1995) argues that texts operate simultaneously in the ideational, that is, the representation of the world and experience; the interpersonal, that is, through social interaction with others; and the textual, that is, examining the organizational units of a text that result in coherence and cohesion (see Halliday & Hasan, 1985). Fairclough (1995) is critical of approaches that he suggests are only concerned with the ideational and cites work by Potter and Wetherell (1987) and van Dijk (1988) as examples of this narrower approach to CDA. His criticism is that they are "ill-equipped to capture the interplay between cognition and interaction which is a crucial feature of textual practice" (Fairclough, 1995, p. 6). However, this criticism is somewhat unjustified because Potter and Wetherell's work, for example, falls within the framework of DP and does not claim to be CDA. DP is firmly grounded in the field of psychology:

> DP asks what is psychology for? Why is there psychology? What are the wide range of categories, constructions and orientations used to do? And the way it goes about studying these things is through considering the ways they figure as issues for the participants themselves. What are people doing with psychology? How are they orienting to psychological displays, claims constructions and so on? (Potter, 2003, p. 2)

DP is an approach that, like ethnomethodology, seeks to understand the individual's own perspective of the world. Fairclough (1995) claims that DP does not focus on ideology (p. 6), yet Potter (2003), drawing on Edwards (1997), suggests that one of the "central themes in discursive psychology is the way that versions of the world and versions of psychological states are linked together in talk for the purposes of action" (p. 6). Therefore, although not overtly investigating ideology, DP does examine how ideologies are linked to the psychological constructs of the individual. Thus, we might suggest that CDA analysis is a top-down process and DP a bottom-up process: CDA starts from a particular ideological position and seeks to show how that ideology is present in the discourse, whereas DP starts with the data and seeks to understand what ideologies and psychological constructs are revealed in the interaction.

Philosophical and Political Roots of Critical Approaches

CDA has drawn on a long line of philosophical traditions and often makes reference to prominent social philosophers and social scientists (e.g., the new Frankfurt school—e.g., Bakhtin, 1981, 1986; Bourdieu, 1991; Foucault, 1984; and Habermas, 1989—have been key figures in CDA; see van Dijk, 2001). Although we would not expect a reader to undertake a course in philosophy or critical theory to read this chapter, it is prudent to be aware of the ideologies that underpin research in CDA, as it is not necessarily a neutral form of analysis (Verschueren, 2001). Indeed, in some respects, CDA presents a problem to the qualitative researcher because of the inherent definitions of some of its basic analytic categories. In one way, the problem is similar to that of classical pragmatics, which presupposes communicative intention and the ability to recognize it; CDA presupposes power dialectics. Therefore, for the qualitative researcher who is interested in, for example, how power relations in the context of disorder are played out, the literature on and approaches to CDA may be useful, but the underlying theoretical positions and the perspective they impose on data have to be acknowledged.

> Critical theory and critical analysis are currently under attack from various theoretical quarters, and many analysts are becoming increasingly hesitant in their use of basic theoretical concepts such as power, ideology, class and even truth/falsity. I see these developments in theory as linked to the defeats and retreats of the left in many countries over the past decade or more.... My view is that the abuses and contradictions of the capitalist society ... give rise to critical theory.... There is therefore every reason to sustain the critical enterprise against its critics. (Fairclough, 1995, p. 26)

Fairclough's (1995) statement reveals some of the fundamental issues that are very important to CDA, which he suggests is a successor to the tradition of European philosophy and critical theory. Much of CDA has been grounded in the Marxist tradition (e.g., Althusser, 1971) of power struggles and in particular, Gramsci's (1971) concept of hegemony "which foregrounds the winning of consent in the exercise of power" (Fairclough, 1995, p. 17).

> Gramsci's theory of hegemony is born from the basic idea that government and state cannot enforce control over any particular class or structure unless other, more intellectual methods are entailed.... according to Gramsci hegemony is political power that flows from intellectual and moral leadership, authority or consensus as distinguished from armed force. A ruling class forms

and maintains its hegemony in civil society, i.e. by creating cultural and political consensus through unions, political parties, schools, media, the church, and other voluntary associations where hegemony is exercised by a ruling class over allied classes and social groups. (Hainsworth, 2000)

Obtaining power, therefore, is easier if you can convince those who give you that power that you are in agreement over fundamental ideological issues. Drawing on Gramsci's (1971) work, CDA suggests that ideological perspectives are embedded within everyday discourse practices, and institutions are held together as much by discourse practices as by constitutional power. Therefore, if one studies the texture (organization) of those discourses, one can uncover how ideologies are constructed and recycled within everyday interactions. CDA has also drawn on the work of Michel Foucault (1984) in showing that "power is a ubiquitous property of the technologies which structure modern institutions" (Fairclough, 1995, p. 27) rather than being the property of a particular group or class of people; that is, power lies in the discourse practices of people rather than in particular individuals or groups (e.g., a monarch or government). Thus, CDA starts from the premise that discourse practices represent the "social power of groups and institutions" (van Dijk, 2001, p. 354) and "rejects the possibility of a 'value free' science ... especially scholarly discourse," which is "inherently ... influenced by social structure" (van Dijk, 2001, p. 352).

DP, on the other hand draws its critical roots from the philosophy of language, particularly the work of Wittgenstein (1953/1958) who suggested that most philosophical problems arise from misunderstandings of the logic of language. Wittgenstein's later work (1953/1958), in particular, his work on "rule-following and private language" suggests that "language involves rules establishing certain linguistic practices. Rules of grammar express the fact that it is our practice to say this (e.g. "half past twelve") and not that (e.g. "half to one"). Agreement is essential to such practices" (J. Fieser, 2004). DP also builds on the tradition of ethnomethodology but "has moved forward" to include "the analytical resources of discourse analysis and conversation analysis" (Potter, 2003, p. 2). DP, unlike CDA, does not start from a position that assumes power is inherently invested in a particular discourse or social group. Thus, although DP may seek to make links to ideologies, it does not posit a priori a specific viewpoint. This is not always the case with CDA, as Verschueren (2001) points out in his thorough discussion of the limitations of CDA:

> The theory being preconceived, it is not surprising, therefore, that 'findings' tend to be predictable and that a gap emerges between textual analysyis and conclusions even for many of those who, like myself, share large portions of the theory-as soon as the question of evidence is asked. Texts are made into simple carriers, as it were, of what one already assumes to be the case. Rather than proceeding from description via explanation to positioning, with inter-

pretation at the core of all stages of the investigation, positioning comes first and interpretation is marginal. (p. 69)

Value Free Science?

In writing this book, it was initially difficult to decide where we would place the chapter on critical approaches, particularly as we wished to avoid framing the book within any specific ideological viewpoint. Van Dijk (2001) suggests it may not be possible to engage in "value free science" (p. 352), but we can attempt, at least, to remain aware of the potential limitations or bias of our analyses. CDA is concerned with (a) the relationship between language, ideology, and power; (b) the relationship between discourse and sociocultural change; (c) the centrality of textual analysis to social research; and (d) the principles and practice of critical language awareness (Candlin, 1995, p. ix). Candlin (1995) further notes "three central constructs of critical discourse analysis" (p. ix) are (a) text and the study of texture, (b) discoursal practices and the concept of "orders of discourse," and (c) sociocultural practices and the concept of culture.

In relation to these definitions, we are indeed concerned in this book with texts and the study of texture. We have also considered sociocultural practices and the concept of culture, but we have thus far avoided the concept of orders of discourse and overt discussion of power and ideology. Prior to this chapter, we have not given any specific viewpoint of dementia precedence over others; however, we are aware that it could be claimed we have taken a covert ideological position by the focus of our research questions. For example, we have noted the institutional identity of the nursing home resident and pointed to potential power inequities in interactions involving people with dementia, but by including the longer transcripts (Appendices B–F), we are attempting to avoid reducing our analyses to "simple carriers" (Verschueren, 2001) of our own subjective opinions. The reader may well wish to draw other interpretations from the data we present here, and we feel that it is part of the academic process (particularly in qualitative research) that the analyst should allow closer scrutiny of their data than has been the case in the past.

THE MEDIA AND DISCOURSES OF FEAR

Despite our wish to remain relatively value-free in our discussion of dementia,[1] we acknowledge that viewpoints put forward in the media constitute a privileged order of discourse, and in Western society, that viewpoint is predominantly negative. Critical approaches to media analysis within the context of AD can be revealing in relation to hegemonic discourse practices, that

---

[1] We acknowledge that it would be impossible to remain totally unbiased or value free when doing discourse; we are also aware that as academics, we inevitably privilege certain interpretations.

is, the social representation of people with dementia. The media operates on the premise that "bad news is good news" (Bell, 1991; Fowler, 1991), that is, that negativity is a strong news value (Galtung & Ruge, 1973) and therefore, stories involving death, disease, or crime gain wider media coverage. The most dominant theme relating to dementia in Western cultural texts[2] is that of loss of self; the person with dementia is portrayed as an empty shell.

Another element of dementia that is both constructed and mediated through our discourse practices is the culture that has grown up around this disease. Much of the public's knowledge about dementia comes via the media in the form of televised documentaries of people living with dementia (which often focus on the negative aspects of dementia because, as noted already, bad news is more newsworthy), health reports (often sound bites of research rather than proper summaries), and health care brochures (often inadequate bullet points). The public is very aware, and indeed very fearful, of the growing threat of dementia, but our work in support groups suggests that people are often initially misinformed about the facts of AD. For example, caregivers and family members begin to attribute every behavior and ailment that an individual manifests as being a symptom of AD, or they perceive the person with dementia as no longer consciously "present," and therefore, they see no point in trying to communicate with them. As one caregiver told the researcher, "you can't communicate with Alzheimer's people" (Guendouzi, 2003). A response to this view is that successful communications in interactions involving people with dementia depends on how one defines communication. Another caregiver frequently informed other caregivers who were new to the task of dealing with dementia that they should expect their family member to become "violent" in the mid-stages of the disease because that was "what people with Alzheimer's did" (Guendouzi, 2003). The generalization of the belief that because "one person with dementia does it, then all people with dementia do it" is a comment commonly heard in support groups.

A recent media example (see below) reveals the themes of hopelessness and negativity within current public discourses of dementia. The article reflects a common assumption about people with dementia-that they no longer possess what is required to be considered human:

Alzheimer's disease, a progressive and frightening neurological disorder … it begins as forgetfulness. As time passes the brain increasingly malfunctions, resulting in profound deficiencies in cognitive thought. This eventually ends in a catastrophe: extreme confusion, loss of judgment, inability to recognize loved ones, belligerency … in the truest sense of the word the advanced Alzheimer's patient has lost all of the qualities that make him or her human. (Gott, 2004, Section G, p. 4)

---

[2] As we have no sufficient working knowledge of Eastern languages, we cannot comment on Eastern cultural texts.

Some might argue that portraying negative images impacts emotionally on the audience, and this in turn gains further media coverage, more public awareness, and therefore, more public pressure for funding for research and treatment. Although there may be some truth in this argument, work examining media images of both individuals and ethnic groups has shown (e.g., Fowler, 1991; Hodge & Kress, 1992) that continual exposure to negative images in the media may result in a general acceptance of these socially constructed stereotypes. Whereas research seeks to question the validity of such stereotypes (e.g., Feil, 1982; Golander & Raz, 1996; Hamilton, 1994a; Prigatano, 2000; Sabat, 2001), there are echoes of similar discourses within academic work whose titles metaphorically reflect the loss of self-awareness, for example, *The Shattered Mind: The Person After Brain Damage* (Gardner, 1974), *The Experience of Alzheimer's Disease: Life Through a Tangled Web* (Sabat, 2001), and "The Mask of Dementia: Images of 'Demented Residents' in a Nursing Ward" (Golander & Raz, 1996).

We do not focus our discussion on the hegemonic discourses inherent in the media portrayal of dementia, but we are aware that this negative image of dementia is a very powerful theme within both the public and private domains. Thus, there is a well-established public discourse underlying any discussion of dementia that includes the following characteristics: (a) loss of self, (b) helplessness (Lubinski, 1995), and (c) fear. In this chapter, we examine data taken from interviews with caregivers (Guendouzi, 2003), interviews involving people with dementia, and a corpus of personal e-mail data from people with dementia to one of the researchers (J. Guendouzi). We show (a) how this dominant discourse is reflected in comments from caregivers and family members and (b) how individuals position themselves in relation to the social identity of being a "demented resident."

CRITICAL APPROACHES TO THE CONCEPT OF SELF IN DEMENTIA

Philosophers from Socrates through to current critical thinkers (e.g., Dennett, 1990) and neuroscientists (e.g., Damasio, 1999) have sought to find ways to explain the phenomenon that is "conscious self." More recently, the debate on self has continued within the fields of genetic research (e.g., stem cell research on embryos) and artificial intelligence (Clark, 2003; Kurzweil, 1999), and although there have been a multitude of books, papers, and academic theses addressing this issue, science still cannot answer the question "what is 'self?'" Is it the result of synaptic interaction (Le Doux, 2002), an adaptive evolutionary mechanism (Barkow, Cosmides, & Tooby, 1992; Wilson, 1978), the product of interaction with others, or is there really a "ghost in the machine," that is, the mind as a separate entity to the biological brain? While the issue of self has traditionally been the question of philosophers and outside the remit of clinical studies, it has also been the focus of much work in neuroscience. For example, in a recent reinterpretation of the duality debate, Schwartz and Begley (2002) apply research from neuroscience to the issue of brain versus conscious mind. They suggest that, although the conscious mind emerges from the physiological workings of our brain, it may also evolve into a "mental force" (the mind) that has agency and that once formed the mind can take "action" to influence the brain. They illustrate this theory with examples taken from Schwartz's clinical work with people who have obsessive compulsive disorder (OCD). Schwartz and Begley's findings show how people with OCD can use their mind to intervene when feeling the urge to enact compulsive behaviors. This action by the mind results in observable (through brain scans) changes to neural structures in the participant's brains.

In the case of dementia, the relation between a biologically functioning brain (one that is still capable of running the autonomic nervous system) and the presence of self (an individual who shows intact[3] goals and intentional action) may become a moral dilemma in the lives of caregivers. Accounts of dementia often use metaphors that suggest that the real individual has departed and is no longer contained within the body. For example, when asked why she did not visit her mother in a nursing home, one caregiver commented "she is no longer my mother she's just an empty shell" (Guendouzi, 2003). For this caregiver the real mother consisted of the memories of her past interactions with her mother. However, the woman's mother, although not able to communicate through speech, did engage with other members of her family through eye contact, hand grasping, and facial expressions (frowns or grimaces). Although the woman's performance of self as expressed in these interactions was not what her family expected or indeed hoped for, the woman did actively acknowledge her visitors, thereby signaling a relationship existed. It is not unreasonable to assume from her actions that she was able to experience both a sense selfhood and agency; that is, she retained some degree of conscious awareness of existing as an individual separate from the family members with whom she was attempting to interact.

Although we fully understand that the daughter's reaction was a psychological coping mechanism, it is a position that ultimately implies that individuals are products of their interlocutor's perceptions and memories.[4] The case cited above reveals a moral dilemma relating to the social obligation of caring (both physically and through social visits) for the person with dementia. If, for example, we take the approach of the daughter who no

---

[3]The ability to make/have/form goals.
[4]There is of course the extreme SCT argument that suggests that as self is referenced through language and therefore located in social interaction, the individual can only ever be the product (perception) of an interlocutor's mind.

longer saw the woman with dementia as being her mother, we could suggest her reasoning was based on the following premise:

If a person with dementia does not meet with my internalized concept of who they *used* to be, as based on my memories and my interactional needs, then it follows that the individual is no longer her former self [my mother] and therefore, if they are no longer "my mother" I am no longer socially obligated to interact with them.

Accepting this reasoning then ostensibly removes moral and social obligation to maintain interaction. Fortunately, most caregivers and family members do not take this approach. Our own experience in observing and interacting with this population suggests that although the ability to express selfhood in a socially accepted form (e.g., coherent conversation and rational behaviors) may be lost, the individual retains a sense of internal self-concept even at a time when her or his communication and reasoning skills have severely deteriorated. As the preceding example suggests, the person with dementia may well attempt in some small way to "voice" their selfhood. Physiological changes in persons with dementia may result in behaviors that are interactionally indexical of "different" persons; however, the individual, although being behaviorally or cognitively changed, should still be accorded the rights pertaining to personhood and dignity that he or she was given predementia. Furthermore, we cannot know to what extent the person with dementia experiences their internal concept of self.

Discursive Positioning of the Person With Dementia

> Unfortunately, for all too long, the focus of researchers' efforts has been through a lens which the late, esteemed, Tom Kitwood (1990) called the "standard paradigm," the medical model, which itself deals with the physical disease process and the behavioral and cognitive effects as measured by standard tests performed in the laboratory and clinic ... such a snapshot most often presents an extremely influential and mainly defectological picture. (Sabat, 2001, p. 93)

The concept of "excess disability" (Sabat, 2001, p. 93) inherent in the standard paradigm reflects Brody's (1971) claim that a "persons functional incapacity is greater than warranted by actual impairment" (Sabat, 2001, p. 93). Sabat (2001) goes on to note that typically, institutions position (Harré & van Langenhove, 1999) people with dementia as "defective." He cites the example of Mrs. L who was unceremoniously wheeled out of a room where she was being interviewed by one of Sabat's students because it was dinner time. Mrs. L continued to tell her story as she was being wheeled away, and the following week she appeared not in a wheelchair but on a walker, an action Sabat suggests may have been motivated by the fact that it gave her more independence-no one could move her without her permission. Certainly, within institutional settings, people are often positioned as dependent and without power to decide their own actions. Sabat, drawing on Kitwood and Bredin (1992) and Kitwood (1998), lists a host of "malignant" social behaviors that people in institutions are subjected to, which in normal circumstances would be seen as being an assault on the "afflicted person's feelings of self-worth and personhood" (Sabat, 2001, p. 97). Although this may be less prevalent in the earlier stages of dementia, it is still a common practice within institutions. BL, a man with dementia who recently spent 2 days in a nursing home to allow his wife some respite time, wrote the following:

Example 7.1

> If you have been keeping up with posts you will realize that I have been imprisoned for two days while J went to a course to learn how to look after me. I will have a report for you about my impressions re institutional care. That will wait awhile as the experience is still very raw and hurting … all timepieces have been changed to military 24 hours style. We get up at 0700 hours, bowels move on command 0730. Showering must be done with minimum water and mess then present for breakfast 0800. We used to just laze in a chair with cereal, toast, a cuppa and the morning paper. This is now not in my interest. It is a place at the table, no reading but in its place, a rundown on what will or will not happen for the day.
>
> Routine and fulfillment are the catch cries. An active mind, spirit, bowels and bladder are the best way of keeping spirits high.… I cannot remember the rest of today's routine, though anything I suggest for doing or no is never on her official list. Tomorrow we are getting one of those whiteboards so I can have no excuse for being in the wrong place at the wrong time. (BL, personal communication, October 2004)

BL, a retired pharmacist, although still being able to communicate, is not able to manage alone when his wife is away. However, despite his obvious linguistic abilities, his comments show he is being treated as if he were severely cognitively impaired. It is difficult to know whether this is an underlying institutional rationale or whether it is just a matter of people in institutions being treated as though they need to be "managed" no matter what their abilities because the institution runs more smoothly if everyone adheres to a common routine. Either way, it is of course no less malignant, and it is interesting that BL introduces his report by saying he was "imprisoned." Kitwood and Bredin (1992) suggest such institutional behaviors represent malignant social psychology. As Sabat (2001) points out, these behaviors do not spring "from ill-will" (p. 97); rather, they are products of institutional settings and the need for order when dealing with a population whose behaviors can be "daunting and exhausting" (Sabat, 2001, p. 97). BL appears to focus on the fact he is offered no choice in the way his day is going to unfold; his personal needs must be regulated to fit in with the institution. His remarks imply that he should at least be allowed to linger over a cup of tea or the morning paper in his retirement years. Yet, as so often happens, the person who has the illness is forced to fit in with the needs of the institution. Institutions are in a catch 22 situation; they need to run their schedules in an organized manner and therefore may find it impossible to manage individuality within the institutional setting.

Sabat (2001) argued that we can view the individual through either the eyes of classic science or the eyes of romantic science. He went on to suggest that classic science creates the "psychometric person" (Sabat, 2001, p. 263; see also chap. 1), someone who reflects the means and averages of the various tests professionals give when assessing impairment. An alternative is to take a 'romantic' science approach (see chap. 1) and look at the person with dementia in terms of the "semiotic or meaning-driven subject" (Sabat, 2001, p. 171), that is, "individuals who can act intentionally given their interpretation of the circumstances in which they find themselves" (Sabat, 2001, p. 171). "Meaning-driven" is understood in this case to be

1. acting out intention-reflection and intention are built upon systems of meaning, as outlined by Geertz (1973) and Shweder (1983);
2. the interpretation of events, and situations; and
3. the evaluation of events, situations or actions (Sabat, 2001, p. 171)

Sabat (2001, p. 227) also suggests that one should view the individual with dementia in terms of Stern's critical personalism (Stern, 1938), examining, for example, whether they still retain (a) intact goals, (b) intentions, and (c) long-standing dispositions.

Certainly in Example 7.1, one can see that BL is acting with intention (to give his account of this experience) by interpreting events in the nursing home and evaluating their impact on both his life and the lives of the other residents. BL has been "positioned" by the institution as a person who needs assistance to carry out the activities of daily living, someone who needs a whiteboard to establish where he is and what he should be doing. His use of a military analogy when describing events that occurred during the 2 days he was in the nursing home does indeed indicate he views the experience as an "assault" on his personhood. Institutional routines are to some extent the product of both the logistic and legal restrictions imposed on the nursing home, but they also reflect the hegemonic ideologies imposed by society when dealing with people with dementia. BL's account of the 2 days in the nursing home reflects his discursive ability to act with intention in describing what he perceives as a highly dehumanizing experience.

Tajfel (1979) has noted that "feelings of self-worth, or self-esteem, may spring forth from that part of an individual's self-concept which derives from his [sic] knowledge of his membership in a social-group (or group) together with the value and emotional significance attached to that membership" (p. 63). BL's use of the pronoun *we* reflects his membership in a social group, the demented, although this is not a membership that accords him self-esteem or a sense of belonging on this occasion. There is another group to which he belongs, a group who "used to just laze in a chair with cereal, toast, a cuppa and the morning paper." His "place at the table" of normal retired people no longer exists, and he is part of a group whose lives are controlled through discourses of dependence on, and in BL's eyes, "obedience" to, an institutional regime. BL, through the use of new medications, has been able to stave off some of the detrimental effects of the disease, and this has given rise, as noted previously, to a group of people with dementia who are more able to speak out about both their condition and their stigmatization by society.

The Social Construction of Self

Sabat (2001) suggests that social construction theory (SCT) (Coulter, 1981; Harré, 1983, 1991) gives one alternative ways of analyzing how the self is projected within daily interactions. As he notes, one way people construct self within their discourses is through the use of linguistic tokens such as the pronouns, *I, me,* or *you*. These pronouns index the individual's awareness of self as a singularity. We could of course suggest that the use of pronouns is a "verbal habit" and simply a "vestigial reflex" (Sabat, 2001, p. 276) stored in the linguistic repertoire of the speaker. We also might wonder whether the "I" is indexical of the individual one has always known or some new "I," and indeed, does this really matter? To the caregiver, family member, or researcher, it may seem as if the person with dementia is a different individual every time they interact with them. For example, a professional caregiver commented about F that "you never know what to expect (.) she varies from day to day." This expectation of unpredictability may become part of the (negatively loaded) persona of AD and dementia. We note, however, that the caregiver also reported that F exhibited behavioral traits that were predictable within the varying stages of her disease; therefore, the caregiver's comments appear to be a way of communicating the state of uncertainty in which she carries out her day-to-day interactions with people with dementia.

Sabat (2001) extended his interpretation of SCT to posit two further aspects of self: Self 2, the self as representative of mental and physical attributes, and Self 3, the socially presented self. Self 2 is the "unique set of mental and physical attributes" (p. 17) that each person possesses. This aspect of self allows for a continuing core self-concept that includes factors such as the individual's spiritual beliefs, politics, and physical attributes (e.g., being tall, thin, blonde, or athletic). Some of these attributes may not be affected by dementia, but others, such as loss of former reading ability or skill at language games (e.g., scrabble), may have to be accommodated into a new concept of self for the person with dementia. The socially presented

Self 3 is not unlike Goffman's (1974) social actor (see chap. 4) in that each individual consists of a "multiplicity of selves," for example, "a respectful child ... the authoritative teacher or the parent" (Sabat, 2001, p. 295). Sabat (2001) suggests that to "construct" any of these selves in interactions, the person with dementia requires the "cooperation of healthy others" (p. 295). He further notes that if the person without dementia orients to the physical attributes of the person with dementia (their dementia dysfunction), he or she may find it difficult to help the person with dementia enact their preferred social role. An example within our own data that reflects Sabat's (2001) interpretation of self is the interaction between B and MA (see chap. 5, this volume; also Appendix E) in which MA redirects B's enquiry about his current activities to refer to his former job as a dairy farmer. Rather than reorient MA to the present, B positions himself as the willing recipient of the identity MA projects, that is, that of an able experienced man. As a result, MA is able to take on the discursive role of mentor in their conversations, and they are able to build up an interactional relationship in which MA appears to show he is acting intentionally and has the ability to draw on "long-standing dispositions" (his expertise in running a dairy) to construct a more able version of self.

Sabat's (2001) third version of self-"the multiplicity of selves"-reflects some of the problems within interactions involving people who have dementia. To play their part, social actors need to be aware of the stage they are on (the particular context), the audience they are playing to (social status and identity of the other participants), and the part they should be playing for this audience, for example, mother, spouse, friend, and so forth. They also need to position themselves within a specific temporal framework, that is, who they are in the present moment. The person with dementia may confuse or misinterpret any or all of these variables, therefore enacting the "wrong" role for the particular context or audience. An example reported to J. Guendouzi involved a daughter interacting with her 60-year-old father. She expected the father to recognize her and to respond accordingly, that is, as if he were her father, but instead, her father enacted a role from his past and mistook her for his wife. She closely resembled her mother at an earlier age, and her visual appearance had cued a response that was a reflection of the man's perceived relationship to the woman. His interpretation and evaluation of the situation in some respects were correct but were temporally displaced; he was enacting his role in the relationship based on knowledge drawn from memories of an earlier stage in his life. The man also failed to recognize his wife whom he saw as a "strange" old woman. Both the daughter and wife were upset by these errors and given the participant roles he had allocated to them, found it difficult to converse with the man-they gave up on the interaction and went home.[5]

---

[5]Caregiver interviews were carried out to obtain background information for this book. Some individuals did not wish to be directly quoted.

This mismatch between expectations on the part of the person with dementia and the person without may result in either (a) overaccommodation, for example, talking to a person with dementia as if they are a child, or (b) underaccommodating, for example, not allowing the person with dementia enough time to process the content of an utterance or giving minimal information, and she or he will infer the illocutionary force of an indirect speech act. For example, in chapter 6, we noted how M, a graduate student, underaccommodated to E when conversing with him, resulting in her taking longer turns than necessary and at times overwhelming E with too much information. The dynamics of social interaction inevitably require that interactional partners recognize each other's social role(s), intentions, states of mind, and so forth, and it is often difficult to know the intentions of a person with dementia. The mismatch in the example above between the man with dementia's understanding of participant identities and that of his family caused the interaction to break down. Caregivers and family members frequently comment (Guendouzi, 2003) that persons with dementia no longer recognize either them or family members. The following two comments were made by family members describing their experience of communicating with people with dementia.

Example 7.2

(a) C: 'Daddy doesn't know who he is anymore '
(b) L: 'She doesn't recognize me'.

Thus, two variables that have an important effect on the dynamics of dementia interactions are (a) the person with dementia's current internal concept of selfhood and (b) the external identity attributed to them by their interactional partner. The problem is that these two versions of the individual do not always match, or to put it another way, there is no way of telling whether they match, or the caregivers just assume there is no way.

The Narrative Self in Dementia.   SCT has also drawn on narrative theory in developing an heuristic to talk about self. Gergen (1991) suggested that self-narratives essentially serve a meaning-making function, that is, rather than seeing one's life as a series of incidental events following on from one another, the individual will attempt to make sense of these life events by making systematic relations between each event.

> According to narrative approaches to self-identity, self-narratives are validated by means of the social context in which they take place. That is to say, one's self-narratives typically require that significant others play a supporting role. One can think of oneself as an honest person if one's story of rejecting temptations or bribes is backed up by a supporting cast. (Botella, 2004, p. 3)

Therefore, the individual is continually in a process of "negotiating" his or her identity with both their audience and themself: Audience reaction acts as a feedback mechanism to our internal concept of self. In fact, the individual engages in a great deal of personal internal debate relating to their own behaviors (e.g., what would my family think of this). This does not mean, however, that a person's version of self is totally socially constructed: "The relationship between … personal and social constructs is likely to be a dialectical one … the person adapts his or her self-theory or self-narrative to social feedback and, at the same time selects what will count as relevant feedback" (Botella, 2004, p. 3).

Narrative analysis involves a first-person account by an individual of his or her experiences and as such is very useful when examining the discursive constructs people use to represent internal versions of self-concept and projecting versions of self to others. We are aware that in undertaking this form of analysis, our assumptions are based on what is manifested in the data, that is, we cannot know what the person with dementia actually thinks. In the case of dementia, however, narrative analysis is a particularly useful way of examining how the person with dementia positions themselves in relation to their own condition. The following examples are taken from a corpus of personal e-mails sent to J. Guendouzi. All those contributing were in the early-to-mid stages of dementia. Unlike face-to-face interaction, e-mail interactions poses less of a face threat to persons with AD. They can use spell-checkers and take their time to formulate replies, and therefore, they often perform better in online contexts than in everyday conversations.

Example 7.3

1. We are all finding ways to "benefit" from what is happening to us and want to live positively. Let's share with one another, because in doing this, in spite of the inroads of the disease, we each still have a valuable contribution to make both here and in our regular life. (S, Australia)

2. Yes the meds do improve some of your abilities such as memory, and thinking skills and maybe even provide you a little more independence for a short while. But during that time other abilities are still declining such as communication and comprehension skills. These two are very important skills because these are the main skills to maintain ourselves. We still loose the ability to say words as we would like, people are easily offended by what we say, our timing is usually off, our short term memory is still a pain in the %and*(! Because we can't remember what we said. Everyday is a struggle to maintain ourselves, a struggle to communicate and a struggle to survive. (T, USA)

3. We don't have much stimulating activities: we are left for more half of time in a room, without nothing to make! … in any event these centers are not organized for people with early stages of AD. (C, France)

4. A lifetime of coping mechanism is slowly being eroded. I try to consciously work at finding other ways to do things … now everything I do requires a lot more pre-planning and rehearsal if it is to come out the right way it used to. (J, USA)

In Example 1, S uses the inclusive pronoun *we* to suggest that membership of this particular online social group can be a positive experience for the members, one in which feelings of self-esteem can be maintained. Although S portrays the disease as an external agent making inroads to the group's lives, she also suggests that rather than being a negative process, they (the group) can "benefit" from their experience and still retain some "value" both in the support group and in the wider social arena (see Shenk, 2001). S's construction of dementia reflects Tajfel's (1979) notion of positive self-esteem gained from group membership. In contrast, T's (Example 2) account of the improvement gained from new medications shows a less positive perspective. Like S, she frames her account from the perspective of group membership and uses the inclusive pronoun *we*, but she claims that although the medications may improve some cognitive abilities (e.g., memory), other skills, such as communication and comprehension, still decline, and she notes that these are the most important skills needed for people with dementia to maintain themselves. Dementia has little positive value for either T personally or the group; her account of dementia is positioned as an insurmountable obstacle against which this group has to "struggle to survive."

In Example 4, J does not attempt to embed himself within a group identity of people with dementia; rather, he uses the first person pronoun *I* to frame his account from a more personal perspective. He talks about making an active effort to cope with his daily tasks, and his opening words—"a lifetime of coping mechanism[s are] … being eroded" reflect the fact that everyone has had to develop strategies for dealing with life. Although J has resisted discursive solidarity with the smaller group of people who have dementia, his statement does invoke membership within another larger group-people without dementia. He notes his attempts to combat the disease by trying to fight the loss of his former skills, and yet this fight is not enough; he still cannot get things to "come out the right way it used to." This comment implies that the way things were represents the "right" state of affairs, and his account suggests he is struggling to maintain membership within the normal world rather than become a member of the dementia community. In Example 3, C's account reflects the larger social discourse associated with dementia. He claims that people with dementia are left alone to fend for themselves and notes that centers for people with dementia are not organized for those in the early stages. Unlike J, C has accepted a group identity that is tied to his dementia, but it is a subgroup of that population, those in the early stages of dementia who are a more able group.

The examples above show that people with dementia portray AD as an external agent attacking their ability to maintain group membership within normal society. Their accounts of their disease also reflect the larger social voice that marginalizes people with dementia and places them outside the boundaries of the normal groups. However, some people with dementia, like S, may attempt to frame accounts of dementia in more positive terms and seek to find personal validation through noting they are still valuable members of society who can contribute in some ways, even if it is only as the voice of dementia. All of these examples show individuals who are acting with intention, retaining intact speaker goals, and further, are able to evaluate and interpret their experience of dementia.

Self in Later Stages of Dementia. The examples examined above were taken from people in early-to-mid stages of dementia. As we discussed earlier, new medications and earlier diagnosis means that some individuals live with a diagnosis and the early effects of dementia for many years, and the rate of their decline of functioning is relatively slow. In the next section, we examine data taken from interactions between J and F, who is in the later stages of dementia (this conversation is not included in Appendix B or C):

Example 7.4

(a)
1	F:	she keeps herself busy year after year
2	J:	who's that
3	F:	a woman who lived here
4	J:	uh huh
5	F:	now she doesn't live here anymore she's in some (.) she's my age (.) very nice person

(b)
	F:	I had this for oh (Xx) depressing you (1.0) I had this with me while till Now (xXx) never get well

(c)
	F:	an er oh: I can't think of all these things now and it is only since I had the er spots was always here on the brain or something

(d)
1	F:	well I haven't been feeling very well
2	J:	uh huh
3	F:	and it took me some deliberation to pull myself together

In these examples, F's comments mark awareness of both her former and current identities. However, in Example 7.4 (a), she appears to be distancing herself from her current self by referring to herself in the third person as someone who formerly "lived here." F describes herself as being a "very nice person" (Example 7.4 (a), turn 5), a comment that might lead us to infer that she does not like her current self. F discursively positions her former self as both temporally and spatially external to her current identity. We might suggest that although her comments mark awareness of both former and current selves, on some occasions, she finds it difficult to equate them as both being the same person—herself. J makes no effort to orient F to the fact that she is talking about herself, and whereas on other occasions, F becomes tearful talking about her dementia, in this example, she is better able to cope with her altered identity by talking about her former self as a separate person, someone who she knew in the past, someone she can refer to with positive descriptors as a "very nice person." It is interesting that she needs to distance herself completely from her current self to talk positively about her own personal characteristics. The internal dialectical tension of being aware of former (positive) and current (negative) selves is in this case resolved by casting herself literally as "other."

However, F does on most occasions show awareness of her own central self-concept as a single person who changes over time. In Example 7.4 (b), F situates herself in terms of her past self ("I had this with me while"), her current self ("till Now"), and her future self ("never get well [again]"). We also note that in another conversation (see chap. 9), F discusses her former role as a dressmaker and that she used to enjoy being active in the household, cooking and cleaning and so forth. She also mentions a contrast between then and now: She used to enjoy dressmaking, but now her eyes aren't so good any more. This decline, although a different form of decline, may be easier to cope with because it is perceived as "physical" and maybe even normal or to be expected in an older person. F is aware that it is her brain that has been affected by dementia and refers to the dementia as "spots" on her brain in Example 7.4 (c). She is aware she has lost her former abilities—"I can't think of all these things now"—a comment that shows she is able to temporally position herself in relation to both past and current abilities. In Example 7.4 (d), F's comment shows evidence of active agency in that she notes it "took me some deliberation to pull myself together," suggesting awareness of her periodic loss of a sense of coherent self. This utterance requires conscious awareness of both an internal and intentional self-concept. Evidence from the data above suggests that beyond the use of personal pronouns, F, a woman in the later stages of dementia, is showing (a) awareness of an internal self-concept; (b) the ability (in moments of intelligibility) to situate current and former selves within both past, present, and future temporal frames; and (c) a concept of agency. If we had chosen Example 7.4 (a) alone to illustrate this section, we might have been tempted to suggest that F had lost her internal sense of coherent self and had projected her autobiographical self not as a singularity continuing through time but as two separate people. However, as Examples 7.4 (b), (c), and (d) show, F's later comments mark awareness of a unified self-concept, and therefore, we might suggest Example 7.4 (a) reflects a narrative strategy F uses to cope with the distress she feels when discussing her current condition.

The interlocutor's role as recipient of another's discursive identity is an important factor in how successful the person with dementia is in projecting a specific identity. For example, we suggested in chapter 5 that MA's projected role as mentor to B, the graduate student, was in part successful because B accepted the interactional role MA allocated to him. In Example 7.5, we examine how J, the researcher, reacts to F's discussion of her dementia. To examine how self is constructed within this example, we first need to examine the conversational moves within the sequence:

Example 7.5 (see Appendix C)

16 J {lento did you have a good <u>Christ</u>mas }
       Information-Seeking Question
17 F well. (.) alright,=
       Appropriate response, potential trouble spot
18 J =it was alright.=
       Clarification-Seeking Question, repair
19 F = m:, (.) didn't (x) do {LV anything, (xx)}=
       Elaboration, potential trouble spot
20 J =did you get any presents?
       Information-Seeking Question, topic shift for repair
       (4.0)
21 F ↓no::. (we've- we're just left here dead,)=
       Appropriate structural response, topic indicates potential trouble spot
22 J =mhm.=
       minimal response, avoidance of face-threatening topic
23 F =↓oh:: wha- what I want is to (4.5) I don't know, (.) what you call it. (2.0)
       I call it when (something changes or) your own brain.
       Topic shift to focus discussion on her dementia
24 J [o:h*
       minimal response, avoidance of face-threatening topic
25 F [{LV (xxx*xxX, xx)}=
26 J = your brain. ((light laugh)) {LV} <u>my</u> brain. <u>my</u> brain is going, }
       Topic shift to mitigate face threat and show solidarity
          (3.5)
27 F but eh, (2.5) wh- when I came in here (1.5) (but I knew xxxx to this xxx
       an it x (2.0) many (1.5) [(xxx)*
       Trouble spot, continues elaborating on her condition

28 J   [your <u>me</u>mory*
        Repair of other -clarification-seeking device
29 F {*pianissimo*} hm (.) but they er (but [maɪə]) well my husband he didn't
        want that. (.) he didn't want me to have any treatment at all
        Elaborates on topic of dementia, potential trouble spot
30 J   =o::h,
        minimal response to mitigate face threat of F's comments

On this occasion, J attempts to draw F into a conversation about Christmas, but although F's responses are appropriate structurally and semantically, they indicate potential interactional trouble. In her first response, the use of the discourse marker "well" followed by a pause qualifies her reply of "alright," implying that she didn't enjoy herself over the holiday. J's first response is to seek further information about F's Christmas, but when F responds negatively (turn 19), J attempts a topic shift to avoid the face threat inherent in a discussion of being stuck in a nursing home over the holiday period. After a long pause (4 s), F finally responds with another negative remark "we're just left here dead" (turn 21). F's responses are structurally appropriate, but the personal nature of her complaints form a potential face threat to J, and she tries to avoid pursuing the topic of F's dementia. When topic shifts fail, J resorts to minimal responses to indicate support as a conversational partner and also to avoid being drawn into a discussion of F's dementia.

F's comments (turns 19 and 21) reflect the negative institutional discourses that are associated with life in a nursing home: "we're just left here dead." The identity she is projecting may be designed to elicit sympathy from her visitor, but it also indicates she is aware that others have some control over her current living status. She finally attempts to indicate to J that she wants to understand her current condition (turn 23), and her circumlocutions and pauses suggest she is having difficulty accessing the information she needs. F's semantic difficulties in some respects make her comments all the more upsetting to her interlocutor; F marks the fact she is changing and that her "own" brain is at the root of the problem. J's discomfort is evident in her minimal response and avoidance of engaging in F's choice of topic. J's next turn shows an attempt to mitigate the obvious face threat of this topic and inject a more humorous tone by offering solidarity with F and claiming her own "brain is going." F, however, is not distracted and continues to elaborate on her account of her deteriorating condition (turn 27). J at this point gives up on trying to divert the topic flow and begins to engage with the topic by seeking clarification of F's remarks (turn 28), and the two women jointly engage in a discussion of F's dementia until J is able to redirect the conversation nine turns later (see Appendix C). J's initial unwillingness to accept F's helpless dementia identity is an interactional strategy based on the face threat of agreeing with F. J is attempting to do what S (Example 7.3 number 1) suggests and find a positive way of showing solidarity with F.

In this example, F shows good use of communication skills; she can act with intention and attempt, at least, to evaluate and interpret what is going on within her brain and ultimately to her sense of self. She is aware of long-standing dispositions (e.g., "when I came in here (1.5) but I knew," turn 27) and is pursuing the conversational goal of trying to get some explanation from J (who she knows is studying people in nursing homes). She is also still able to use implicature (turn 17) by answering J's question about Christmas with the minimal information and an intonation pattern that suggests her Christmas was not "alright." The trouble spots within this exchange are related to potential face threats to F's self-esteem; J does not wish to pursue F's discussion of her dementia because she knows it might end in F becoming upset. Again, this raises questions of what constitutes trouble in conversations: On this occasion, it is the fact that J does not wish to elaborate on F's choice of topic rather than real unintelligibility that leads to J's attempts to redirect the conversation, a strategy that F might find confusing.

Having looked at the organization of the conversation, what can we say from a critical perspective? First, as noted earlier, F's initial remarks reflect common public discourses relating to dementia and nursing homes, particularly her comment about being "left here dead." It is interesting that when voicing these opinions, her intelligibility is generally better than when she is trying to talk about her own current cognitive abilities or how dementia is affecting her life. We have noted elsewhere (Guendouzi & Müller, 2002) that F performs better on what appear to be formulaic utterances (e.g., "it's a lovely day" or "he's marvellous to me"), and this may also be true of utterances that represent common public discourses such as political views and stereotypes about people or behaviors. Certainly, her remark reflects a common stereotype in Western culture that implies the elderly and infirm are shut away in institutions and left for dead. However, when she starts to construct discursive representations of her inner psychological state or tries to rationalize what is going on in her mind (or brain), her language becomes much more dysfluent (turns 23, 25, 27). F becomes more intelligible when she abandons her attempt to discursively project a coherent version of current self and becomes the author (see chap. 4) of her husband's words (turn 29). It appears that for F, using public discourses and the voice of others is an easier task than constructing an individual account of self. Of course, many people find it easier to voice the opinions and words of others, to reiterate common stereotypes and religious or political dogmas, but in the case of dementia, it becomes more marked because these formulaic accounts may be the only lucid segments in a conversation and in fact may not truly represent the opinions or intentions of the person with dementia. As we have already discussed, people with dementia are often very compliant communicators and will make a great deal effort to keep a conversation going (see chap. 8). Therefore, we need to be aware of communicative behaviors that may be manifestations of cognitive deficits rather than manifestations of the person's identity; that is, the person with dementia may make comments that seem out of character or hurtful to their caregivers, but these may be the only utterances they can access and produce within the interaction.

CRITICAL APPROACHES AND CLINICAL RESEARCH

Critical approaches to discourse often follow an analytical route that focuses on the hegemonic processes that construct institutional identities and then point to the inequities arising from these discourses. Verschueren (2001) challenges critical discourse analysts to discuss other possible interpretations of data, but another issue in relation to taking a critical perspective when examining data is that if we deconstruct things, we also need to offer approaches that can not only reveal inequality but also suggest solutions or show how they might be useful in applied contexts. In the next section, we suggest a metaphor we have found useful in approaching the topic of selfhood in dementia.

Self as a Complex System

The current view of dementia in Western society is rather like the notion of closed and open systems in systems theory, an approach that is a further example of the dialectical approach. An open system is a system that receives input from its environment; it then interacts with input and passes output back to its environment. A closed system is a system in which there is no interaction with the environment; this lack of interaction results in internal chaos, disintegration, and finally death (Littlejohn, 1999). The person with dementia is often portrayed as isolated within himself or herself, a victim of a state of being that is not unlike the definition of the closed system. For example, it is often assumed that there is no "true" interaction with demented people and therefore no growth or learning (informational feedback from the person with dementia to the person without dementia); the person with dementia is perceived by others as experiencing internal chaos and slowly deteriorating until finally there is death (Guendouzi, 2003).

A complex system[6] exists in a continual state of dynamic flux responding to feedback from its environment. As the system adapts to this feedback, it attempts to create a state of homeostasis. The self can be represented as a complex system that exists within a dynamic environment of social interac-

---

[6]Language, for example, is a complex system relying on feedback from many subsystems (linguistic, paralinguistic, and contextual variables).

tions. The dynamic system (the self) has to access and respond to many sub-systems to project a version of self on the world. These subsystems would include, for example, the context of the interaction, interlocutor feedback, an individual's memories of past experiences, his or her past and current social roles (e.g., teacher, mother, engineer, etc.), interactions with others, an internal concept of mature self, current cognitive ability, and awareness of agency, that is, being able to act on the world.

In their daily interactions with others, individuals rely on feedback from these subsystems to maintain a sense of homeostatic self, a state in which the individual experiences self as a "stable structure that endures in time" (Ben-Yishay, 2000, p. 133). By making adjustments in response to feedback from these subsystems, individuals discursively adapt their performance of self to present a cohesive version of self to the world. However, in dementia, these feedback loops often misfire and may be misinterpreted by either the person with dementia or his or her interlocutor. In interactions involving people with dementia, the adjustments and adaptive strategies used by either party may not be appropriate for the participants or the context (see chaps. 5 and 9). Therefore, as a result of misinterpreting feedback cues, both the person with dementia and her or his interlocutor may contribute to communicative breakdown within the interaction. Therefore, interactions involving people with dementia are rather like a complex system with "entropy," that is, a system existing in a state of unpredictability.

Confusing situations or experiences may cause persons with dementia to go into "fear" mode, and they may produce behaviors associated with stress or fear. Similar responses occur in normal populations during stressful conditions; however, the default reaction in dementia is that the behaviors manifested are a symptom of the dementia itself. Caregivers, for example, often mistakenly assume that once an individual has been diagnosed with dementia, they will begin to exhibit aggressive behaviors-this is not necessarily true. Many behaviors manifested in dementia are symptoms of the fear and confusion the individual experiences in losing memories and the skills of language and communication. Friedell (personal communication, March 2003), a sociologist diagnosed with early stage dementia, suggested that this is not unlike the trauma suffered by holocaust survivors. He suggested being given a diagnosis of dementia may result in pretraumatic stress in which the anticipation of decline and fear of loss of self can cause depression and physiological symptoms similar to those experienced in posttraumatic stress (PTS). Despite the potential traumatic nature of a diagnosis of dementia, both caregivers and persons with dementia have reported receiving very little support or information at the time of diagnosis. Often counseling is implemented but not necessarily targeting PTS. This aspect of dementia not only exacerbates the dementia symptoms but also gives rise to symptoms that may be part of the trauma rather than the dementia.

It is interesting that in the context of dementia, there appear to be more support groups for caregivers than for people with dementia. One reason for this is the health profession's view (in some areas) that a support group for people with dementia would need qualified paramedic or nursing personnel available. Caregiver support groups are often supported by institutions that are in the business of dementia, for example, assisted living facilities. It is the caregivers who make decisions about putting someone in assisted living and/or a nursing home, not the person who has dementia. Therefore, the support group industry targets its potential market, and the social construction of the person with dementia as dependent, helpless, and incapable of making their own decisions plays right into the interests of the caregiving industry.

CONCLUSION

There are many reasons why we decided to include a chapter on critical approaches in this book, but probably the most relevant was that CDA is a useful tool when raising awareness and deconstructing the possible motivations behind public discourse. People with dementia are not a homogeneous group; they are individuals with whom we can have meaningful interactions and who retain a degree of personal independence (if not physical independence) and sense of self far into the course of the brain pathology of dementia. To care for people with dementia, we need to be able to interact with them, and, as was shown above, the individual with dementia may have an unstable perception of self. An individual's "sense of self, or ego-identity, though capable of enduring in time, cannot be taken for granted.... There are a number of situations in life when the sense of continuity can be disrupted, with severe consequences to an individual's life" (Ben-Yishay, 2000, p. 233). Dementia is one such situation; it disrupts an individual's sense of continuing ego identity. Ben-Yishay (2000) calls for clinicians to seek appropriate therapeutic techniques when dealing with individuals whose brain impairment has disrupted their coherent sense of ego identity and suggests it is possible, in some cases of brain impairment, "to reconstitute the individual's ego identity" (p. 134) and help them gain acceptance of their disability.

Perhaps in the case of dementia, this might mean helping the caregivers and family to accept disability but also to acknowledge abilities and realize that although the disease has altered some of an individual's traits and behaviors, it has not necessarily taken away awareness of her or his internal concept of self. Through detailed qualitative studies that view the person with dementia as an individual, we can seek ways to support communication in dementia and begin to help the person with dementia express their own identity. Malinowski (1923/1972) pointed out that phatic communion (small talk) may appear to be aimless or meaningless talk, but it is also a means of maintaining interpersonal contact with others (and thereby exhibiting evidence of retaining intact goals). This same notion applies to dementia discourse. Even if the words uttered appear to have little semantic meaning or informational content, there is a need/drive and motivation to communicate, and in that sense, the speaker is signaling a coherent message to his or her interlocutor—keep engaging with me, I am here!

Prigatano (2000) encourages clinicians to consider the following principles when working in the field of neuropsychological rehabilitation:

> 1. The clinician must begin with the patient's subjective or phenomenological experience to reduce their frustrations and confusion in order to engage them in the rehabilitation process.
>
> 2. The patient's symptom picture is a mixture of *premorbid* cognitive individuality characteristics as well as neuropsychological changes directly associated with the brain pathology. (p. 118)

Currently, there is no means of "curing" or reversing the progress of AD, although new drugs are helping some people with dementia to alleviate or control some of the dementing symptoms. The progress of pharmaceutical intervention and earlier diagnosis has given rise to a new aspect of the dementia experience, the fact that the early stage of dementia is extending over a longer period. Persons with dementia are able to maintain higher levels of physical and cognitive function for a longer period and therefore have longer to anticipate their coming trauma, but they have also a longer "run-up" time to a less independent state and therefore more time to come to terms with the prospect of their disease. A more positive side to this aspect of dementia is the possibility that this population might be more responsive to intervention. Researchers in the field of communication and its disorders can play a role in this process by carrying out detailed qualitative analyses of communicative patterns in dementia interactions, particularly longitudinal studies (Hamilton, 1994a, 1994b; Ramanathan, 1994). Interlocutors without dementia need to actively work toward accommodating to their partners' interactional needs. Rather than trying to orient the person with dementia to reality, the non-AD interlocutor should seek to validate the role the person with dementia is presenting within the interaction. Furthermore, the partner without dementia needs to be aware that certain aspects of self are socially constructed through our interactions, for example, we often overlook the individual in front of us and address the stereotype of AD.

Studying conversational data from a critical approach serves two very important roles in dementia research. As noted earlier, it gives us more insight into how (at times hegemonic) institutional discourses frame interactions with people with dementia and position them into an identity associated with helplessness, lack of choice, negativity, and fear. Second, it allows us some insight into the experience of dementia, and following on from this, we can involve a new voice into the discourse of dementia-the voice of those who actually have dementia and who like BL may not appreciate our well thought out life aids and interventions. For too long discourses of dementia have marginalized those who are most affected.

Final Thought

The issue of self-concept in dementia is not unlike the process of horror Kafka portrays in his novel *Metamorphosis* (1915/1988), a story in which the protagonist Gregor Samsa awakens to find he has become a giant cockroach unable to be understood by others and no longer recognized by his fearful family and friends.

8

Repetitiveness in Conversations With Dementia

REPETITIVE VERBAL BEHAVIORS
IN DEMENTIA-AND ELSEWHERE

In this chapter, and chapter 9, we take an approach that is somewhat different from that in chapters 3 to 7 : Whereas chapters 3 to 7 are each dedicated to a specific theoretical or philosophical approach or method, our point of departure here is a frequently encountered issue in conversations with dementia. The various approaches already encountered will inform our data analysis.

Repetitive verbal behaviors (RVBs) in neurogenic communication disorders are the subject of a substantial amount of literature frequently based on cases investigated in experimental or test-based paradigms. Table 8.1 gives an overview of categories and definitions (from Wallesch, 1990, p. 134).

TABLE 8.1
Repetitive Verbal Behaviors

Type and Definition:	Sources
Echolalia	
"The automatic and compulsive repetition of words by the patient in the absence of the understanding of their meaning."	Brain (1965, p. 105)
"A reflex automatism of verbal response, providing an empty, stereotyped quality to speech."	Hecaen and Albert (1978, pp. 74–75)
"Repetition of the investigator's utterances with or without mild changes in position and choice of words."	Huber, Poeck, and Weniger (1982, p. 80)
Iteration	
Repetition of parts of words (sounds or syllables), included in Ludlow, Polinsky, Caine, Bassich, and Ebert's (1982) definition of palilalia.	Machetanz, Schönle, and Benecke (1988)
Palilalia	
"The involuntary repetition two or more times of a terminal word, phrase or sentence."	Critchley (1970, p. 201)
"A disorder of speech characterized by compulsive repetition of a phrase or word that the patient reiterates with increasing rapidity and with a decrescendo of voice volume."	Boller et al. (1973, p. 1117)
"The reiteration of single or partial syllables or combinations of syllables many times with increasing rate."	Ludlow et al. (1982, p. 353)
Perseveration	
"The recurrence, out of context and in the absence of the original stimulus, of some behavioral act."	Buckingham, Whitaker, and Whitaker (1979, p. 329)
Recurring/recurrent utterances	
"A subgroup of speech automatisms which consist exclusively of syllables or sequence of syllables which are linked up in their production."	Huber et al., (1982, p. 81)

(continued)

TABLE 8.1   (continued)

Type and Definition	Source
"An utterance made up of either real words or a non-meaningful string of speech sounds which some aphasic patients produce either every time they produce speech or just sometimes."	Code (1982, p. 141)
"The term recurrent utterance is most usually reserved to describe repeated and unchanging utterances made up of recognizable words which some aphasic individuals produce either every time they attempt speech, or almost every time they attempt speech."	Code (1989, p. 155)

Stereotypy

"A permanent stereotyped verbal expression with or without linguistic meaning unconsciously and involuntarily uttered."	Alajouanine (1956, p. 6)
"Set phrases that are used recurrently but usually communicatively adequate."	Huber et al. (1982, p. 82)

Speech automatism

"A constantly recurring utterance which is formally rigid, consists of neologistic sequences of syllables, interchangeable words or phrases, does not fit into the linguistic context either lexically or syntactically, and which the patient produces in contrast to the intention expected by his interlocutors."	Huber et al. (1982, p. 81)

Speech tics

(a) Coprolalia: "All unprovoked swearing using single words or phrases."	Ludlow et al. (1982, p. 353)
(b) Word tics: "Any meaningful word interjected into speech and not part of communicative speech or hesitation phenomena."	Ludlow et al. (1982, p. 353)

*Reproduced with permission from Psychology Press, Ltd; www.psypress.co.uk/journals.asp

The categories in Table 8.1 give an idea of the wide range of RVBs that have been investigated and classified; they also show that labels may be used differently in different studies. As Wallesch (1990) points out, "different authors classify the phenomena in different ways and use a wide variety of terms" (p. 138). Literature on RVBs in dementia reports the frequent occurrence of echolalia in the more advanced stages of the dementing disease (Cummings, Benson, Hill, & Read, 1985; Wallesch, 1990, p. 143) as well as of perseveration, which again is reported as common in the advanced stages (Sjogren, Sjogren, & Lindgren, 1952) although uncommon in the early stages (Shindler, Caplan, & Hier, 1984; Wallesch, 1990, p. 149). Shindler et al. (1984) define perseverations as "immediate inappropriate repetition of a prior response" (p. 149) and distinguish these from intrusions defined as "inappropriate repetition of responses after intervening stimuli" (p. 149). Bayles, Tomoeda, Kaoszniak, Stern, and Egans (1985, p. 103) distinguish between continuous and discontinuous perseverations and in the latter category, between perseverations that occur after an intervening response (ideational perseveration) and those that occur after an intervening stimulus (impairment of switching). Much of the available literature is concerned with the search for neuropathological and motor correlates leading to the cognitive and behavioral manifestations of RVBs. Thus, Bayles et al. (1985) speak of multiple potential factors causing perseverations in dementia, that is, "lack of cortical inhibition of new memory and poor recent memory, persistent neural excitation, and paucity of ideas" (p. 115).

As well as repetitive behavioral patterns-such as the repetition of utterances, parts of utterances, or motor sequences (as in the definitions in Table 1)-there are studies that focus more on the repetition of ideas, redundancy of information, or perseveration of topics in dementia (see Ulatowska & Chapman, 1995, and further studies discussed there), which in turn will of course tend to be expressed by means of more or less fixed verbal expressions. Repetitiveness, be it of ideas, topics, or their verbal expression, is also a concern that is frequently cited by caregivers (see Powell, Hale, & Bayer, 1995).

Some Terms and Definitions

The brief introduction above shows that multiple terminologies are used in the literature on RVBs and that the same terms are at times used with slightly varying definitions. Thus, under the wide umbrella of repetitiveness, we distinguish various subcategories. First, there is the repetition of ideas or conversational topics when a speaker insists on leading a conversation back to talking about, for example, a long-lost relative, or football, or political likes and dislikes. We use the term *topic bias* for this type of repetitiveness (see, e.g., Body, 2005; Perkins, Body, & Parker, 1995). Topic bias may express itself in the use of repetitive linguistic structures, when the same content is expressed repeatedly in the same words or with very little variation. However, repetitive use of the same or of near-identical utterances does not necessarily amount to topic bias. Most of the categories in Table 8.1 would not be expressive of topic bias, but perseverations and stereotypies might. Likewise, discourse markers such as "well," "actually," and "as a matter of fact" are by their nature repetitive but do not represent topic bias. We continue to use the term repetitive verbal behavior (RVB) for any utterance or part of an utterance that is used in a repetitive pattern, either verbatim or with little and systematic variation. In due course, our data may lead us to various subcategorizations.

RVBS IN CONVERSATIONS
WITH AND WITHOUT DEMENTIA

As we pointed out earlier, much of the literature on RVBs is concerned with their potential symptomatic nature in various disorders of communication and cognition. We are more concerned with the potential role that RVBs have to play in either the maintenance, or indeed disruption, of conversational interaction. One question that comes to mind at this stage is how to operationalize the notion of repetitiveness, or, in other words, how many repetitions make an RVB or a topic bias? A conversation that was all novel and contained no repeated verbal behaviors at all would be a strange conversation indeed. Likewise, much of day-to-day interaction relies on prefabricated chunks of language, so-called formulas (we return later to a discussion of formulaicity in our data), for example, in greetings, leave-takings, and apologies, but we also rely on predictable collocations for many descriptive tasks. Human conversation thus has a certain tolerance for repetitiveness and therefore predictability and, it can be argued, a need for it (see, e.g., Wray, 2002, and earlier publications by the same author for a detailed discussion; also Body, 2005). Similarly, the perseveration of an idea can be socially supportive as in the repeated reassurance that a speaker is committed to assist a listener in some task, for example, or in the repeated assertion that a listener did the right thing when making a difficult decision.

What, then, makes repetitiveness noticeable or "above normal"? At this stage, preanalysis as it were, we can speculate that the tolerance for repetitiveness may be linked with the information content of the RVB in question, its length and linguistic complexity, and its persistence (not necessarily its frequency): The repeated use of "as a matter of fact" or "I have to tell ya" may be noticed as a feature of a speaker's idiolect but will not usually be considered disruptive or counterproductive to continued interaction. The repeated narration of a whole episode of a speaker's life or the persistent return by a speaker to a particular topic of conversation, on the other hand, will.

Data: FM and the Repetitive Use of Questions

Our data for this chapter consist of an informal conversation between three participants, FM, R, and MH.[1] At the time the conversation was recorded, R and MH had been visiting FM in the nursing home at weekly intervals for approximately 2 months. FM does not, from one visit to the next, appear to remember R's and MH's names or any factual details about them that she has been told before, but she does not treat them as total strangers.[2]

The most prominent repetitive pattern in FM's conversation is the use of certain questions, most often slight variations on the theme of "where y'all from." These questions represent both a topic bias because they (re)introduce the topic that the question is about into the conversation and RVBs because there is little variation in their content or form (there are other RVBs in FM's talk, and we look at some of them below). In this particular conversation, there are 5 repetitive inquiries and thus five "favorite" topics. At this stage, a few words on the topic of counting instances of behaviors in qualitative research may be in order. We do, in this chapter, give numbers of instances. This is intended to give readers an idea of the prevalence of RVBs and topic bias in this conversation. Although we understand that many qualitative researchers are very wary of counting instances, numbers do help in the description of a recurrent pattern (see Silverman, 2000, for further discussion of this topic).

Topic A: "Where Y'all From."   In this conversation, FM uses 19 instances of a question asking where her interlocutors live or come from. Altogether, 159 turns in a 561-turn conversation are taken up by repeatedly negotiating this information. The most common variants are *where PRONOUN (COPULA) from* and *PRONOUN from where/here*, occurring considerably more frequently than the variants *where PRONOUN live*, *PRONOUN live here*, and *what/where is PRONOUN's home*. Four out of the five instances of the variants containing *live* occur as the last four examples of this construction in this conversation, which leads to the question whether we may see a clustering effect here or a priming effect (more of which below, in the discussion). We also note that many of these questions occur after pauses in the conversational flow. While this is also true for other utterances (and as can be seen from the full transcript, measur-

---

[1] Excerpts from this conversation have already been discussed in Müller and Guendouzi (2005).
[2] This is, of course, a very impressionistic statement. We have not formally tested FM's recall of factual information or indeed recognition.

able pauses also occur within utterances), we note this pattern now for future reference.

Within the conversation passages initiated by "where y'all from" or similar questions, we find more repetitive patterns. Questions set up a range (typically, a small range) of possible answers; thus, the answers themselves potentially become RVBs. Indeed, the principle of adjacency, such that one conversational turn not only forms the context for the following one but also constrains it in form and content, is one of the basic tenets of CA (see chap. 5). The extended repetitive sequences initiated by "where y'all from" are illustrated in Example 8.1. FM's request for information, often preceded by a pause, is followed by a relevant response from one interlocutor (R or MH); FM follows up with a comment, often a repeat variant of *X is (not) far (from here)*. This uptake may in turn prompt a comment, typically a confirmation, from the present interlocutor. Then FM directs either a repeat request for the same information or a reduced form (such as "and you,") to the other interlocutor, which receives a relevant response that in turn may be taken up by FM by a comment, again often a variant of *X is (not) far (from here)* or a statement relating to FM's place of residence.

Example 8.1 (see Appendix F)

61 FM: =oh no, teaching is not a easy job. *((all chuckle)) ((indrawn breath))* (2.0) and
         I'm getting <u>old,</u> you know? *((all chuckle)) ((indrawn breath))* I'm <u>old,</u> sugar.
         (2.0) (xX,) (1.5) tryin' to take a little care of myself so,
62 R: mhm,
         (2.0)
63 FM: where y'all from.
         (3.0)
64 R: u- me? I'm from C.
65 FM: C?=
66 R: =yea.
67 FM: oh yea. you're not from here at all.
68 R: {LV <u>yea.</u> *((laughs))}* a very different country.
69 FM: uh?
70 R: C, em. I mean-. it is very far,=
71 FM: =ye:s. and where you from honey.
72 MH: O.
73 FM: oh yes. O is not (.) not too far.

TABLE 8.2
Topic A: "Where Y'all From"

Turn (No. on Topic)	Utterance
32 (3)	… not too far from L (1.5) where y'all from.
63 (11)	(2.0) where y'all from
91 (2)	mhm. (2.5) and that's where you live. m:?
131 (15)	…… (2.0) no I haven't been here (x: xxx), *((chuckles))* very short time. (10.0) y'all live around here?
164 (12)	(4.0) where y'all- where you live.
194 (6)	what is your home,
	((note 12-s pause in F's previous utterance (193)): (12.0) and when you leave from there you're goin' home.))
209 (5)	(just as well to-) (.) ye:s. (7.0) (x the truth an' everything) (24.0) where y'all from.
229 (11)	(xX) (.) longer. (13.0) and y'all's from (.) where.
255 (16)	(24.0) where y'all from.
273 (3)	(they moved xxxxxx xx) I'm talkin', *((light chuckle))* heh. (I don't know who're you) (10.0) where you say you're from,
312 (2)	'm not tired sugar. (3.0) just sittin round. doin nothin. (20.0) y'all not from here huh.
314 (5)	where y'all from.
333 (18)	(10.0) where y'all from.
	((Note also: 338: and who you (x) from here, ; 345 where she's from?;))
374 (11)	where's your home.
394 (10)	*((chuckles))* m::::. (2.0) but you- your home is (2.0) in whe- where.
438 (6)	m:, (.) oh yes I'm goin home next week, *((chuckles; announcement over intercom interrupts))* (4.0) where you live honey.
479 (10)	……(3.0) they still in school they're not (1.5) out of school yet. (14.0) and where you live,
546 (6)	(4.0) you live here?
552 (4)	where you live.

Topic B:"You like it Around Here." FM's inquiry "you like it around here" occurs eight times altogether, and question, response, and follow-up sequences account for 26 turns of the conversation. Example 8.2 illustrates how topic B is negotiated:

Example 8.2:

525 R: yea. I'm just a student.=
526 FM: =student.=
527 R: =uhuh,
528 FM: at what school.
529 R: uh, the university of L
530 FM: ye:s:. (7.0) and you like it over here?
531 R: yea. sure.
532 FM: ((chuckles)) m:. (2.0) and you like it too.
533 MH: ((laughs)) yea,
           (11.0)

TABLE 8.3
Topic B

Turn (No. on Topic)	Utterance:
145 (5)	(4.0) and you like it around here?
186 (2)	(31.0) and y'all like it over here?
354 (2)	right. (5.0) and you like it here honey,
372 (2)	an' you like it?
392 (2)	oh ye:s:. you like it so far?
404 (4)	and you like it to be around here,
497 (5)	m:. and you like it sugar.
530 (4)	ye:s:. (7.0) and you like it over here?

A further pattern that appears to emerge are topic sequences. In all but two instances, FM's *you like it (over here / so far)* is preceded by either the assertion that F or R is a student, as here, or by the negotiation that R's home is far away.

Topic C: "Have Any Children," and Topic D: "You're Married." There are four instances of *(PRONOUN) have/got any children*, two of which are in close proximity to two out of three instances of "you're married"; see Example 8.3:

Example 8.3

176 F:	have any children,
177 R:	no,
178 F:	you're married.
179 R:	yea.
180 F:	{LV and you are married.}=
181 MH:	=no,=
182 F:	=oh you're not married.
183 MH:	{CV no not yet.}
184 F:	{LV you don't [have any-*}
185 MH:	[I'm only* twenty-one, ((R laughs))

TABLE 8.4
Topic C

Turn (No. on Topic)	Utterance:
95 (5)	got- got children?
107 (6)	{piano (xxX,)} ((chuckles)) ((indrawn breath)) (3.0) yes:, (7.0) you have any children, huh,=
176 (2)	(6.0) have any children,
184 (2)	{LV you don't [have any-*}

TABLE 8.5
Topic D

Turn (No. on Topic)	Utterance:
93 (2)	(4.0) you're married?
178 (6)	you're married.
540 (6)	… if I do I'll marry again. somebody else can take care of me. (3.0) both of y'all married. huh,

The sequencing of Topic C (having children) and Topic D (being married) is on the face of it not surprising because there is an obvious real-life (although culturally conditioned, no doubt) relationship here that makes the sequencing of these inquiries acceptable and possibly even expected. As an aside, what is interesting for those working with persons with AD is that FM has apparently preserved, thus far, the real-world and cultural knowledge that links the two questions and is able to use this knowledge very skilfully in her conversation. Another example of following one repetitive inquiry with another once the first one has run its course is FM's use of Topic E, below.

Topic E: "You're Visiting?" The three instances of *you ('re) over here / here (just) visiting* all follow on sequences introduced by Inquiry A, as illustrated in Example 8.4, which also shows an instance of FM using yet another repeat inquiry, reintroducing Topic B:

Example 8.4

384 FM: you far from here. (4.0) ye:s:. (2.0) but you're here visiting.
              (1.5)
385 R: not visiting.
386 FM: you goina be here a while?
387 R: a:h I'm here to study.
388 FM: a what?
389 R: I'm a student (.) here.
390 FM: oh you a student here.
391 R: mhm,
392 FM: oh ye:s:. you like it so far?

TABLE 8.6
Topic E

Turn (No. on Topic)	Utterance:
277 (2)	and you're over here just visiting,
384 (3)	you far from here. (4.0) ye:s:. (2.0) but you're here visiting.
489 (6)	and you visitin too?

Overall, around 40% of turns in this conversation are taken up by turn sequences introduced by the repeat inquiries discussed above.[3] Moreover, there are other repetitive turn sequences. For example, FM frequently uses "huh?" or a similar minimal request for clarification, which induces R or MH to repeat their previous utterance. FM also uses other RVBs, namely, many partial or verbatim repetitions on of R's or MH's preceding utterance and self-repetitions of her own utterances; see Example 8.5 for an illustration of all three patterns. We have already noted in our discussion of Topic A that the turn sequences introduced by repeat inquiry are in themselves repetitive in nature and that we find repetitive topic sequences, too, such that one favorite topic follows on from another one:

Example 8.5

255 FM: where y'all from.
256 MH: from- (.) about half an hour from (.) L.

---

[3]A total of 37 repeat inquiries and their follow-up account for 225 out of 561 turns.

257 FM: yes. (1.0) that's all?
258 MH: mhm,
259 FM: oh well you can almost see you from L eh,
260 MH: ((laughs)) {LV not quite.}
261 FM: {piano m::::.} (4.0) 'bout an hour from [L,*
262 MH: [half an* hour.
263 FM: about an hour from L?
264 MH: half an hour? you know?
265 FM: oh a half hour. (3.0) wh- what's the name of it.
266 MH: O?
267 FM: oh yes. I know where is O. (15.0) an' you live in O too.
268 R: no, (2.5) I live very far from here.
269 F: huh?
270 R: far from here, I mean C. I'm from C.

A VIEW FROM EC

At this stage, it may be advisable to take a step back from the individual instances of RVBs and topic bias and consider the speech situation in which the interlocutors find themselves (see chap. 3, on EC). In chapter 3, we introduced the SPEAKING grid, and a brief application here may afford some pause for reflection on the RVBs and topic biases we find in this conversation. Our speech situation is R and MH's visit to the nursing home in which FM is a resident, which embeds the speech event under investigation, namely, the conversation. The SETTING is FM's room in the nursing home, thus confirming or underlining the status and roles of the PARTICIPANTS: FM is on home ground, whereas R and MH are temporary visitors who can be assumed not to be entirely familiar with the communication patterns they may find including the ways in which dementia may impact on the conversation. However, as well as having overt roles as social visitors vis-à-vis FM, R and MH also have a role that comes with both of them being students and R being obviously a foreigner; both circumstances are repeatedly referred to in the conversation. Thus, they may be understood and may actively place themselves in the position of learners, whereas F may be seen as being the local expert who has a greater ownership, and possibly implied control, of the situation. In chapter 3, we discussed the problematicity of defining the ENDS in conversations with dementia, especially in situations in which some of the participants have known covert as well as overt goals. Although R and MH are studying dementia, and their covert goal is thus to use this interaction as a learning experience about interactional patterns in dementia, their declared goal (explained to FM before the recording started and including a request for permission to tape record the situation) is to learn about nursing home residents including their lives and memories. Whether this declared goal remains in FM's conscious awareness throughout the conversation is doubtful given her obvious problems with short-term memory and anterograde amnesia. Thus, it is more likely that she derives an END for the conversation from its setting and participants: She has two visitors and treats the social event of the visit as an end in itself. The ACT SEQUENCES are the narrower focus of our analysis here or at least those act sequences that result in repetitive patterns. We return to them in a moment. As we may expect in a social visit, the KEY of the interaction is informal throughout in keeping with the GENRE, a friendly chat between (differentially) unfamiliar participants on the occasion of a social visit. The predominant INSTRUMENTALITY is speech; and of course, our audiotape does not permit us to analyze nonverbal aspects of the interaction. We may add here, however, that the vast majority of the spoken language used in this interaction is highly intelligible, which is not a trivial fact in the presence of dementia. The NORMS operating in this situation can be described as consisting of various overlapping sets of conventions relating back to the setting and the participants and their relative positions and status vis-à-vis each other. The norms of polite conversation appear to be operational: throughout the interaction, there are very few instances of interruptions or overlaps and interestingly, no utterances that would be inappropriate in a conversation between three adult females from two different generations who do not know each other intimately. Thus, the ACT SEQUENCE that is of interest to us here-that is, all of FM's inquiries into her interlocutors' lives and her follow-up comments-is linguistically and interactionally polite (see chap. 4) in that they express an interest in R and MH and their lives but only to a degree that would not be face threatening by either revealing or requesting information that could be perceived as too personal in a conversation between relative strangers.

There appear to be two main constraints on the ACT SEQUENCE in this conversation (strictly speaking, we should maybe say that these constraints operate on the topic choices that in turn determine acts). The intact norms of polite conversation just discussed represent one of these constraints or constraint complexes,[4] and R and MH's covert ENDS are another. Compared to many other interactions between persons with and without dementia, R and MH may be somewhat atypical in their conversational behaviors because they do not insist on either their earlier acquaintance with FM nor on information that has been imparted previously but rather are content to adjust their conversational pace to FM's questions and thereby initiative and

[4]Again, the fact that these norms appear to be operational here is not a trivial circumstance in the presence of dementia.

to reiterate information as many times as requested. A further influence on the progression of the conversation we mention here is in fact the absence of a constraint: There is no pressure on any of the participants to convey any particular content; there is no information that must be conveyed, no action that has to be taken.[5] Given this particular bundle of constraints, participants, and context, one may well come to the conclusion that it is not surprising that a conversation of some 40 min becomes repetitive and keeps recycling the same topics, which in turn are likely to be expressed by means of the same ACT SEQUENCES. What else, indeed, would this particular group of people have to talk about? It is important to keep in mind that as far as FM is concerned, R and MH are relatively unfamiliar social visitors, and because they do not attempt to reorient FM to their reality of having met her several times before, they take their lead from FM in how their roles are shaped and projected.

Our view from EC gives a first inkling that topic bias and RVBs of the type we observe here-specifically, repeated inquiries and repetitive act sequences that are replayed several times with little and predictable variation-may in fact be an emergent characteristic of a speech situation given a favorable constellation of factors. Among these factors is, of course, dementia and therefore memory problems (among others). However, we must also consider in our analysis of RVBs the contribution of intact conversational politeness on the part of FM, that is, the intact social knowledge that allows her to appropriately negotiate this situation to her apparent satisfaction and the overt satisfaction of her interlocutors. Furthermore, repetitive ACT SEQUENCES in conversations are by their very nature collaborative achievements. Thus, R's and MH's uptake of FM's questions, their responses to her questions, show little variation of expression because the information requested does not permit much variation within the constraints of (Gricean) cooperation (see chap. 6). Furthermore, their determination to leave the conversational initiative with FM makes no attempt to avoid or derail the spirals of repetitiveness.

Although a full discussion of discourse samples collected in assessment paradigms would lead us too far afield, it is worth considering whether some of the RVBs and topic biases produced in such situations may also be at least in part due to the constraints of the situation. For example, Bayles et al. (1985, p. 108) discussed verbal perseverations produced in oral description tasks in which a participant is asked to tell an examiner all they can about common objects such as a nail or a marble. While the task obviously challenges participants' word finding, remaining on task, sentence formulation, and other linguistic and nonlinguistic skills, we should not forget

---

[5]Compare, for example, interactions that have as their END that a patient accept medication, or a resident consent to come to lunch, or see the doctor and be examined.

the overall situational demand, namely, that the speech situation is one of assessment, the setting may be a laboratory at a university or hospital or the participants' place of residence, but in either case, the communicative task is not one that is altogether natural. Therefore, the overall demand becomes one of producing language in a situation in which, for example, a long pause, which may be tolerated in a conversational setting, would be counterproductive (as in, e.g., prompting the examiner to move on to the next task prematurely). It would be interesting to compare how language elicited in assessment settings compares to, for example, conversational language as regards the occurrence of RVBs and topic biases (see also Hamilton, 1994a, and Perkins et al., 1998).[6]

A VIEW FROM CONVERSATION MANAGEMENT

In the previous section, we looked at RVBs and topic bias as arising within the constellation of factors making up a speech situation or in other words, the macrocontext of RVBs. Here, we examine FM's repetitive questions from the angle of conversation management and take a closer look at the microcontext of some of FM's repetitive questions. Due to space limitations, we restrict our discussions to several instances of the question "where y'all from." The first one of these occurs in turn 32; see Example 8.6.

Example 8.6

32 FM: {piano it's not right- close- close, but ('dyou know what) not too far from L}
         (1.5) where y'all from
33 MH: O,
34 FM: O. I used to have (.) relatives in O. (1.0) but I don't know if they still there.
         (2.0) I don't hear from them they must be gone somewheres else.
         (2.0)

In this example, the question "where y'all from" represents a shift to a related topic: In the previous 10 turns, FM, R, and MH establish the location of the school where FM used to be a teacher (see Appendix F). We further note the linguistic disfluency in turn 32 preceding a measurable pause and the fact that the utterance up to the pause is produced with noticeably

---

[6]See Perkins et al. (1998, p. 46) for a brief discussion of repetitive questions by conversation partners with DAT and Lewy bodies. Recurrent, repetitive questions are interpreted as a strategy to avoid difficulty (e.g., the inability to identify a person talked about) by handing the turn back to the conversational partner to maintain conversation flow. Perkins et al. (1998) describe the use of repetitive questions initiating a topic as ideational perseveration, which in turn can be explained "as arising from the persons's inability to monitor his or her own speech output or from inability to change mental sets" (Perkins et al., 1998, p. 46, referring to Shindler et al., 1984, and Bayles et al., 1985; see also Müller & Guendouzi, 2005).

lower intensity. This we can interpret as a trouble indicating behavior (TIB), namely, an indication that FM is finding it difficult to establish the location of her old school (turn 26) with any degree of precision. The pause of 1.5-s duration is a transition space, that is, a potential completion point of FM's turn, but R or MH do not take advantage of it. The turn reverts back to FM and with it the obligation to keep the conversation going. Thus, the change to a related topic, "where y'all from," after a measurable pause, represents a repair move, a self-initiated self-repair within her own turn to be precise. The question sets up the first half of an adjacency pair, and MH's response in turn 33 half fulfills the demands of adjacency by contributing the relevant response concerning her own home. In turn 34, FM makes MH's response the topic of her utterance and provides a comment from her own experience. The topic of O (MH's home town) is pursued for another 4 turns.

The second occurrence of "where y'all from" occurs in turn 63 (see Example 8.1). Again, the question occurs after a measurable pause and after a minimal turn on the part of R. This time, the shift is to an unrelated topic. From R's and MH's point of view, it is of course also a return to a topic that has been covered before. We cannot be sure, given FM's dementia, whether this is not the case here. What is important, though, is that all three participants treat the topic as new. The question again follows a multiclause utterance on the part of FM. We again note measurable pauses and two unintelligible syllables that may represent an attempt at a word. The final sentence of FM's turn 61 is incomplete (indicated by the intonation and the conjunction *so*) and is not completed after R's minimal turn "mhm," (with a slight rise of intonation). Instead, there is another measurable pause and the topic shift by means of the question. The two unintelligible syllables followed by a pause and an incomplete syntactic structure can again be interpreted as trouble, but R and MH do not attempt to repair. Instead, it is, again, FM herself who initiates repair by means of the question in turn 63. R provides the first completion of the adjacency pair in turn 64, and FM's uptake of her response consists of a minimal request for confirmation, which sets up another adjacency pair. That completed, FM confirms understanding by making a comment, which in turn is confirmed and commented on by R in turn 68. R's utterance represents another trouble spot (possibly due to R's laughing voice quality) indicated by FM's minimal request for clarification (turn 69: "uh?") and apparently successfully repaired in turn 71 by R. Once this is established by FM's "ye:s," she returns to the topic initiated in turn 63 and follows up with the question to MH, which in turn gets duly responded to and followed up on by FM.

The third instance of "where y'all from" in turn 209 (see Example 8.7) confirms a pattern of a troubled turn followed by a measurable pause and the topic shift by means of the question. The pause here is considerably longer than in the other instances, and note the occurrence of another long pause (7 s) in the same turn:

Example 8.7

206 MH: it's pretty outside today.
207 FM: oh that what she's saying.
208 MH: mhm,
209 FM: (just as well to-) (.) ye:s. (7.0) (x the truth an' everything) (24.0) where y'all from.
210 MH: O.
211 FM: O, that's not very far from here,=
212 MH: =no.
213 FM: I have (Xxxxx) up there. (3.0) yea they live in O.

The preceding turns (from turn 201) have been spent establishing that "it's pretty outside." FM's turn 209 appears to be a comment on MH's confirmation of what R has said, but it is impossible to be sure of the thrust of her utterance (due to a combination of syntactic incompleteness, lack of content-rich words, and decreased clarity of the speech signal) or whether the part of the utterance after the 7-s pause is an attempt to continue her previous comment or a fresh start. There are two transition points, represented by the pauses, that MH and R do not take advantage of, and again, it is FM who repairs, continues the conversation, by means of the question. Likewise, we again find her taking up MH's response with the by now predictable comment "that's not far from here" and a further elaboration, relating the new topic 'O' to her own experience.

FM's question "where y'all from" makes up the whole of turn 255 (see Appendix F). Note again that a long pause, 24 s, precedes the question, which in turn follows after another topic (establishing that all interlocutors know Ms. B from down the hall) has been exhausted; the question thus represents another topic shift to an unrelated topic. This time, we interpret FM's question as other-initiated, other-repair, dealing with the long silence following both R's and MH's minimal responses to FM's question "y'all know her to" in turn 252. Thus, although R and MH do not treat the long silences in this conversation as trouble, interestingly, FM does and makes an attempt to fill them (see also chap. 5, this volume, for a discussion of the ownership, or lack thereof, of pauses in this conversation).

In turn 314, the question "where y'all from" is set up by means of a variant in turn 312 (see Example 8.8). This functions as a pre-s (using Levinson's 1983, p. 345, terminology), a prequestion, as it were.

Example 8.8

312 FM: 'm not tired sugar. (3.0) just sittin round. doin nothin. (20.0) y'all not from
         here huh.
         (2.0)
313 MH: nn:,
314 FM: where y'all from.
315 MH: O,
316 FM: O. (2.0) that's not very far from here. huh,
317 MH: n:o,

The prequestion setting up the question "where y'all from" follows a 20-s pause (turn 312) and again is a switch to an unrelated topic. This time, there is no TIB in terms of, for example, incomplete syntactic structures (at least not beyond what is acceptable in casual conversation) or diminished articulatory clarity. However, it is another instance where MH and R do not fill a lengthening pause, but FM does, this time by means of a prequestion followed by the question itself after a minimal response from MH.[7]

In our final example, turn 3343, the question "where y'all from" again makes up FM's whole turn and follows a measurable pause (10 s). The topic shifts to an unrelated topic; turns 327 to 332 accompany FM drinking a milkshake and R putting the empty packet on the window ledge.

It would appear, then, that RVBs of the type used by FM in this conversation (and in many others we have had with her over the course of 2 years) are a useful tool in the management of a conversation. Questions set up incomplete adjacency pairs, and it is up to the conversation partner to complete the preferred sequence with a response. FM skillfully uses this structural tool to continue the conversation at points where there is a potential danger of discontinuation or breakdown: We have observed instances of troubled turns on FM's part, with a fluent question completing the turn, and instances of long pauses. It is an interesting feature of this conversation that it is FM who fills the pauses, rather than her two interlocutors. Further, the triadic structure of the conversation also contributes to the topic bias, since FM shows a pattern of addressing either the same question, or a shortened version, to the second interlocutor after the first one has answered it.

RVBS, FORMULAS, AND NONPROPOSITIONAL SPEECH

The linguistic, specifically the neurolinguistic, nature of RVBs has exercised researchers for some time. On the basis of our data, we cannot hope to answer questions of where or how RVBs are generated (see, e.g., Wallesch

---

[7] Note that in turn 318, FM maintains the topic of "O" and expands it with a comment from her own experience after a 35-s pause. Thus, a pause is not always filled with a topic shift.

& Blanken, 2000) or explore their neuropathological correlates. Therefore, we do not pursue the ongoing psycholinguistic and neurolinguistic debate further here. However, we can examine some indicators of a possible formulaic character of the RVBs we find used by FM, in particular, her repetitive questions. Wray (2002) offered a "working definition" of a *formulaic sequence:* "a sequence, continuous or discontinuous, of words or other elements, which is, or appears to be, prefabricated: that is, stored and retrieved whole from memory at the time of use, rather than being subject to generation or analysis by the language grammar" (p. 9). It is of course tempting to regard any RVB that is used with little or no variation as a formula. However, as Wray (2002) pointed out, there is a great danger of circularity here.

Referring to Pawley and Syder (2000), Wray (2002, p. 35) lists "overall fluency, intonation pattern and changes in speed of articulation" as indicators of prefabricated chunks of language. We can note that FM's repetitive questions are generally produced fluently, without hesitations or false starts. This, of itself, is not necessarily a strong indicator in favor of formulaicity because most of FM's short turns are produced fluently. However, there are a number of turns where a repetitive question closes a troubled turn (see the discussion of conversation management above) and where the question is articulated more clearly than the rest of the utterance, which may point toward the fact that it is easier to produce because it is a fixed expression (see, e.g., turns 210, 274).

On the other hand, it is possible that the long pauses preceding the question in these examples provide enough planning time for FM to produce a fluent, problem-free utterance. In addition, the greater part of FM's utterances is fluent; in contrast with, for example, F, discussed in other chapters (see Appendixes B and C and chap. 9), FM does not exhibit many fluctuations in speech intelligibility. FM's questions are produced with no notable variation in intonation contour or in speed of delivery, but they are not exceptional in this regard in as much as FM's speech does not, overall, show many prosodic fluctuations.

Van Lancker-Sidtis (2004) distinguishes between compositional-propositional and holistic-nonpropositional language, with various subcategories of each, visualized as points on a continuum ranging from novel to reflexive constructions. Toward the more novel end of the continuum but still containing some prefabricated linguistic material, we find, for example, sentence stems (as in "I'd like you to meet ...") and indirect requests ("it's getting late") or collocations ("fast asleep"). Toward the other end of the continuum, there are pause fillers ("ya know"), or expletives ("son of a gun"; Van Lancker-Sidtis, 2004, pp. 3–4). The continuum is described as a "schema [that] offers a non-exhaustive, heuristically presented overview of the selected categories and properties of formulaic utterances and possible relations between them" (Van Lancker-Sidtis, 2004, p. 4), with the caveat that "questions remain about how the categories differ or group together and whether or not transition at the endpoints (reflexive and novel expression) is continuous" (p. 4). The main concern in Van Lancker-Sidtis's discussions are what she describes as two modes of language competence and their interaction with each other, namely, the processing of formulaic, fixed material on one hand and of novel linguistic constructions on the other. An illustration of the interaction between these two language-processing modes is the widespread use of so-called schemata or phrasal lexical items,[8] defined as "fixed forms with at least one open lexical slot" (Van Lancker-Sidtis, 2004, p. 28) such as "you've seen one _____, you've seen them all" (p. 29).

We do not make a decision here into which category of RVB or nonpropositional speech FM's repetitive questions fall. As discussed earlier and in some detail by Van Lancker-Sidtis (2004), taxonomies are manifold and not unproblematic. Part of their problematicity lies in the fact that any definitive categorization of RVBs makes definite assumptions as to the nature of the language processing involved, and this is not justified on the basis of our data. However, Van Lancker-Sidtis's timely reminder that the use of expressions of various degrees of flexibility or fixity is an important part of linguistic competence (and by implication of course, performance) is useful for our discussion. As we pointed out above, much of the literature on RVBs and topic bias in neurogenic disorders is concerned with their symptomatic nature relative to the underlying disorder. Our data does not permit us to draw any conclusions along these lines. We can note that RVBs of certain types are a common occurrence in conversations with FM; we can note their patterns, both in terms of the macrocontext of the speech situation and the microcontext of the turn sequences in which they occur.

EMERGENT REPETITIVENESS?

With the above discussion in mind, we can ask the question whether the use of RVBs (rather than their nature) is as much symptomatic of certain interactional constellations as of a neuropathology. In other words, can we speak of emergent repetitiveness? Our view from EC showed that the speech situation here embodies a number of factors that are conducive to the recycling of topics, among them, FM's dementia; the relationship between the participants; the overt, covert, and inferred (as regards FM) ends of the participants; as well as the fact that conversational politeness and social knowledge are intact to the extent that she can negotiate a friendly chat among relative strangers successfully. Our view from conversation management confirms the conclusion that repetitiveness can be seen to emerge

---

[8]The terms are from Lyons (1968) and Kuiper and Everaert (2000), respectively.

from a combination of speaker-internal and situation-internal factors. In terms of conversation management, FM's intact turn-taking behavior is crucial. We saw that FM takes the initiative in filling pauses, in other words, in supplying repair moves when there is a danger of conversation breakdown, whereas R and MH typically do not. On the other hand, R and MH are collaborative as regards the preferred completion of adjacency pairs and supply answers to questions whenever required to do so. Thus, what appears at first sight to be a single, easily isolable utterance type, an RVB, appears rather to be the result of a complex interplay of many factors, of skills, deficits, behaviors, and situational factors, a product of multiply embedded contexts.

9

Intelligibility and Mutual Understanding in Dementia Discourse

UNDERSTANDINGS OF INTELLIGIBILITY

This is our second issues chapter, and as in chapter 8, we shall make reference to various methods, concepts, and points of theory that we introduced earlier in this book. As we mentioned in chapter 2 on data collection and transcribing, it is rare in nonclinical discourse studies that intelligibility becomes the focus of analysis. However, in clinical contexts, the abilities of interlocutors to understand each other and to signal their understanding is of course a central concern. We need to deal with fluctuations in speech intelligibility, deteriorations, and indeed improvements thereof; and of course, intelligibility may be a focus of therapeutic intervention. In the context of dementia, speech intelligibility per se, the improvement of the clarity of the speech signal, will very rarely be a prime target in rehabilitative activities. However, the ability of persons with dementia and their conversation partners, be they carers, health care professionals, or others, to make themselves understood to each other is of course a key factor in the maintenance of communicative functioning.

In the speech-language pathology literature, intelligibility is defined and conceptualized in various ways depending on the goals and foci of the research or intervention in question. For example, one may define intelligibility as the measure of the degree to which a person's speech can be understood by a listener (e.g., Weismer, Jeng, Laures, Kent, & Kent, 2001) or as a measure of the accuracy with which an acoustic signal is conveyed by a speaker and recovered by a listener (e.g., Kent, Weismer, Kent, & Rosenbeck, 1989; also, Hustad & Beukelman, 2001, 2002; Kent 1992a, 1992b; Kent, Miolo, & Bloedel, 1994; Yorkston & Beukelman, 1978; Yorkston, Beukelman, Strand, & Bell, 1999; Yorkston, Strand, & Kennedy, 1996). Thus, especially in the literature on speech disorders (as opposed to disorders of language or cognition), intelligibility is typically and sensibly treated as an issue of measurement of accuracy. At times, intelligibility, or identifiability of the speech signal, is distinguished from comprehensibility of the spoken language produced (e.g., Hustad & Beukelman, 2001, 2002; Yorkston et al., 1996). Kent (1992b) speaks of a multidimensional complex and a joint property of a speaker–listener dyad. This conception of intelligibility comes very close to our own take on this aspect of interaction. Kent (1992b) distinguishes auditory, perceptual, linguistic, acoustic, and physiologic dimensions to which we can add others, for example, informational, contextual, and attentional ones.

Given the focus of this book, our definition of intelligibility is based in conversational interaction. Conversation is collaborative and context bound, and participants typically strive for mutual understanding. Thus, *intelligibility* in interaction is, for our purposes, defined as the potential to achieve mutual understanding. Mutual understanding, and indeed the potential to achieve such a state, cannot be measured or observed directly. Interactants in a conversation cannot make objective claims as to whether mutual understanding has been achieved. They can and do, however, assert and bring to bear on the interaction their own perceptions. Because perceptions are accessible only through introspection (own perceptions) or by interpreting another's signals, the signaling of mutual understanding (or rather the interpretation of said signaling) is of course of prime importance (see also Wilkinson, 1999).

The assumptions that a potential for mutual understanding exists and that interlocutors strive to fulfill this potential are not trivial ones in the context of dementia. As we have shown in our own data throughout this book and as discussed in Berrewaerts et al. (2003), the impairments and preserved abilities that come with DAT present quite a heterogeneous picture across individuals and across the progression of the disease, although rough generalizations can be drawn (see chap. 1). Although we have, of necessity, treated our data extracts as static records, snapshots of interactional skills and problems, it is of course important to keep the progressive nature of DAT in mind. The skills and impairments of both persons with dementia (whether DAT or other) and their carers and other interlocutors change over time; the disease and its communicative sequelae impose dynamically changing demands on all those affected by it. As cognitive and communicative abilities of a person with dementia deteriorate and are in part compensated for both by that person and by interlocutors, interlocutors without dementia experience their own communicative impairments and are continually presented with new challenges.[1] However, dynamic challenges, fluctuations in mutual understanding, are also present within the microcontext of a single conversation as we show in our data sample below.

SOME METHODOLOGICAL ISSUES

Investigating intelligibility through the use of recordings and transcripts of conversations throws up some interesting methodological issues. These are closely related to the methodological problems we encountered and discussed in connection with CA as a method for the investigation of the complexity of conversation (see chap. 5). In essence, we are attempting to investigate the complexity of processes unfolding in real time by accessing a limited product from these processes, namely, a conversational recording, and subjecting it to another complex of interactive processes, namely, those of transcription and analysis. If we are interested in, for example, fluctuating intelligibility and communication breakdown or compensatory strategies to cope with such fluctuations over the course of an extended conversation (or even over the course of the progression of dementia), we have to live with these methodological issues, and we need to acknowledge them. What this boils down to, of course, is a core issue of qualitative research of whatever method: We need to be capable of distinguishing between patterns observable, describable, and categorizable in our data and any inferences we draw from these observations.

Conversational (Online) and Analytic Intelligibility

As we briefly noted in chapter 2, in our discussion of data gathering and transcribing, we need to distinguish between intelligibility for the purpose of interaction and intelligibility for the purpose of transcribing and data analysis. In other words, the potential for mutual understanding present in the conversation and its participants does not necessarily map perfectly onto the potential inherent in the interaction between data and transcriber

---

[1]See, for example, the discussions in Sabat (1991, 2001) and Perkins et al. (1998) on the crucial role of the interlocutor without dementia in managing and facilitating interactions.

to re-create a representation of the conversation. Thus, transcribers/analysts need to acknowledge that they are not analyzing intelligibility as experienced by an interlocutor (conversational, online, intelligibility) but rather intelligibility as experienced by the transcriber (analytic, post hoc, intelligibility). The latter can serve, with some reservations, as a basis on which to build inferences about the former. In cases in which the transcriber is also a participant in the recorded conversation, he or she can supply some introspection as to how analytic maps onto conversational intelligibility. However, post hoc introspective insight can of course not be taken as equivalent to the online process it comments on.

The shift from live, real-time, online involvement in a face-to-face interaction to the interaction between a live analyst and a recorded medium involves of course a dramatic shift in the distribution of all the skills (e.g., cognitive, perceptual, and productive) and factors (contextual and interactive) involved in realizing the potential for understanding. The live interaction affords access to contextual embedding and a wealth of interacting signals that are lost in a recording (especially if the recording is audio only). As well as that, online repair strategies are available; for example, requests for clarification can be implemented as necessary (see chap. 5). On the other hand, a recorded interaction removes the constraints of real-time processing; in practical terms, a transcriber/analyst has access to potentially unlimited replay. Further, analytic understanding, in the case of transcribing, also involves a medium transfer from a predominantly spoken interaction to a graphic medium (see again chap. 2). Thus, the demands on the analytic interlocutor (or transcriber) are quite distinct from those on the live interlocutor. In a live conversation, one may choose to let a lack of understanding pass unrepaired to avoid an FTA or to avoid a potential disruption of a fragile conversational flow. Leaving a section untranscribed may be viewed (although of course it shouldn't) as an admission of defeat on the part of the transcriber. What both live interaction and analytic interaction have in common is of course the fact that both are, essentially, about meaning construction on the basis of the available resources.

With these caveats in mind, we treat analytic understanding and the potential underlying it, that is, analytic intelligibility, as a basis for inferences about conversational understanding and intelligibility over the course of a conversation.

THE TRANSCRIBER'S VIEW

The conversation illustrating our discussion is between J and F (see Appendix B for the full transcript). At the time of recording, J had become a regular visitor, fulfilling roles both of a friend and of sociolinguistic interviewer, gathering information from F about her life and experiences.

As we briefly discussed in chapter 2, the process of transcribing yields a categorization of degrees of intelligibility that essentially emerges from the manageability of the data for the transcriber. This manageability constrains the categorization: The transcribers (in our case, both of us worked on the data) attempt, at various times, to have a productive dialogue with the data that results in a readable, understandable product. One of the demands imposed on transcribers is that of consistency. It follows that levels of intelligibility (in the sense of the transcribers' ability to make sense of a recorded spoken message) also need to be categorized in a recognizably consistent and reliable fashion. In a collaborative effort of transcription, this is not a trivial fact: Because one of the transcribers (J) was also a participant in the conversation, her recollection of what happened necessarily results in a perspective on the data that is different from the other transcriber's. Furthermore, repeated listenings result in a gradual refinement of the transcript (see again chap. 2).

What makes this conversation so interesting for our purposes are the marked fluctuations in the clarity of F's speech. This was a recurrent characteristic of her speech and not limited to this conversation. Some turns afford a very clear potential for understanding, whereas others utterly defeat the transcriber's attempts at interpretation. Example 9.1 illustrates these fluctuations:

Example 9.1 (see Appendix B)

7   J: m::. (4.0) does your husband take you to the shop does he,
         (2.0)
8   F: does he takes me (.) shopping.
9   J: mhm,
10 F: (xxXxXx around.)
11 J: *((brief laugh))* (2.5) uhum.
12 F: (when he was a x [kem].) at first he was out shopping (there) and it was a nice day out. (xx and we got [ə] the essentials. you know,) (1.5) and then[e] (we xxxx maybe (3s unintell.) and then (we would x, x closest Sunday, half eleven off to- we're off to- we were going to the[ə] mass xxx.)
13 J: mhm,

For our purposes, we are less interested in quantifying the proportions of the conversation that are, from the transcriber's perspective, fully intelligible versus in doubt versus unintelligible than in any patterns that may manifest themselves in the fluctuations of intelligibility. As ever in qualitative research, our first questions is what's happening here? By categorizing the manageability or translatability in the transcript, we are in essence operationalizing the doubt of the transcriber as a tool for further analysis. Thus, the question becomes, where does doubt arise?.

Overlapping Talk

One such property is represented by overlapping talk. While in face-to-face conversation, talk in overlaps is often readily understood by the interlocutors (especially in a two-party conversation), it often presents a problem for a transcriber. There are some instances of overlapping talk in this conversation (e.g., turns 44–45, 157–158). However, these account only for a small proportion of doubtful turns or parts of turns. A further observation is that by and large, turns that are problematic for the transcriber are typically spoken by F rather than J. On the face of it, this would appear a less than exciting pattern: this is, after all, what we tacitly expect in a conversation in which one partner has a communicative impairment. However, this assumption may lead us to overlook the possibility that turns that are unproblematic for the transcriber/analyst, for example, the majority of J's turns, are also unproblematic for the conversation partner, which is certainly not a given in conversations with dementia. Furthermore, translatability into the written medium, typically a function of clarity of the speech signal, does not necessarily equate with intelligibility in the sense of a potential for mutual understanding.

Clarity of the Speech Signal

F's speech exhibits marked fluctuations in clarity and distinctness. Transcriber doubt as to the intended speech is more often due to lack of articulatory precision than lack of intensity, although the latter also occurs at times. These instances of doubt are captured in the transcript in the manner discussed in chapter 2. Turn 12 illustrates all categories of transcriber doubt we distinguish: no doubt of interpretation (conventional orthography, no parentheses), transcriber's best guess at meaning (conventional orthography in parentheses), best guess at speech segments (phonetic transcription), best guess at numbers of identifiable syllables (use of "x" for each syllable), and timed sequences where no further analysis of speech is possible. The use of "[kem]" in turn 12 is an instance of the transcribers erring on the side of caution. It might very well be justified to interpret this string of sounds as "came," and the pronunciation pattern (realization of the vowel as a monophthong) would fit in with F's native accent of English. Whether a transcriber errs on the side of caution, as here, is of course in part determined by factors other than the clarity of the speech signal. Like interlocutors, transcribers rely on multiple clues for constructing meaning, one of which is an area that again is not unproblematic in F's turns, namely, sentence structure and linguistic fluency.

Sentence Structure and Linguistic Fluency

Problematic sentence structure presents less of a problem for the process of transcribing but is certainly an impediment to further analysis. At times, however, clarity of speech signal and syntactic irregularities combine to reinforce transcriber's and analyst's doubt as in turn 12. If we interpret "[kem]" as "came," then the preceding two syllables "was a x" represent a false start, and "[kem]" as the recovered item that completes the subordinate clause introduced by "when," which can be constructed as making sense together with the following main clause "at first he was out shopping (there)." Thus, an interpretation at the level of speech clarity leads to an interpretation of syntactic structure.

THE ANALYST'S VIEW

Although transcribing is a first step in analyzing a recorded interaction, analysis rarely stops with the process of transcribing. As the next step, it is worth returning to the question we asked above, namely, where problems arise for the transcriber; in other words, are there any patterns to the fluctuating clarity of the speech signal? For the sake of this discussion, we have included any talk that can be transcribed orthographically-in other words, anything that the transcriber can make sense of-with clear speech, assuming that this would also be treated thus in the live conversation (keeping in mind the caveat raised previously that the transcriber's and the interactant's perception of intelligible speech do not necessarily map onto each other perfectly).

Turn Length

Another look at Example 9.1 gives us some pointers to a possible pattern, which we can check against the rest of the conversation. A starting point is turn length: Turn 12 can be separated into five t-units; see Example 9.2[2]

Example 9.2: t-units in turn 12 (Example 9.1)

1. (when he was a x [kem].) at first he was out shopping (there)
2. and it was a nice day out.
3. (xx and we got [ə] the essentials. you know,)
4. and then[ə] (we xxxx maybe (3s unintell.)
5. and then (we would x, x closest Sunday, half eleven off to- we're off to- we were going to the[ə] mass xxx.)

---

[2]A t-unit is commonly defined as a main clause including all its arguments and any subordinate clauses depending on it (see, e.g., Hunt, 1965).

There are several factors that present a problem for meaning construction on the part of the analyst (and, we may assume, the interactant) here: first of all, the fluctuating clarity of F's speech, as discussed above, which affects all t-units but the second one here. Unclear speech pairs at times with incomplete syntactic structures as in t-unit 4. One is tempted to describe this incompleteness as a result of deteriorating speech clarity, but we can of course not be entirely sure that the unidentifiable part of t-unit 4 represents its syntactic completion. From this example, it appears that what is unidentifiable is new content, as in t-unit 4 where the narrative link is established by means of "and then," and we can identify the subject *we*, which represents given information, but not any new information, which F appears to attempt to produce. Further, there are linguistic disfluencies and false starts, as in t-unit 5, which result in stranded and incomplete phrases as in "closest Sunday" (if indeed this is to be taken as a noun phrase rather than *Sunday* being used as an adverbial noun), or prepositions without a following noun as in "off to-," which is rephrased and completed after the third attempt.

On the face of it, turn length as a factor in terms of identifiable, intelligible talk should not surprise us: the lowest common denominator being that in a longer turn, more can potentially go wrong because the speaker is attempting to produce more talk. Nor is it the case that all short turns (of 1 t-unit or less) are clear; see, for example, turns 10 or 16. However, it is the case that in this conversation, F produces very few turns of more than 1 t-unit in length that are unproblematic in terms of intelligibility. Turn 96 is disfluent but clear both in terms of speech and meaning; turn 86 contains unidentifiable speech only in the third and last t-unit, but there are problems with reference (to which we return later); turn 307 contains only two instances of two unidentifiable syllables,[3] and although there are false starts and self-corrections, the intended meaning is clear.

Turn Length, Illocutionary Acts, and Information Content

If turn length points to a first pattern in the increased likelihood of a breakdown in intelligibility, we need to keep in mind that turn length does of course not just happen. Rather, a speaker constructs a turn in response to the demands of the conversation and according to her intention in making a contribution. This leads us to a consideration of illocutionary acts and of the novelty (or otherwise) of information that is contributed. In this section, we focus on the first 100 turns of this conversation and particularly on F's contributions (40 analyzed turns altogether; those that involve overlapping speech are not taken into consideration here, neither are

---

[3] It is not entirely clear whether all unidentifiable syllables represent attempts at words, which of course adds to transcriber's, analyst's and interactant's uncertainty.

"nonword" requests for clarification such as "huhh" in turn 6). About three quarters of F's turns are short turns consisting of up to 1 complete t-unit (although many are shorter such as one-word responses), and about two thirds of those are unproblematic in terms of intelligibility. Unproblematic short turns represent a variety of illocutionary acts: requests for clarification or confirmation (seven instances; see turns 2 or 8 in Example 9.1), assertives that are responses to questions (five instances; see, e.g., turns 20, 42), an assertive that is confirmation of a preceding utterance by J (turn 32), assertives that elaborate on a topic introduced in a preceding turn (four instances; see, e.g., turns 34 and 81), and a question (turn 18). On the face of it, it is not surprising that a short turn that consists of a confirmation expressed by means of a simple "oh yes" (as in turn 32) or a one-word request for clarification as in "pardon?" (turn 30) should be unproblematic. In addition to being short, such expressions are formulas (see chap. 8), and both their forms and their functions are fixed and thus easily accessed. One could also argue that an expression such as "oh it's beautiful yes" (turn 34) is of a more or less formulaic nature, a fixed expression of approval or positive evaluation, but such a claim would be more difficult to defend in turn 26; see Example 9.3 for the relevant extract from the conversation:

Example 9.3

23 J: it's grown very big C, hasn't it.
24 F: pardon?
25 J: C. it's grown a lot bigger.
26 F: u::↓o:: yes. (it was just a sad little place when I came out here)=
27 J: =m::.=
28 F: =(and the Xxx here)
        (2.0)
29 J: I think it's- it's looking very nice now,
30 F: pardon?
31 J: it's looking very nice now.
32 F: oh yes.
33 J: they've done all the docks up an-=
34 F: =oh it's beautiful yes,=
35 J: =instead of being- (.) a mess.=
36 F: (if they're having one of the? Xx, (.) X, xx- xXxxxXxx must be a [mæd],
        XX?)
37 J: yea.
38 F: but if he (should have XxxX, he) could be (anyway), (2.0) but (not), (4.0)
        oh you came that way.
39 J: {piano mhm }, (3.0) did you ever work, (1.5) did you ever go out to work,
40 F: dressmakin.

This short extract shows two examples of F contributing an elaboration of information presented by J, in both cases with a repetition. Turn 23 introduces the topic of the city of C having grown big, which information is repeated after F's request for clarification in turn 24, and in turn 26, elaborates with contrasting information from her own experience: "It was just a sad little place when I came out here." Note that in turn 28, after J makes a minimal, content-free contribution ("m::."), what appears to be another attempt at elaboration on the part of F breaks down and becomes unintelligible in that what would seem to be the only new content word (or words; a noun completing a the noun phrase introduced by the definite article) is unidentifiable. J's turn 29 initiates a similar turn sequence. Here, J elaborates on the topic of the city of C; again, F requests clarification, which is met by a repeat from J, confirmed by F, and again elaborated by J; and then (turn 34) by F, with an utterance that rephrases J's repeated assertion "it's looking very nice now." Note that again, F's apparent attempt at elaborating further on this topic (if "they" in turn 36 is coreferential with "they" in turn 33) breaks down and that again, it is the new information (noun phrases) that are unidentifiable.

In this context, it is interesting that F's problematic short turns are all assertives, often responses to J's utterances (five instances, e.g., turn 10; note also that F's request for clarification in turn 8, which consists of a partial repetition of J's turn 7, is fluent and fully intelligible). In the first 100 turns of this conversation, F produces only 2 turns of 1 complex t-unit or more that are unproblematic in terms of containing unintelligible items. In turns 46–8, the main clause is a response to J's preceding question, and the subordinate clause represents an elaboration containing new information relating to F's own experience. In turn 93, the first main clause is again a response to a question; the second t-unit remains incomplete; the third one appears to represent a self-correction (including a disfluency), elaborating on the initial response.

Problematic turns of 2 t-units or more are assertives throughout. The link between t-unit and illocutionary act should, again, not surprise us: questions (requests for information), confirmations, and the like are more typically expressed by means of brief turns. However, what is interesting is a link that appears between illocutionary act and information content, which in turn is linked with utterance length. The clarity of F's speech frequently deteriorates when she attempts to contribute new information to the conversation, often in the form of an elaboration on the current topic (see again turn 12, Example 9.1 above).[4]

---

[4]The difficulty in introducing information may also be linked with F's use of pronouns without adequately introducing or reintroducing their referents. For example, it is likely, although not certain, that "he" in turn 38 refers back to F's husband, last mentioned in turn 12 (in which case turn 38 also represents an unsuccessful topic shift). The referent of "she" in turns 73 and 75 is eventually identified in turn 80 as S, one of F's daughters.

Given our data, we can of course not make any firm assertions as to the nature of F's information-processing deficit or the competition of all mechanisms involved in the production of a spoken utterance that compete for limited resources. However, we can make observations as to how such a deficit is managed or compensated for in the interaction.

Collaboratively Negotiating Mutual Understanding

To appreciate the collaborative negotiation of mutual understanding, we have to recall the goal or end of this interaction (see chaps. 3 and 4): While J has a covert end of gaining information from F as regards her experience of life with AD and as regards her conversational skills, this is not the overt, joint end of the conversation. Rather, as in many social visits, the end of the conversation is the conversation itself, and this end is achieved to a remarkable degree; witness the 311 transcribed turns. Given that there are no particular transactional constraints on the conversation in that there is no content that absolutely has to be transmitted from one interlocutor to the other, the ACTS SEQUENCES and the topics negotiated are essentially subordinate to the overall end of the conversation (namely, that the conversation continue), and thus, the negotiation of mutual understanding becomes an end in itself. Below, we comment on several behavior patterns that appear to serve the purpose of either reestablishing mutual understanding or moving the conversation in a new direction once mutual understanding is lost, namely, topic shifts, educated guesses, and a watch and wait strategy. We are not discussing straightforward requests for clarification here beyond already having mentioned that a considerable number of F's short turns serve this purpose.

Topic Shifts.   In a casual conversation, topic management is typically rather flexible, and frequent topic shifts are not uncommon (see chap. 5). Both participants in this conversation use topic shifts as a tool to continue the interaction either when turns have become too troubled for repair or after measurable pauses when a topic appears to have either been exhausted or become unmanageable (see also chap. 8 and the use of repetitive questions as topic reintroducers after long pauses). We interpret F's utterances, for example, in turns 18, 38 (see Example 9.3), 67, or 73 as such topic shifts. In turn 38, a topic shift to the here and now comes after F's utterance breaks down after an incomplete subordinate clause (introduced by "but") and a 4-s pause. In conversation analytic terms, we can say that J does not take advantage of the transition relevance place represented by the extended pause (which is at odds with the syntactic structure, and this may be the reason why J does not initiate a new turn), and thus, the turn reverts to F who rather than attempt to complete the clause she started, shifts to a different topic altogether. Of course, a perspective more focused on communicative skills impairments consequent to AD could interpret this example as an instance of F getting distracted, forgetting her earlier utterance, and commenting on a circumstance in the here and now instead. Of course, both interpretations may be accurate. It is interesting that J, in turn 39, does not comment further on this new topic other than by means of a quiet, minimal acknowledgment but in turn, after a measurable pause, introduces a new topic herself, which is taken up by F in turn 40 and maintained as far as turn 56.

Educated Guesses. Example 9.4 illustrates J's introduction of new topics when F's preceding turn has become troubled beyond repair or when F does not take advantage of a transition relevance place represented by an extended pause (turns 57 and 62). It also contains examples of another strategy at repair, namely, that of making an educated guess as to the content of a preceding utterance and thus inviting confirmation or correction:

Example 9.4

49 J: it's hard.
50 F: oh yes (xx. you XxxXxX:xx), and. (2.0) XxxX. [sə?ə]-,)
51 J: seamstress. (.) seamstress.
52 F: eh- (X wasn't my style).
53 J: oh the style. yea,
54 F: ([əmlə], [aɪv wɪl] everything I ever- making xXx makin my clothes for myself xXxx. {LV xxXx, })
        (3.0)
55 J: {piano that's true, }
56 F: (and quite after xxx, clothes x, when we were, xXxX?)
57 J: {piano u::m, } (6.5) do you sit <u>out</u> in the garden in the summer. (2.0) in the summer. do you sit <u>out</u> in the garden.
58 F: (to the father,)
59 J: in the <u>gar</u>den.
60 F: sit out in the [gar*den, (why, no [xx*), not thisX),=
61 J: [yea,*   [in the summer*
62 J: ={piano no, } (5.5) does your husband miss Ireland. (1.5) does your husband- does M does he like- does he miss Ireland or does he like C now.
63 F: does he?
64 J: {lento <u>miss</u> Ireland. }
65 F: iron.

In turn 51, J makes an educated guess as to F's intended meaning based on what is identifiable of the sound sequence of the final word and on the topic of "dressmaking." Her guess of "seamstress" is not accurate, but F can, in turn 53, correct J's guess and thus reestablish, or at least improve, their mutual understanding. In turns 58 and 66, J uses the same strategy, equally unsuccessfully, and again, mutual understanding can be established through correction of the guess in the latter example aided by an additional request for clarification from F. It is worth keeping in mind that while F's speech clarity deteriorates at times and thus presents less than ideal input for J, F herself is hearing impaired, and thus, J's utterances are not necessarily as intelligible for her as for J herself and of course for the transcriber (hence, we may assume, the wrong guesses in turns 58 and 66, which unlike J's turn in turn 50, were not aided by an established topic).

Watch and Wait.   The permission of a long pause or contributing a content-free minimal turn and handing the turn back to the other interlocutor shows different patterns of success depending on who uses this behavior. We may assume that in J's use of this strategy, her covert end in this conversation manifests itself (even if we may assume that at the time of utterance, this end was not necessarily at the forefront of her conscious thought), namely, to gain knowledge about F's interactional, conversational, and language skills. Consider turn 11 (see Example 9.1) where J's brief laugh, followed by a measurable pause and minimal "uhum," is followed by F's attempt at a narrative sequence. In fact, the basic narrative structure (marked by repeated use of "and then") is intact, but the content is problematic. In turn 13, J again adopts the watch and wait strategy, but F's utterance in turn 14 adds to the trouble rather than resolve it by containing an unidentifiable sequence and a pronoun whose referent is unclear. At this stage, J attempts to realign the conversation by leading back to the "shopping" topic. F's response is largely unintelligible, and again, J opts for a minimal turn (17, "mhm"), which, however, does not allow F to complete the repair and provide the required information. Rather, after a measurable pause, she shifts the topic to a present concern ("you want us to stay").

On the other hand, when F does not fill a pause, eventually J will respond and either expand on a previous topic (turn 29) or change the topic and ask a question to which F may be able to respond or by repeating or rephrasing a former utterance, which may scaffold F's response (turn 39 illustrates both).

Repeat or Rephrase and Invite Confirmation.   Partial repetitions or recasts of the other interlocutor's preceding utterance is another strategy whereby mutual understanding can be monitored and if necessary, reestablished. Two such examples are turns 8 (see Example 9.1), where F rephrases J's question, and turns 19 to 22 (see above). When J, in turn 19, insists on the "shopping" topic after a minimal uptake of F's topic switch (see above), F responds with a relevant contribution by rephrasing part of J's utterance. This in turn is repeated by J ("right into town") and confirmed by F.

INTELLIGIBILITY AS A POTENTIAL

If our discussion of the various ways in which F and J negotiate mutual understanding has shown anything, it is (we hope) the circumstance that the behaviors or strategies used by both interlocutors do not differ widely with the exception of the watch and wait strategy mainly employed by J. Furthermore, all the strategies employed are perfectly at home in normal conversations; that is, F shows, in the presence of dementia, a considerable arsenal of conversational skills. It will also have become apparent that much of this conversation is taken up by negotiating mutual understanding by way of requests for clarification, rephrasings, educated guesses, or the conversation is realigned by sending it down a different path and shifting the topic. We mentioned previously that given the overt end of this speech event, namely, having a conversation, negotiating mutual understanding becomes an end in itself. What is (we think) remarkable is that mutual understanding is pursued with such relentless zeal in the face of so many trouble spots. This and many other conversations with persons with dementia have led us to the view that it is helpful to look at intelligibility as a potential inherent in a conversation and its context rather than as a property of a speaker or of the speech produced.[5] The realization of this potential is dependent on the many factors that together make up the contextually embedded conversation. Our understanding of intelligibility draws on the following assumptions.[6]

Assumption 1: Humans Have Evolved as Social Beings, and Social Interaction Is a Basic Human Need: Social Conversation Is the Locus Classicus for the Fulfillment of This Need (see also Schegloff, 2003). In the context of a disease that progressively destroys cognitive, linguistic, and motor functioning, it is not trivial to observe that some patterns of conversational behavior are comparatively robust. The conversational data we have used throughout this book demonstrate that even in persons whose memory and cognitive capacities are severely disrupted, we find many intact conversational skills: Turn taking happens and is appropriate; there are attempts at repair; there are topic shifts that may be abrupt and repetitive (see chap. 8); linguistic and interactional politeness is intact, to name only a few aspects.

Assumption 2: Not Only Does Conversation Fulfill a Basic Human Need, But There Is an Assumption on the Part of Interlocutors That Mutual Understanding Is Achievable. Of course, we don't assume that interlocutors assume that anything that has been said will be understood, but rather that interlocutors

---

[5]Whether implicitly assumed or stated explicit, the idea of a potential for mutual understanding is of course an underpinning of the many studies of clinical discourse that draw on CA (see chap. 5).

[6]Parts of the discussion in the remainder of this chapter and part of the data used here and in chapter 8 have already been included in Müller and Guendouzi (2005).

sharing common communicative tools (e.g., a language or compatible non-verbal signals) expect to be able to negotiate mutual understanding at some level. This is the way we read Clark's (1996) discussion of joint actions and also classical pragmatic approaches such as Grice's principle of cooperation (see chap. 6). Whether mutual understanding has been achieved at any given point of a conversation is of course a matter of perception on the part of all interlocutors. For the sake of brevity, we use the term *order* for the perception of mutual understanding. Further, it is important to keep in mind that order has to be renegotiated at each turn because each contribution (whether verbal or nonverbal) has the potential of becoming, in CA terms, a trouble source. The assumption that order is possible is of course not open to direct observation and neither are the perceptions of order or its absence. However, data from conversations with dementia (and, of course, from any human context) consistently show supporting evidence of this underlying assumption: Even casual conversations, as the ones reported here, are not "about nothing." Topics are introduced and developed (sometimes unsuccessfully) and changed, sometimes to maneuver the conversation out of what threatens to become or has become a dead end. In addition, as we saw above, both interlocutors employ various strategies to renegotiate mutual understanding because for the conversation to be able to continue, it has to be "about something." Therefore, even when the end of the conversation is the conversation itself, there is a drive toward mutual understanding.

Assumption 3: Because Order Is a Matter of Perception, Monitoring an Interaction as It Evolves in Its Context Is an Integral Part of the Interaction. Monitoring encompasses the whole conversational complex: participants' actions, environmental factors, and participants' reactions to actions (see also Clark, 1996, on monitoring and establishing common ground). Furthermore, monitoring extends into time: Local or online monitoring operates moment by moment as the conversation takes place. Memory-based monitoring involves several "extensions" of memory. Minimally, one could distinguish the following: holding utterances in working or processing memory as they are produced and perceived and feed into planning of the next positioned utterance; also, events in the contexts as they happen; turn-exchange length memory that, for example, permits the completion of second-position or third-position repair sequences; conversation-length memory that, for example, allows interlocutors to refer back to contents already presented; and longer term memory, extending as far as an interlocutor's remembered life span.[7] Local, online monitoring and time-extended

---

[7]Note that although we find it helpful to distinguish these categories of memory, we do not wish to imply a strictly 'modular' understanding of them. However, encounters with AD show that different aspects of memory are differentially impaired (see Bayles & Kim, 2003, for a summary).

monitoring of course interact with each other and together extend into the future in that monitoring is the basis for prediction, expectations, and therefore planning (e.g., utterance planning).

Assumption 4: Monitoring Is a Mutual Affair and Relies in Part on Signaling and in Part on Expectation. In other words, interlocutors monitor not only their own understanding but the other interlocutor's. Thus, what emerges is an evolving model of another's understanding. This dynamic model (dynamic in the sense that it changes through time, that is, turn by turn) is based in part on the perception of signals sent but also on expectations based on prior experience: People tend to converse more effortlessly with familiar interlocutors.

The expectation that order is achievable, coupled with monitoring as an integral part of interactions, is, ironically, one of the major potential sources of frustration in dyads in which one interlocutor has dementia. In the context of a progressive dementing disease, interlocutors are progressively less secure (or reliable) in their monitoring of each other's mental state and contributions because the discrepancies between each other's mental faculties become ever wider and the fact that joint memories (as shared, e.g., by family members or friends) and abilities of recognition, as well as the ability to lay down new memories, gradually erode and eventually disappear in the person with dementia. As our data extracts in this chapter show, F has preserved structural conversational skills. However, she does have severe memory impairments, which makes the monitoring of the conversation over time problematic. In addition, there are problems with speech clarity, which as we saw appear to be patterned with higher demands of message formulation as when she attempts to elaborate by introducing new information. If we consider order as an emergent property of interactions, we need to acknowledge that the impairments of dementia also result in communicative impairments on the part of interlocutors who can only imperfectly monitor the other's understanding. Thus, order is disrupted, and the potential for mutual understanding remains in doubt.

CONCLUSION

The communicative challenges presented by a progressive dementing illness such as AD are dynamic in nature in that they change over time. Communicative impairments in AD emerge from the interaction of many factors: The underlying brain pathology affects multiple levels of neurological functioning and therefore multiple levels of, for example, cognitive, linguistic, affective, sensorimotor, and thus communicative skills.[8] Moreover, the communicative (or indeed pragmatic) impairments that become evi-

---

[8]See Perkins (2000) on the cognitive and sensorimotor bases of pragmatics.

dent in actual, contextually situated communicative events cannot be derived from progressive underlying neurological deterioration in a linear fashion because communication by its very nature is a process in which interactants jointly distribute and make use of all available resources. In the typical dyad consisting of a person with dementia and a caregiver, the need to interact and the expectation that order should be achievable (at some level) enters into a sometimes frustrating dialectic with the increasing difficulties of mutual monitoring that arise out of the changing constellation of factors in this context.

Given the dynamic and emergent nature of communicative impairments in dementia, the challenges they present need to be met by equally dynamic skills and strategies. As we have shown, communicative strategies may be productive or counterproductive depending on the turn-by-turn constellation of factors in the interactional dyad; thus, the compensatory nature of communicative behaviors is also an emergent property of the interaction as it unfolds. One goal of studying discourse in dementia has to be to explain at least some of the communicative successes and failures between cognitively normally functioning persons and persons with dementia. Any such explanation needs to acknowledge the context bound, multifaceted, complex nature of every communicative event and thus the emergent character of successes or failure, of order and breakdown.

10

Epilogue: Future Directions

Much remains to be learned from and about people with dementia and their interlocutors. For example, there is to date little work that looks at how people with dementia, for example, in institutional settings, interact with each other on a day-to-day basis. In many residential care facilities, bedrooms are shared, and there is little room (literally and conceptually) for privacy. Therefore, coping not only with one's own but with others' varying interactional skills and impairments is a matter of social survival in the nursing home. An investigation of mechanisms and strategies, ranging potentially from withdrawal to aggression, should prove interesting.

Another area of interest is the progression of DAT and other dementias in bilingual persons. Although the beginnings of greater research activity are visible at the time we write this, there is still little work readily available. Anecdotally, one of us has heard repeatedly from caregivers of bilingual people with DAT that in the later stages of the disease, they begin to use a language that is not shared by their caregivers, often their first language, but one that was not passed on to younger generations. The introduction of another language of course increases the potential for communication breakdown considerably, and the ability to control switching between languages in a manner that is conversationally appropriate and cooperative is one of the skills that appears to be affected in DAT (Hyltenstam & Stroud, 1993; Obler, DeSanti, & Goldberger, 1995).

For those with critical leanings, the image of AD and dementia in the media, the public, and policy making will surely remain an issue of lasting interest. The constellation of aging populations in the industrialized world, the race for new therapies that improve cognitive functioning (not only in those with dementia but potentially for anyone who would like to enhance their cognitive armamentarium), and rising health care costs, which in turn raises questions of equitable access to therapies, will produce texts (in the sense of CDA and DP) that will warrant critical examination. Although we did not foreground CDA procedures as a frame for this book, anyone working in the field of dementia needs to be aware that public and institutional discourses will impact their work in multiple ways, ranging from funding for research and teaching to public information (or indeed misinformation).

Within the field of communicative disorders there has been some resistance to qualitative research approaches, although there are also some devoted followers (see chap. 1). Qualitative approaches do not reveal macrotrends or generate numbers that might back up theories or show the efficacy of therapies. Indeed, it is difficult to claim robust findings when dealing with case studies or individual behaviors. However, this should not deter one from using these methods: After all, people are not means or standard deviations; they are individuals, and as such, we need to have more evidence of how specific communication skills work or do not work in real-life conditions. People do not generally live out their lives by taking part in experimental tasks; rather, they engage with the world through their daily interactions with others. Our selves are projected through our daily narratives and accounts of events. For the clinical student or researcher, a great deal of insight can be gained from applying ethnographic approaches and microlevel analysis of data samples taken from naturalistic situations. If the job of the communication specialist is to enhance and facilitate communication, then we need to know more about both typical and individual language deficits and interactional skills in dementia. Furthermore, we cannot engage in experimental tasks or therapy without interaction, and thus, a deeper understanding of, for example, conversational organization, collaborative meaning creation, or communicative acts can only improve both the research of dementia and the delivery of therapeutic services. Discourse analysis offers multiple tools that can aid clinicians to both carry out their own job and also help to educate the caregivers of people with dementia. Furthermore, the various methods available under the umbrella of DA can afford the clinician a better understanding of the needs of a person with dementia. Increased longevity coupled with early diagnosis means that we have a growing population of people living with dementia. Caring for this population is going to be a major health issue over the next decades. While there is undoubtedly a need for experimental research, we also need better insight into both the experience of dementia and the discourse practices of this speech community. DA and other qualitative methods can be used as a clinical tool to deal with the many implications for social and communicative interaction arising out of the presence of progressive brain pathology.

Appendix A

Notations and Conventions for Transcribing

The Basic Layout

Orthographic transcription of all utterances produced by the participants.

Turns are numbered.

((coughs))	Double parentheses and italic type indicate behaviors or events other than speech that are relevant to the interaction or comments made by the transcriber

Prosodic Information Integrated Into the Orthographic Transcription

.	falling intonation
,	level, or continuing intonation (can be a slight rise or fall)
?	rising intonation
↑↓	a marked rise or fall on the syllable following the arrow
<u>Christ</u>mas	underlining indicates a marked added emphasis

Pauses Within Utterances and Silences Between Utterances

(.)	brief pause; shorter than 0.5 of a second (brief pauses at the end of utterances are not indicated)
(3.0)	timed pause, 3 s

Overlaps and Interruptions and Latched Speech

[	overlap begins
*	overlap ends
=	Latching, that is, the end of one utterance is followed immediately by the beginning of another, without overlap, but also without any pause

Levels of Intelligibility (Transcriber's Perspective)

did you have a good Christmas	No parentheses: no transcriber doubt; fully intelligible
(did you have a good Christmas)	Transcriber's best guess at meaning; confident enough to identify intended meaning, but some doubt remains
(did you have a [gʊˈkɪçmɛ?])	Use of phonetic transcription indicates that the transcriber can identify a sequence of speech sounds but is not confident enough to ascribe word meaning
(did you have a xXx)	The transcriber can identify unstressed ("x") and stressed ("X") syllables
(2.5 s unintell.)	2.5 seconds unintelligible speech

Voice Quality and Intensity

{LV }	The voice quality associated with a light laugh during speech
{CV }	Creaky voice
{W }	Whisper
{TV }	A "tearful" voice; the voice quality sounds as though the speaker is about to start crying
{piano }	Noticeably quieter than surrounding speech
{pianissimo }	Very quiet
{forte }	Noticeably louder than surrounding speech
{fortissimo }	Very loud
{allegro }	Noticeably faster speech rate than surrounding speech
{lento }	Noticeably slower speech rate than surrounding speech

Gaze and Gesture

Gaze and gesture are usefully accommodated on separate lines of transcript, especially where they become a focus of analysis. Where both gaze and gesture lines are used, the gesture line is situated immediately above the orthographic transcription line and the gaze line above that. The only transcript in this book that uses separate gaze and gesture lines is Appendix D.

Gaze line:

″	A change in gaze direction happens at this point.
---	Gaze direction is maintained in the direction specified
bec	briefly breaks eye-contact
ghl	gaze half left
ghr	gaze half right
ghd	gaze half down
gm	gaze toward M (the other participant in the conversation)

Gesture line:

(( ))	Any gesture is enclosed within double parentheses
fh	Folds hands
hn	Head nod(s)
hs	Head shake(s)
lf	Leans forward
htf	Head tilt forward

Discourse Line

Keys to the abbreviations used in the discourse line in data extracts in several chapters in this book are given with the relevant examples.

Appendix B

Conversation Between F and J

The setting is F's room in the nursing home; F is seated in her wheelchair. The tape recorder and microphone were placed on a table close to F.

The transcript starts 6 min, 15 s into the conversation (the earlier part was not transcribed due to the presence of high levels of background noise).

1 J: it's noisy again. (.) (let me shut this). (4.5) (have to) wait until they finish the hoovering.

2 F: pardon?

3 J: they're <u>hoovering</u> a lot, aren't they.

4 F: (eighty-six) [(Xx)*

5 J: [Every-* everywhere they're going they're hoovering.

6 F: {*piano* huhh. }

7 J: m::. (4.0) does your husband take you to the shop does he,
       (2.0)

8 F: does he takes me (.) shopping.

9 J: mhm,

10 F: (xxXxXx around.)

11 J: ((*brief laugh*)) (2.5) uhum.

12 F: (when he was a x [kem].) at first he was out shopping (there) and it was a nice day out. xx (and we got [ə] the essentials. you know,) (1.5) and then[ə] (we

xxxx maybe (3s unintell.) and then (we would x, x closest Sunday, half eleven off to- we're off to- we were going to the[ə] mass xxx.)

13 J: mhm,

14 F: (xxxXx to them, while {LV on the road, I was asleep there?) }

15 J: where did you use to go shopping, (.) where did you do your shopping.

16 F: ehm, (.) M (xxXxxxXxx, (1.5) well,)

17 J: mhm,

18 F: ehm, (1.5) (you want us to stay, do you?)

19 J: yea. (3.5) did you use to go into town to do your shopping or did you go (.) A [Rd or (.) W* Rd.

20 F: [uh- uh no.* (right into town,)

21 J: right into town.

22 F: mhm,
        (2.0)

23 J: it's grown very big C, hasn't it.

24 F: pardon?

25 J: C. it's grown a lot bigger.

26 F: u::↓o:: yes. (it was just a sad little place when I came out here,)=

27 J: =m::.=

28 F: =(and the Xxx here,)
        (2.0)

29 J: I think it's- it's looking very nice now,

30 F: pardon?

31 J: it's looking very nice now.

32 F: oh yes.

33 J: they've done all the docks up an-=

34 F: =oh it's beautiful yes,=

35 J: =instead of being- (.) a mess.=

36 F: (if they're having one of the? Xx, (.) X, xx- xXxxxXxx must be a [mæd], XX?)

37 J: yea.

38 F: but if he (should have XxxX, he) could be (anyway), (2.0) but (not), (4.0) oh you came that way.

39 J: {piano mhm }, (3.0) did <u>you</u> ever work, (1.5) did you ever go out to work,

40 F: dressmakin.

41 J: uhuh, (.) did you just make everyone's clothes. or your daughters'.

42 F: yea. (would I) make clothes, (.) (like) kids' and wedding dresses, an-=

43 J: =wedding dresses. did you make the wedding dress.

44 F: no. xxXxxx (because they're) too far away. [(xXxX:,)*

45 J: [oh yea.* (1.5) do you enjoy doing that.

46 F: I used to do. but me eyes are not- (.)

47 J: no,=

48 F: =very good now,

49 J: it's hard.
50 F: oh yes (xx. you XxxXxX:xx), and. (2.0) XxxX. [səʔə]-,)
51 J: seamstress. (.) seamstress.
52 F: eh- (X wasn't my style).
53 J: oh the style. yea,
54 F: ([əmlə], [aɪv wɪl] everything I ever- making xXx makin my clothes for
        myself xXxx. {LV xxXx, })
        (3.0)
55 J: {piano that's true, }
56 F: (and quite after xxx, clothes x, when we were, xXxX?)
57 J: {piano u::m, } (6.5) do you sit <u>out</u> in the garden in the summer. (2.0) in the
        summer. do you sit <u>out</u> in the garden.
58 F: (to the father,)
59 J: in the <u>gar</u>den.
60 F: sit out in the [gar*den, (why, no [xx*), not thisX),=
61 J: [yea,*   [in the summer*
62 J: ={piano no, } (5.5) does your husband miss Ireland. (1.5) does your
        husband- does M does he like- does he miss Ireland or does he like C now.
63 F: does he?
64 J: {lento <u>miss</u> <u>Ire</u>land. }
65 F: iron.
66 J: Ireland. (2.0) his home.
67 F: oh- oh (it were never (.) hugely xXx, now we have xx xXx job), ((light
        laugh)) (XxxXXxxxxxXx), (2.0) (the next Xx decorations [ɪs] Xx on here).
        (2.0)
68 J: oh yea. who put those on.
69 F: my husband (I'd say),=
70 J: =mhm,=
71 F: =(on the way home from- from I don't know).
        (2.0)
72 J: and on the wardrobe,
73 F: (she:[bɑ] XxxXx extra. I've never seen these two fellows before. have
        you?)
74 J: uhm no. (1.5) it's quite thick isn't it.
75 F: mhm, (as soon as she got home, she'd start picking xxXx up, and left xx
        alone, and sayin that xXxx) she should be home for Christmas. she-=
76 J: =oh that's good.
77 F: she:ə =
78 J: =is that P.
79 F: no the other one.=
80 J: =S.=
81 F: =the gay one,=
82 J: =oh.=
        (2.0)

83 F: *{LV* (we're ok, she's happy.) *}* *((light laugh from both))* (1.5) um:, (1.5) she
        wa- she was Xx (except for a few days, but [ə] (1.5) to his Xx. and so she
        were X, and if he doesn't wait, until then) (3 s unintell.)=

84 J: =mhm:,-

85 F: =(it's his flesh. you know,) (1.5) so we've got to do that. (there's only a
        couple of pieces left in the *{LV* house you know,) *}* (2.0) (but we tried to get
        XxX over here xXx),

86 J: mhm, (5.0) it's a nice room,

87 F: m::, (3.0) it's a (beautiful) place,

88 J: yea. it is, (3.5) it's very close to your home isn't it. so M can [come,*=

89 F: [oh yea. yea.*

90 J: =it's just up the road,

91 F: mhm, (2.0) yes,

        (6.0)

92 J: does he come every day, (1.5) does he come <u>every</u> day.

93 F: I think so. I don't know (whether he) he's- he uhm he likes a pint. *((light
        laugh from J))*

94 J: where does he go.

95 F: to XXxxx I <u>think</u>.=

96 J: =a:h.=

97 F: =that's where he used to go (where I was going),

98 J: what about the Catholic (.) Social Club.

99 F: yea?

100 J: on W Rd,

101 F: *{LV* (xXx here takin me out some x), *}*

102 J: m:.

103 F: yes, he[ə] (.) (I don't know xxx find out (2 s unintell.) xxxx were children. I
        blamed him [tə]. and she left),

104 J: m::, (6.5) *{piano* mhm, *}*

        (6.0)

105 F: (but what will he do <u>here</u>).

        (2.0)

106 J: m:. what do you do.

107 F: e:h.

        (3.0)

108 J: watch TV,

109 F: (xX to[ə] X up on the masses. [ə]m,) (20.0) I don't know what (doctor)
        says. xxx *{lento* (<u>and</u> <u>my</u> home), *}*

110 J: mhm,

111 F: and (another) one, with (a football, xxX around) here.

112 J: uhuh,

113 F: and, (I can't- can't find xXxx *((background noise))*)

114 J: maybe it's at home. is it at home.

        (6.0)

115 F: m:, p- pardon?

116 J: you said you can't find it. (1.5) you can't find it,

117 F: (but who's put them there),

118 J: I don't know.

119 F: oh.

120 J: maybe the nurses put them there.

121 F: mhm. (XxXx [dɛsk]).

122 J: mhm,

123 F: (and [ə] xXx xXxXx, x possibly, (.) and he can have) that,

124 J: o::h,=

125 F: =(and poor xXxx, Xxxxxx that) he wanted this one here. (XxxxxxXxxX. uhm so XxX xXxX I don't know),

126 J: mhm, (3.5) does he like football.

127 F: who.

128 J: MA.

129 F: yes. and [ə] (2.0) w- they all like it.

130 J: what team do they support.
    (2.0)

131 F: I don't know but it's somethin to do with Oxford.

132 J: a:h, Oxford United,

133 F: that will be it (X I think) yes.

134 J: what about you. do you support Leeds? (1.5) which do you support. Leeds?

135 F: I don't support any (of them) ((overlapping light laugh from J)) (I have to remember (.) once (.) playin little what's-it Xx (2 secs) xX) tellin me he's now on the way. I (wondered why (.) everybody's laughin at me),=

136 J: =m::.=

137 F: =(xXxx XX, take an interest, Xx boys xXX, there's little I can do (2 s))

138 J: did you use to go and watch MA play football.

139 F: yea, (3.0) (I don't ever listen xXx. just X,)

140 J: m:. (4.0) it's cold watching football,
    (6.0)

141 F: (unintell.) ((recording interrupted at this point))

142 J: sorry?

143 F: what did you say (Xx) ((overlapping background noise))

144 J: M is going to Mass.

145 F: oh yes. (down.)=

146 J: =mhm,=

147 F: I won't go (but I, I don't know Xx I go xx to mass,) but[ə] (.) I can't hear properly.

148 J: o::h yea.

149 F: (that's Xx.) so:: I feel I would rather (say xX quiet and listen.)

150 J: mhm,

151 F: {LV and I don't see what's going on. }

152 J: uhuh,

153 F: have your parents (XxxX xXX your parents xXX,)
154 J: no my mother's dead.
155 F: a::h.
156 J: yea. she died when she was thirty. (.)
157 F: [(Xx)*
158 J: [yea. she* was very young. (.) hm::.
159 F: m::,
          (3.0)
160 J: and my father lives in P. (.) in Western Australia.
161 F: {W oh yea}
162 J: have you been to P.
163 F: no.=
164 J: =m, no.=
165 F: I've been to (.) Canbe- (1.0) what's thea capital. [Canberra?*
166 J: [Canberra.*
167 F: Canberra?
168 J: yea.
169 F: I've-I (2.5) and a- all the places I've been to but I can't {TV think about
          (them now), } (3.0) (and it ge- (.) have I- XxX, have I met the XxxxX,)=
170 J: =a:h. (2.0) well M will be in in a minute won't he when he's finished mass,
171 F: (they're already) starting it aren't they.
172 J: yea. how long does it last?
173 F: (XX that last,)
174 J: mhm, (.) be an hour. (.) maybe, half an hour?
175 F: {piano huh- }
          (4.0)
176 J: do you go on Sundays to mass.
177 F: (anybody) can go evening, Saturday, Sunday,=
178 J: =mhm,
179 F: and[ə] I used to go every Xxxx practically. but I don't have any pleasure
          {TV from it? }
180 J: oh. don't you? no.
181 F: ((3 secs vocal creak.)) {B [I said this*} {T xXxXX, }
182 J: [your hands are cold.* {W it's alright } (1.5)
          you're cold.
183 F: yea,
184 J: need to warm them up. ((background noise drowns rest of utterance;
          3sylls))
185 F: can I see your watch.
          (2.0)
186 J: it's my daughter's. ((light laugh))
187 F: o:h yea.
188 J: I borrowed it. I broke mine and I borrowed hers.=
189 F: =mhm.=

190 J: but it's very hard to see because-

191 F: yea, =

192 J: =you can't see the num[bers. (.) that's- yea.*

193 F: [(Xxx xXxX,* XxxXxxxXx watch. Xxx I can't see it
         Xx,)=

194 J: =oh it's over here. there.

195 F: mhm,

196 J: that's much clearer.

197 F: oh [yes* it is.

198 J: [see*, ((light laugh))

199 F: mhm, (2.5) (XXxx looking for-) =

200 J: =sorry?=

201 F: =(of- of M. (1.5) av-) (.) sister got hold of M.

202 J: yea.

203 F: a:h.

204 J: well she's- he's gone to mass.

205 F: ahah.

206 J: mhm, (2.5) and then he'll come back.
         (2.0)

207 F: ahah. (2.0) {W (they still don't care) }

208 J: sorry?

209 F: they still don't (give us a XxXX) ((background noise))

210 J: they don't give you a,

211 F: cup of tea.

212 J: o:h. do you <u>want</u> a cup of tea.

213 F: (yeyea,)=

214 J: =I don't drink tea.

215 F: you (XxXXx you got to clear your X yourself,)

216 J: o:h.
         (8.0)

217 F: yea, I've never had (1.0) <u>green</u> and <u>red</u> (.) together before like that.

218 J: m::.

219 F: looks rather nice. you don't need anything else,=

220 J: =very Christmassy,

221 F: uhuh,
         (2.5)

222 J: I have to buy a Christmas tree,

223 F: oh yea.

224 J: {piano m:. }

225 F: and I'm surprised at my family this year, they- oh, (have I got me tissue.)

226 J: here it is.

227 F: oh, {LV thank you. }

228 J: ((too quiet to transcribe))

(23.0)

229 F: m:: (and) (6.0) *((coughs))* (and all the kids and all you know xXx) two or three weeks before (2.0) and tree decorating and whatnot. and this year still they're at school, (.) at college.

230 J: mhm,=

231 F: = (the two Xost, and[ə] (2.5) theyə (2.0) in the evening Xx, there were (.) X parties and dances and things but Xx x this any (.) xXX,)

232 J: (Xxx) it's busy when people start- when they go to college they start going out a lot don't they.

233 F: yea,

(2.0)

234 J: is she a nurse your s- your daughter.

235 F: pardon?

236 J: doing nursing. (1.5) *{lento / forte* doing nursing. your daughter. *}*

237 F: yea, the second one is. mhm,=

238 J: =S.

(3.5)

239 F: she got her[ə] (.) degree a couple of years back. in out in (.) Au[stralia.*

240 J: [Australia,*

(3.0) what made them go to Australia.

241 F: *{?LV/TV ((unintell.; background noise)) }*

242 J: they didn't know anyone out there they just decided it might be a nice place to go.

243 F: mhm,

244 J: m:.

245 F: that's it.

(6.0)

246 J: it's what my parents did yes. thought the weather was better so *{LV* off they went. *} ((light laugh; F joins in))*

247 F: but you know it's (.) strange, after the two wedding days, (2.0) the first one we got (my xx xx everyone, XxxxX properly,) this year, (.) and[ə] (.) it rained (.) all day long.

248 J: o:h.

249 F: the other one, (5.0) (xx XxxX) it was so hot (xxX) they *((swallows))* couldn't keep dry. it was so[ə] (.) <u>hot</u>.

250 J: right,

251 F: so, (neither day, were nice wedding days.)

252 J: m::. *((light chuckle from F))* ah that's a pity, (10.0) did <u>you</u> go,

253 F: *{W* no *}* no (not X bein) (.) this year,

254 J: a:h.

(9.0)

255 F: (there seems to be a Xx- x parted up.)

256 J: mhm,

257 F: (xxx lovely xxXxx, (2 s unintell.) probably enjoyed it,)

258 J: mhm, (4.0) that's good. (1.5) did they send photos. {*lento / forte* did they send photos. }
(2.5)

259 F: did they,

260 J: {*lento* <u>send</u> <u>phot</u>os. }

261 F: oh yes. (so) lots on there,
(7.0)

262 J: mhm, (1.5) this one here. (1.5) the big one.
(3.0)

263 F: yes. Xx bri- bring em over- over here.
(12.0) *((sound of rummaging))*

264 J: was that this year.
(3.0) *((sound as of person shifting around))*

265 F: mhm,

266 J: was <u>this</u> one this year.

267 F: this is (.) our daughter (.) in=

268 J: =this one.=

269 F: =(her husband.) yea. yea. (.) (that's Xx but) she didn't get her photograph taken the same day as=

270 J: =m:m,=

271 F: =that wedding. (her) sister's. decided to take it (XxX,) but they're lovely photographs aren't they.

272 J: yea. (2.5) nice smiles. *((light laugh))*

273 F: {*piano* m:, } (8.0) and she can't keep her fingers still. she's (always Xx makin something for her X or somebody or other)=

274 J: =m:,

275 F: even when she comes in here (.) *((gulps))* pardon me, she brings some things (that x XxXxx (2 s unintell.) that, Xx Xxx that,) =

276 J: =m:,=

277 F: (Xxxxx up,) I[ə] I (.) (always used a-) (1.0) a model. [(xXx)*

278 J: [which one's* a model? (2.5) this one?

279 F: that one yes.

280 J: ah. she's tall.

281 F: yea, (2.0) but[ə] (3.0) {*piano* that one's a model. }

282 J: o:h this one.
(3.0)

283 F: {*piano* (Xx thing about her,) } that's my daughter,

284 J: mhm,

285 F: that's (.) her husband, (.) that's our son, (2.0) and this one=

286 J: =is that your granddaughter.

287 F: yea (XxXx got) so that I can't tell, (now Xxxxx go by X,) (.) the flowers.

288 J: m:,

(5.0)

289 F: (been X [dɛ] yet,) (4.5) that's my son-in-law, (2.5) that's her son, (3.0) that's my (.) daughter (2.0) (-in-law) {LV oh (there's a lot of XX), } ((light laugh))

(3.0)

290 J: could be friends couldn't it.

291 F: uhuh.

(18.0) ((noise of rummaging))

292 J: are you getting tired,

293 F: tired,

294 J: m:,

295 F: {LV (I am hardly young,) } (2.0) just lie down just a couple of minutes,

296 J: m::.

297 F: (tell him to come and call xxx don't have to go and look for him).

298 J: mhm, oh he'll be back in a minute, won't he.

299 F: you think so?

300 J: yea. (4.5) when mass finishes he'll be back. (12.0) he said you're in charge.

301 F: pardon?

302 J: he said you're in charge.

(3.0)

303 F: who said,

304 J: M.

305 F: he said (xXx large).

306 J: he said you're in charge. (3.0) at home.

307 F: {LV o:h. } ((light laugh)) (when my mother died Xx) (1.5) she was [ə] (.) (thirty-nine), (.) and (there were) (.) sev- a sem-, (.) six children- seven children. and they were grown up. (.) most of them, (1.5) and [ə] (.) when she died I got (xxx) took over and (helping with the (.)) kitchen and things you know.=

308 J: =yea.=

309 F: and I liked it.

310 J: mhm,

(2.0)

311 F: I (loved to) [ə] (.) washing and ((recording ends))

Appendix C

Conversation Between F and J

The participants and setting are the same as in the conversation in Appendix B with the exception of N, who is a nurse in the nursing home where F resides.

Approximately 2 months have elapsed between the earlier conversation and this one.

1 F: (Friday,)=
2 J: =It's Friday today.
3 F: (really,)=
4 J: =hmm=
5 F: =I never know what day it is (.) [a Monday* or (.) anything [here* (.) (is the date,)
6 J: [hmm*   [(((light laugh))
7 J: that's because when you don't work anymore you don't have to worry <u>do</u> you. (.) about what day is what. ((F sniffs)) {forte when you don't work anymore you have to- [you* don't need to [worry about what* day is what,}
8 F: [yeah*   [(xxxx)*
9 F: (xxxxxx) (they don't-) they don't change their ([ʃoː]) for this (you know,) (2.0) (xxx)=
10 J: =did you have a good Christmas?
11 F: pardon?
12 J: did you have a good Christmas?

222

13 F: *((sniffs))* ([wi.autʃad])
14 J: m?
15 F: (what we- what were [(xx)*
16 J: {*lento* [did you* have a good <u>Chris</u>tmas. }
17 F: well. (.) alright,=
18 J: =it was alright.=
19 F: = m:, (.) didn't (x) do {*LV* anything, (xx)}=
20 J: =did you get any presents?
        (4.0)
21 F: ↓no::. (we've- we're just left here dead,)=
22 J: =mhm.=
23 F: =↓oh:: wha- what I want is to (4.5) I don't know, (.) what you call it. (2.0) I call
        it when (something changes or) your own brain.
24 J: [o:h*.
25 F: [{*LV* (xxx*xxX, xx)}=
26 J: =your brain. ((light laugh)) {*LV* <u>my</u> brain. <u>my</u> brain is going, }
        (3.5)
27 F: but eh, (2.5) wh- when I came in here (1.5) (but I knew xxxx to this xxx an it x
        (2.0) many (1.5) [(xxx)*
28 J: [your <u>mem</u>ory*
29 F: {*pianissimo* hm (.) but they er (but [maɪə]) } well my husband he didn't want
        that. (.) he didn't want me to have any treatment at all.=
30 J: =o::h,
31 F: (xxxxbət) (.) and it was (just) (.) he hhh [(xx)*
32 J: [he didn't* want you to have treatment
        no, (.) he didn't want you to have <u>treat</u>ment.
33 F: (that's it) (2.0) he wants me to be just kept here.
34 J: mhm,
35 F: not (this xx xxxxx 1s unintell.) and he's good to me, (1.0) [əmə] my eldest brother (.)
        (thought) what he wanted to be (.) kept here, (.) and ([ətəʔəməwɛɪəm əmə]) (.)
        (xxx) he- he's marvelous (.) to me (xxx),
36 J: <u>M</u>. (.) or your brother. (.) {*lento* <u>M</u>,} (.) or your brother.
        (15.0)
37 F: my brother (.) ([βɪkʃəne:]) *((sniffs))* (.) but [ə] (.) my brother w- would like me
        to come out (xx waiting me) jus bein (.) bein kept well an everything,=
38 J: =m:::,
39 F: and my own ([bəl] brother xxxx (.) xxxxx)
        (2.0)
40 J: what's your brother's name?
        (4.0)
41 F: {*pianissimo* my brother}. my brother (10.0) (xxxxx)=
42 J: =where does your brother live,
43 F: {*pianissimo* a::h (3.0)} {*sigh* oh dear}
44 J: Y?
45 F: no?

46 J: oh. *{allegro* doesn't live in Y.*}* (2.0) does he live in C̲,

47 F: no? (2.0) (XX there) (3.0) oh (it had been taken away with me,) (.) an they want me to (make xxXXx [tʊk]),

48 J: *{pianiss.* aːh riːght.*} {forte* who took it away.*}*
   (10)

49 F: I get (X[xxx)*

50 J: [what've* you done to your le̲g̲
   (1.0)

51 F: who? (xx)

52 J: mːːː.

53 F: (xxX,)

54 J: it's on this side. (3.0) no it's this one he̲r̲e̲, (0.5) did you bump it.

55 F: I would've bumped it wi' bein pu̲s̲h̲ed.

56 J: mhm,

57 F: (xXx)(2.0) my mind's *{LV* (over XX)*}* *((light laugh))* (.) ([waivmɪsɪsɪn]). (1.0) (an then (2.0) xxxx ask would they)? (xxx together),=

58 J: =did your chi̲l̲dren come at Christmas?

59 F: yea. aːll of 'em, sixteen,

60 J: six̲te̲en̲.

61 F: (but em basically (.) me (6.0) sixteen (xxx). no, (1.0) (xX children, (.) an then [xxx*

62 J: [and their* children

63 F: *{LV* (their children) *}*
   (1.0)

64 J: did they all fit i̲n̲ here.

65 F: yea, (they climbed on the bed an everywhere,) (3.0) (I'm surprised that xx xx on the bed). (.) (that they *{LV* Xxxxx over me).*}*

66 J: what do they do at C̲h̲ristmas here. do they have a pantomine.

67 F: eh? (2.0) (x me I think now,) (1.5) (I feel awfully X). (I am [ə]),

68 J: *{piano* mhm,*}*
   (6.0)

69 J: have you been we̲l̲l̲ over Christmas (.) have you been well.

70 F: eh?

71 J: have you been okay over Christmas.

72 F: *((sniffs))* yes I seem to keep well and (2.0) (Xxx)

73 J: mhm,

74 F: can you make me some er (1.5) (in waːter), (.) me orange juice.

75 J: do you want some orange. okay. hang on,

76 J: (if you can) fiːːnd it
   ((4 s sound of rummaging))

77 F: *((brief utterance; too quiet to make out; turned away from microphone?))*

78 J: there's no uhh cup.

79 F: (x) (anything that x 'll hold it.)

80 J: uhm, (.) no. (3.0) no cup. m:. (5.0) let me go and ask. (3.0) *((to nurse:))* um she wants a glass of squash but there's no cup or anything

81 N: I'll get some I'll get some I'll get a glass of water or,=

82 J: =okay. thanks very much.

    (1.5)

83 J: she's gonna bring a glass of water. (4.0) they'll bring a glass of water.

84 F: (I hope she's knows it long before.)

85 J: *((light laugh))* mhm (.) did sh- did they come from Au<u>stra</u>lia at all.

86 F: [ə]::

87 J: not yet,

88 F: well the first one's arrived,

89 J: the <u>first</u> one.

90 F: m:: (arrived) last week, (.) ↓ooh (1.5) ([waːɪ] I haven't got em x)=

91 J: =you haven't got your <u>teeth.</u>

92 F: mm?

93 J: your <u>teeth.</u>

94 F: yeah (.) will you call for them (.) (Xx xx) (1.0) (oh he's tickled to be Xx if you ask a fellow)?

95 J: mhm? (5.0) so was it S came or P.

96 F: P that's come from Australia, she should be here this week, (.) now she's [ə] (3.0) she (.) is [ə] (3.0) she should be here sometime this week.

97 J: m:hm:?

    (3.0)

98 F: ah well (xx) (.) things have been bakin, anyway she'll be getting so excited (.) I can't be bothered with anybody or (XxX). and I don't want to grieve (it would be awful) but how can I when they don't want me here.

99 J: <u>who</u> doesn't want you here (.) who doesn't want you here. (3.0) you don't <u>want</u> to be here.

    (3.0)

100 F: no::, (4.0) no::, I (0.5) would like to be (Xx). I would like to live out<u>side.</u>

101 J: mhm,

    (2.0)

102 F: and (3.0) as a normal person.

103 J: you <u>are</u> a normal person. (1.0) {LV yes you are, you're a <u>nor</u>mal <u>per</u>son (0.5) of course you are} *((both laugh))*

    ((sound of knocking on door))

104 N: *((comes in with water))* alright?

105 J: do you want squash in it?

106 F: yes

107 J: okay, *((35 s; sounds of glass being filled etc.))* oops your foot there, (.) right. hang on.

108 F: *((13 s; sounds of F drinking))* that's lovely. oh-?

109 J: do you want me to put it down? (1.0) okay.=

110 F: =no I'd like some more,

111 J: oh you want some more. okay,

112 F: *((35 s; sounds of F drinking))* {W a:h that's beautiful.}

113 J: okay. I'll put it on there. *((to nurse:))* she wants some more (xX)? (12.0) *((sounds of J returning to chair, sitting down))* *((to F:))* you get uh (.) quite thirsty 'cause of the heating probably, [central* heating makes you dry,

114 F: [yea,*

115 F: yeah it makes you dry and (.) me lips dry (2.0) but [ə] (.) we never go out of this ↓room.

116 J: m:,

117 F: not even for half an hour or hop or skip about [ə],

118 J: *((laughs))* {LV can you hop or skip about?}

119 F: well I would {LV try if I (ever felt like it.) }

120 J: m:. (.) have you got a <u>prob</u>lem with your legs.

121 F: no? I I didn't have,

122 J: m:.

          (3.0)

123 F: I think that's different colors through (x it bein [ə])

124 J: the <u>tights</u> are different.

125 F: mhm?=

126 J: =those are white tights and those are <u>brown</u> tights.

127 F: oh well. (gulps)=

128 J: =well there you are. *((handing F a tissue))*

129 F: they have mixed uh (tissups).

130 J: m:.

          (6.0)

131 F: *((belches softly))* excuse me,

132 J: m:.

133 F: I would just to come for a walk with you.

134 J: it's <u>rain</u>ing today though, (.) that's the only problem, maybe- maybe next week when its not raining, (.) <u>if</u> it's not raining, (.) there's gonna be a bit of a storm today,

135 F: oh yeah=

136 J: =it's getting win[dier*

137 F: [(xxXx*xxxx <u>nice</u> xxx,)

138 J: the weather forecast said there's gonna be a big storm I think,

139 F: I like to get out when its sunny. (.) and the- (2.0) e- when its (xx) sunny like that. (2.5) eh- (6.0) *((coughs))* (Xx) (6.0) <u>he</u> (he's) boss. my boss.

140 J: your <u>boss</u>. (.) who's your boss your <u>hus</u>band. (.) who's your boss?

          (6.0)

141 F: {piano m:. m:. the <u>boy</u>friend. you know.} (.) wha- wha- (what will be,) (.) (xxx) my husband (x),=

142 J: =M? (.) ↓M

143 F: yes. (.) he (would) take me out for uh (.) twenty minutes (.) round the green the grass, you know (what you know the [ə] patch of grass there.) (.) he [ə], he

would take me out there but if I think he's going out, (.) and around (xxx on the ground) or shopping, (.) oh.

144 J: do you <u>like</u> going shopping?

145 F: I used to do, (1.0) but I don't {LV know now,}

146 J: what sort of shopping do you like. clothes shopping? or [food shopping*

147 J: [I like the window*
shopping yeah,

148 F: m:.

(1.5)

149 J: where did you use to do your shopping.

(2.0)

150 F: we used to do it in [ə] (2.0) {LV its so long (been)} ((light laugh))

(2.0)

151 J: A Rd ?

152 F: yes I like (there) (3.0) but its so so long ago::. and I wouldn't know {LV where to start, }((light laugh))

153 J: ((indrawn breath)) {piano I know.} well you get lost in the shops the[se days they're* so big.

154 F: [o:h yea:h*

155 J: and <u>Tes</u>cos, they've got a <u>new</u> Tescos,

156 F: m::?

157 J: by, (1.5) by the <u>ri</u>ver.

(1.5)

158 F: I don't know where {LV it ↓↑ i:s }=

159 J: =um (2.0) it used to be a Co-op,

160 F: oh yeah,

161 J: an its Tescos now,

162 F: uhu=

163 J: =an its so big, (.) they have (.) people with roller skates to go and fetch the {LV stuff for you.} ((light laugh)) they have lots of- they have [ə] boys and girls with roller skates on, who rollerskate up (.) [to find the* prices

164 F: [are they* {LV (really)} it sounds {LV like a (Xxxx)} (3.0) uh huh (2.0) I I don't think I should {TV ever get back (to do that again)?}

165 J: {piano oh no.(.) that's a bit dangerous wouldn't it be.} that would be a bit <u>dan</u>gerous I think roller skating, (1.5) {forte <u>ska</u>ting would be dangerous,}

(2.0)

166 F: (Xxx I haven't even got {forte (proper leavin)?} (2.0) you know what I mean?=

167 J: =mm:m:=

168 F: =I think if I (were) let out my legs (.) exercise [(.) it would* eventually

169 J: [ah do you want to,*

170 F: come to it. we we we we're (Xx) (1.0) be (xXx floppy. did I bore you.) (1.0) (get) another drink please.

171 J: oh yea. ((12 s; sounds of drink being prepared))

172 F: thank you,

173 J: {*allegro* you okay like that?} ((25 s; noise of drinking)) {*piano* (do you want) a tissue.}

{W}

174 F: ((25 s; sound of F: drinking)) ((gulps)) {W pardon me } ((10 s; sound of F drinking))

175 J: you {*LV* <u>are</u> thirsty aren't you.}

176 F: m<u>hm</u>, yeah, (.) (xxx no tissues) about?

177 J: sorry?

178 F: no <u>tissues</u>.

179 J: uhm? right.

((2 min; sounds of person moving; things being rearranged; murmuring in background;))

180 J: (x its) not a very nice day today actually, (1.5) its very <u>dark</u> out there,=

181 F: =mhm. (3.0) yeah. it was lovely to go out with (her over xx) water, which is best (way x day xx you for take walkin) (.) {*lento* which would be the best time you (w- could) take me.}

{LV}

182 J: well on a Friday when its <u>not</u> {*LV* raining though, } [((*laughs*)) *as long as its not

183 F: [yea.*

184 J: raining (.) can't go out in the rain can [we, no*

185 F: [no:,*

186 J: did you use to like <u>wal</u>king. (2.5) did you use to like <u>wal</u>king,=

187 F: =I used to love it yeah,

188 J: mhm, (15.0) where did you use to go.

(10.0)

189 F: everywhere (x to see some) flower I don't know (where {*LV* xxx may be),}

190 J: did you use to walk up the river? by the T?

191 F: no. [ə] it was {*LV* [ə] wild grass up there,} ((*light laugh*))

192 J: I went to L (.) [Cathedral.* (.) and that's lovely.

193 F: [Cathedral*

194 F: ↓really.

195 J: m::.

196 F: beautiful (xx there)=

197 J: =I didn- I'd never been before, I went <u>last week.</u>

198 F: oh yeah,=

199 J: =an its like a little country village in the middle of C (.) it's lovely.

200 F: beautiful.

201 J: m::.

202 F: yeah.

(1.5)

203 J: {*piano* nice houses as well }

204 F: I I think C were <u>beautiful</u>. (.) but what's it like now with all the concrete?

205 J: m::. it's getting bigger. they're building new=

206 F: and (.) harbor (.) still near.

207 J: m. they're doing all the- the- the docks aren't they.

208 F: m:.

209 J: but that looks nice now actually,=

210 F: =oh yea.=

211 J: =it looks a lot better. (.) because it was (.) looking very [Xx xx*

212 F: [xxx Xx x*.

213 J: m:. they said theyr're going to have (.) <u>water</u> taxis.

    (2.0)

214 F: (xxx up in the [hɑvs]? are you {LV going to xX?}

215 J: they're goin to have <u>taxis</u> that go from (.) by the castle, (.) by CA Park down the
    river to the docks. (2.0) little boats that are goin to be taxis. they're goin to have
    <u>boat</u> <u>taxis</u>.

    (4.0)

216 F: are you xx X on, (.) ((light laugh from J)) have you?

217 J: {LV no,} ((laughs; F joins in))

218 J: {piano m:,}

    (5.0)

219 F: and what about my poem. has it come to a stop or (xx soon xx).

220 J: ↓o:h it's still going,

    (2.5)

221 F: {LV am I in?}

222 J: yes, (3.0) do you like poetry.

    (2.0)

223 F: (there's some kind of) pieces I ↓li:ke but, ((coughs)) I don't seem to be
    interested in any(thing) lately.

224 J: do you- do you- (.) do you like reading. did you use to like reading.

225 F: I used to but,=

226 J: =what sort of books.

    (9.0)

227 F: uhm, (4.0) ([stɪrɪŋ]. [bə bə] basing x [dum]. (.) old famous (.) thing, (.) x. (up
    to xxx)=

228 J: =↓o:h. autobiographies of famous people.

229 F: {piano mhm.}

230 J: who- whose- whose autobiography. <u>whose</u> autobiography. (2.0) which people
    were you interested in.

    (12.0)

231 F: (xxXxxxx say?)

232 J: actors actresses {LV or politicians.}

233 F: (no more religious people.)

234 J: o:h reli[gious people.*

235 F: [xxxxxx,*

236 J: uhu,

237 F: I (x) see (x) name (xX), (2.5) (xxxx). (3.0) no, (45) (xx Saint Wilberforce).

238 J: ↓o:h. William Wilberforce.

239 F: mhm. (.) I don't know many of them just- just-

240 J: did you use to like watching films?

(2.0)

241 F: only occasionally,

242 J: what sort of films do you like.

243 F: (the X [mɛ]).

244 J: a:h. religious ones

245 F: yes, I think so, (xXx move), (2.5) [ə] I don't- (Xx lot and lot of people. or used to do in the same x.) (.) and I don't seem to bother much (xxx 3 s unintell.) (2.0) ye:s. (Xx happens and xx {LV and that's your lot,)}

Appendix D

Conversation Between E and M

The setting is an interview room in a university-based, speech-language pathology clinic. The participants sit on comfortable chairs facing each other but offset from each other by about 30 degrees. The interaction was video recorded with a fixed camera positioned behind M such that E's non-verbal behaviors were captured in detail but not M's.

```
      ghr---------,, -gm -----------------------------------------------
1   E: (5.0) man, (.) I guess my wife got (.) got a job here.
```

```
      gm----,,bec,,gm----------------------------------------------------
2   M: oh, kay. (1 2) wh- uh does she work on campus?
```

```
      ---------------------------------------
                                          ((lf))
3   E: yes, she works in the library.=
```

```
      ----------------
4   M: =oh really,=
```

```
      -----------
              ((lf))
5   E: =yes=
```

```
      -----------
6   M: =oh no,=


      ---------------------
7   E: = J--, (.) J-- C---?


      ---------------------------------------,,ghd----------------------------------------------------------
                                             ((turns head right))                                    ((fh))
8   M: (1.5) okay, I'll ha- next time I go there I'll have to (.) check out see who's here- there, (.)


      ------------------------------------------,,gm------------------------------------
      ((lf))
      were you in librarian (.) science, [(.) prior* to re[tire*ment?


                                                -----------------,,ghd--------
                                                ((hs))
9   E:                                          [no*                          [no*


      ------------------------------
10  M: what did you do.


      ---------------,,ghr-----------------------------------,,gm-----------------------------------------
11  E: I was- (1 2 3 4) man. I gotta think now (1.0) uh I guess I was responsible for


      -------------------------------------------------------------------------------------------
                                           ((frown))
      (.) for getting out the work, (.) getting out- (.) I was in industry.=


      ----------
12  M: = o::h.=


      --------------------------------
      ((points right index finger))
13  E: =before I came [here.*


                        ---------
14  M:                 [okay,*


      ,,ghr---
      ((fh))
15  E: =and,=


      ----------------------------
16  M: =like an expeditor?


      -----
      (2.0)


      ,,gm----------
             ((hn))
17  E: n:ot really.


      -----------
18  M: oh okay,
```

```
„ghd---------------„gm--------------------------------------------------------------
              ((hands half open))                    ((hn))
```
19 E: uh:, (6.0) man. that- that's a good question (.) I was in industrial

```
--------------------
```
management.=

```
-------------„ghd
```
20 M: =okay, okay,

```
--------------------------„gm-----------------------------------------------------------------------
              ((shifts body forward))
```
21 E: and (4.0   ) they gave me (.) at one place in H (while xxxx) company=

```
----------„ghd
```
22 M: =oh okay,=

```
----------------------„gm----------------------------------------------------,ghd
                                            ((hn              ))
```
23 E: =in H. (.) I was responsible for all the production they put out

```
-----------
```
24 M: oh ge:ez.

```
-----
```
25 E: and
```
-----
```
    (3.0)

```
---------------------------------------------------------------------
```
26 M: like in the administration or were you out on the floor? or=

```
------„gm--------------------
```
27 E: =I was out on the floor.=

```
----------„ghd
```
28 M: =oh okay,

```
-------
    ((hn))
```
    (1.5)

```
---------------„gm----------------------------------------------------------------------,ghd
                    ((hn; opens hands))                            ((folds hands))
```
29 E: and (.) handling all the problems and (.) everything anything that came up. (1.0)

```
-----------------------------------------------------
        ((lf))
```
    and man that was the last time I <u>work</u>ed.

```
---------------------------------------
```
30 M: how long ago was that then.

```
---------„ghr----------------------,,gm-----------------------------------
                              ((lf; unfolds hands))
```
31 E: {*piano* oh} (5.0) it's been (3.0) how long have we been in L.

```
-----------------------------,,ghl------------------------------------------,,gm----------------------,,bec,,gm
                                              ((smiles
```
32 M: now that I don't know I thought she said something like a couple of years,

```
----------------------
                                 ))
```
33 E: three, (.) maybe?=

```
,,ghd-------------------
```
34 M: =is that what it is?

```
,,ghrm-----------------------------------------------
           ((hn; unfolds/refolds hands;           hn))
```
35 E: I, (.) I I guess it's been about three years.

```
-----------------------------------
```
36 M: how long were you in H?

```
--------------------,,ghr--,,gm---
```
37 E: {*piano* oh man.} (2.5) fifteen?

```
------------------------------------------,,ghd-----------------------------------------------------
```
38 M: fifteen, (.) how d- how d' you like it? (3.0) It's too big for me. (.) but then if you're

```
--------------------------------------------
```
from N maybe- maybe it's little.

```
---
```
(2.0)

```
------------------------------------,,gm-------------------,,ghd-----------gm----------------------
                                                                            ((points))
```
39 E: I liked it. (2.0) but (.) it's, (.) to me it- it was like, (2.0) well you get off your block (2.0)

```
----------------------
```
((unfolds hands))
you're lost.

```
----------------------------------------------------------------------,,ghr-----------------------
                                      ((hn                 ))
```
40 M: ((*laughs*)) yeah you're right that's how I see it too. (.) I've never been able to

```
--,,gm----------------------------------------------------------------------------------
```
drive to H to see somebody. (.) and find it without ending up (.) way::

```
-------------------------------------------
          ((hn              ))
```
over there somewhere. ((*laughs*))

```
     ,,bec,,gm--,,ghr-
     ((smiles; hn   ))
41  E:  that's it. (1 2) uh:,
```

```
42  M:  it's got some interesting neighborhoods though I found the last time I was

        ,,gm----------------------------------,,ghd--------------,,gm----------------------------------------
        there. (.) different little niches in town, (.) it's not just big buildings. ((light laugh))
```

```
                                ((hs      ))
43  E:  I haven't even- (.) I haven't bothered to look around like that.
```

```
        --------------------,,ghr-------------------------
44  M:  ((laughs)) (2.0) too busy probably huh?
```

```
        ---------------,,gm-----------------------------
                                ((htf))
45  E:  *well, (5.0) my honey is a driver.=
```

```
        -------
46  M:  =o:h.=
```

```
        ----------------
                        ((htf; half unfolds/refolds hands))
47  E:  =she drives.=
```

```
        ,,ghr-----------------,,ghrm----
                                ((smiles; hn
48  M:  =oh:. you're (lucky) [((laughs))*
```

```
                                --------------------------------------------------------------------------------
                                hn ))
49  E:                          yes I am.* (.) I think I'm very lucky. (.)anyway, (.)
```

```
        ,,ghr---------------------------------------------,,gm--------------------
                hn ))
        anyway, (.) other than that (1.5) uh (.) I'm legally blind.
```

```
        -----------
50  M:  you are.=
```

```
        ---------
51  E:  =yeah.=
```

```
        --------------,,ghd----------------------------------------------,,ghrm------------
52  M:  =oh okay, (.) that was the trouble getting in here. (1.0) a little bit,
```

```
        -------,,ghl---
        ((hn     ))
53  E:  that's, (4.0)
```

```
                      ------------------,,gm------------------------------------------,,ghd
54  M: have you always- n– o you haven't always been. (.) have you?

       --gm---,,ghd------------------------------------------------------,,gm--------------
55  E: n:o. (1 2 3 4) I'm trying to think. (3.0) I guess it's been about five years.=

       ------------
56  M: =oh wow=

                      ------------------------------,,ghr-------------------,,gm------------------------------
                            ((hn              ))
57  E: =since they uh (.) they uh told me that. (.) but I had an eye test (2.0) you know

       ,,gh---,,gm------------------------------------------------------------,,ghr----------------,,gm
             ((gest. r. in.fing.))
       and. (2.0) they determined (.) the doctor determined (.) that I was legally blind.

       ,,bec,,gm.-------------------------------------------,,ghd---------------------,,gm-------------
58  M: I see. can y- you can you wear glasses and that'll help, or (.) at close range or

       --------------
       [anything?*

       -----------------------
       ((hn   ))
59  E: [I read,* yeah.=

       ---------------------------------------
       ((hn                             ))
60  M: =yeah (.) so you can still read.=

       ------
       ((hn))
61  E: =yes.

       ----------------
62  M: that's good.

       ,,ghl-
       (1 2)

       ,,gm------------------------------------------------------------------------------------
                                                              ((turns head right; frowns))
63  E: and, (.) I do wear glasses when I read. I guess they're magnifying glasses?

       ---------,,ghd----------------------,,gm----------------------------------------------------
64  M: oh okay yeah. that's what I use I can't be without mine now. (.) ever since I

       --------------------------------------------------------------,,ghr----------------------,,gm-----
                                                              ((smiles))
       turned 40. so I have these for reading. and it's getting worse and worse ((laughs))
```

```
„ghr-------------------------„g shirtpocket----------------------
                                  ((takes sungl. out of shirtpocket))
```
65 E: but uh, (.) well I have- well these are my sunglasses

```
--------------------------------------------------------------,,gm--
```
66 M: are they prescription? (.) they must be prescription [no?*

```
                                                  ----------------------------
```
67 E: [no*, no they're just (.)

```
    „g to glasses/pocket-----------------------------------------------------
```
68 E: regular (.) as far as I know they're regular (.) sunglasses (4.0)

```
----------------------------------------------,,gm-------------------,,to to glasses--------------
```
69 M: yeah they look regular, (.) I can't- I don't know how to tell (2.0) I know I can't

```
                                                              -------------,,gm--
```
    be without mine. (.)*well (.) uh heh did you grow up in N or

```
    ----------------,,g to pocket---------------------------------------
```
    another part of New York state. (.) [I'm curious about that.*

```
                                        ------------------------------,,gm-------------
```
70 E: [I was in New York State.* I was in N.

```
    ------------------
```
71 M: whereabouts?

```
    -----------------
```
72 E: upstate N.=

```
    ---------------------------------------------------
```
73 M: =upstate N where it's pretty huh?

```
    -------------------------,,g to pocket
                ((hn          ))
```
74 E: yeah where it's nice.

```
    ---------,,gm----------------------
```
75 M: um, (.) you grew up there?=

```
    -------
```
76 E: =yes.

```
    ----,,ghr------------------------------------
    ((folds hands))
```
77 M: what was it like growing [up* there.

78 E: [um*

```
    ------
```
    (3.0)

```
-------------------------------------------------------------
```
79   M: what are some of your favorite things about where you come from.

```
------
```
(2.0)
```
------„gm------------------------------
                                    ((htf))
```
80   E: well I come from the A-----area.

```
--------
```
81   M: okay,

```
----------------------„ghr
((unfolds hands;sphere shape))
```
82   E: C, (1.0): and the- =

```
----------------------„ghrm-------------------------------------------
```
83   M: =I don't know it. I don't know it. I wanna- I'd like to <u>know</u> about it though, (.)

```
„ghr-------------------------------------------------------------
                              ((smiles ))
```
I hear it snows a lot up there, ((laughs)) I'm a swamp rat. I'm from here in L

```
------------------------„gm-----------------------------------------------„ghr---------
```
so (.) I don't know too much. I have been to the city once (1.5) N--- City.

```
„gm
```
(2.0)

```
-------------------------------------------------------------
                              ((unfolds hands; right h. rises 4"))
```
84   E: well, (1.5) has that changed at all? because when I was growing up, (.) everyone

```
-------------------------------------------------
                              ((folds hands))
```
said you only went to N---- (.) if you had to.

```
-------------------------------------------------------------
         ((smiles))
```
85   M: oh ((laughs)) well. (3.0) I guess where I came from a lot of people would go:

```
------------------------------------------------------„bec„gm-------------------„ghd---
                              ((hn                                ))
```
to N to try and make it in some field, (.) I never had that (1.0) feeling

```
----------------„gm-----------------------------------------------------------
```
but I went- I had a friend who lived in N, (.) and who lived near there and who

```
-----------------------------------------------------„ghd---------------------„ghr-------
```
took me for a day there walking around the city. (.) It was interesting (.) I liked it (3.0)

```
---------------------------------------
```
So what was it like <u>U</u>pstate.

```
------
```
(3.0)

```
,,gm--------------------------------------------------------------------
                                                        ((htf))
```
86 E: I can remember, (.) the thing I remember is being cold.

```
----------------,,ghr-----------------------------------------------------------
((smiles ))
```
87 M: ((laughs)) (1 2 3) did you have sleighs? [and go ice-skating and-*

```
                        ----------------,,gm---------------------------
                                            ((hn))
```
E: [there were* there were ice skating,

```
----------------------------,bec,,gm----------,,ghr----------------------------------------,,gm-
                ((hn))
```
88 E: and snowing, (.) and s- s- sleigh riding (2.0) and (3.0) I can remember, (.) during the

```
-------------------------------------------------------------------------------------------------
                                            ((hn))
```
summer there was enough dew (.) that (.) we used to sleigh ride down this hill.

```
----------------------------------,ghd------------------,,gm,,ghd
```
89 M: ((laughs)) my goodness. (2.0) that's interesting,=

```
-------
((hn))
```
90 E: =and,

```
,,ghrm----------------------------------------------------
```
91 M: did- did you have many brothers or sisters?

```
,,ghr----------------,,gm----------------------------------
```
92 E: I have (.) I have one brother (1.0) and two sisters.

```
--------------------------------------------------------------------------------
```
93 M: and where were you in the (.) configuration there (.) were you=

```
--------------------------------------------
                                    ((opens right hand))
```
94 E: =I was- I was the oldest one.=

```
--------------------------------
```
95 M: =oh you were the oldest.=

```
---------,,g straight ahead---------------------------------------------------------------------,gm---
                (( r.h. to ear; r.h. straight at head height; punctuates 'sister' w. r.h.))
```
96 E: =I w- yeah. it's me, (.) then (.) then I had a sister, and I think she and I s- are are the only

```
--------------
```
ones alive.=

```
     ---------------------------
97  M: =oh my goodness.=


     --------------------
98  E: =of our family.=


     „ghr-------------------------------------------------
99  M: wow. (.) and you're the oldest though.


     „gm-----------------------------,,ghr
     ((hn                            ))
100 E: yes. yes I am the oldest.


     -----------------------------------------------------------------------------
101 M: so what was that like. did you have to- (.) did you have more responsibility than


     ---------------------------------------------------------
     the rest of them and all that kind of thing?


     ---------------------------------------,,gm-----------------------
102 E: well, (2.0) we grew up, (3.0) some of us grew up,


     ---------,,bec,,gm
103 M: ((laughs)) (2.0)


     --------------------,,ghr--,,gm-------------------------------------------------------
     ((htf))
104 E: we get older. (1.5) and I'm trying to- I'm- I grew up- I (.) was in a small town.=


     --------------
105 M: =oh okay,=


     --------------------------------------------------
                              ((htf))
106 E: =I was living with my grandmother.=


     -----------------
107 M: =oh really.=


     ----------------------------------,,bec,,gm--------------------------
                         (htf))
108 E: =and my two aunts. (3.0) who are very religious.


     --------------
109 M: oh really?=


     ------------------------------------
     ((hn                        ))
110 E: =born-again Christians.=


     --------------------------
111 M: =oh my goodness.=
```

Appendix E

Conversation Between MA and B
(With Contributions from C and an Unidentified Resident)

The setting is a common room in the nursing home in which MA, C, and X reside. MA, C, and B are seated around a circular table with MA and C in their wheelchairs; other residents sit nearby, and there is much coming and going. The tape recorder and microphone were placed on the table between the participants.

1 B: so what d'you feel like talking about today.
2 MA: huh?
3 B: what do you feel like talking about.
4 MA: huh?
5 B: how's your week been.
       (3.0)
6 MA: (x x?)
7 B: how was your week.
8 MA: oh it's alright,
9 B: it was alright?
10 MA: oh ya.
11 B: yea?
12 MA: oh ya.

13 B: where is your wife today,
14 MA: ([ɪ iː dɛ], y-) over there.
15 B: she's over there?
16 MA: he goin take his bath.
17 B: ah, take a bath. (18.0) so's she goin- be coming out soon,
18 MA: huh?
19 B: is she going- be coming out soon?
20 MA: who,
21 B: your wife?
22 MA: ya, pretty good. thank god.
23 B: thank god,
((1 min untranscribed; conversation with third person))
24 B: so what do you normally do l- here.
25 MA: huh?
26 B: what do you normally do here in- in a day.
27 MA: huh?
28 B: what do you here in a day.
29 MA: who.
30 B: you.
31 MA: what I used to do?
32 B: yea.
33 MA: for my livin?
34 B: yea.
35 MA: I run a dairy.
36 B: you run a dairy?
37 MA: eh: sell the milk, (xxxx) creamery. (3.0) hello cher.
38 C: how are you doin.
((2:28 to 4:00 untranscribed))
39 B: how long were you a dairy farmer.
40 MA: huh?
41 B: how long were you a dairy farmer.
         (2.0)
42 MA: how long I- I run a dairy,
43 B: yea. how long did you run the dairy.
44 MA: sixteen years.
45 B: sixteen?
46 MA: sixteen years. (send) the milk (xxxx) creamery.
         (2.0)
47 B: wow.
48 MA: oh ya. I don't work for nobody. I work for <u>my</u>self.
49 B: that's right.
50 MA: (x) you make a dollar for you I make a dollar for me. eh: make a dollar for
         you, that not good for me, is for you, *((chuckles; B joins in))* oh ya. (4.0)
         anybody can do that, (2.0) when started (x) I didn't have nothing. (x) people

give me credit, 's I'm goina pay. (1.5) and if I (x) got ten dollar go pay. after a while, everything is for me. but uh- I want to run the business straight. crooked business you know what is, (.) goin to jail.

51 B: yea, *((chuckles))* {LV you gotta keep it a straight business. }

52 MA: oh ya.

((9 s pause; untranscribed until 5:58; other speakers))

53 MA: if you see, come whatever. two three week, (1.5) let me tell you. if you not (crazy), you be smart.

54 B: yea?

55 MA: you understand?

56 B: I understand.

57 MA: if you come over there. and you- you got you not crazy, 'bout three week in (there) {LV you won't be crazy. }

58 B: really *((MA laughs; B joins in))*

59 MA: mais ya, (3.0) oh well. (3.0) the best thing you do. take all you save.

60 B: yes.

61 MA: huh,

62 B: definitely take care of yourself.

63 MA: and you take care of the- the (xxxx), you have got nothing. that's true eh?

64 B: very true.

65 MA: oh ya. {CV o-o-oh}

66 B: you seem to have taken care of yourself,

67 MA: mais that the best thing,=

68 B: =yea,=

69 MA: =if you can take (what you have,) if you can, let me tell you. you goin be (crazy.) *((both chuckle))*

70 B: yes.

71 MA: oh ya. (3.0) {W oh well,} (4.0) oh well, the love is something. I tell the love is something.

72 B: love,

73 MA: ya.

((7:20; silence, then interruption by coffee server; 7:33))

74 B: you get your morning coffee in here?

75 MA: huh?

76 B: you get some coffee. today.

((intercom announcement in background))

77 MA: oh, don't worry. (xx gon' miss that.) (1.5) you don't drink coffee?

78 B: oh no. not much.

((7:46; intercom announcement continues until 9:09))

79 B: is your coffee good,

80 MA: yes, you- you don't drink coffee?

81 B: no. I try not to.

82 C   you don't drink coffee?

83 B: no. not normally.

84 C   (xxx you used to.)

85 B: yea I used to a little bit.

((shouting in background))

86 MA: well, y- you better start drink, (1.5) because (1.5) you (lo- lose all that) if you
          don't (xxx) no drink no coffee, y: you (x), you lose that. *((shouting stops)) ((B
          chuckles))* let me tell you, (1.0) take (everything) you got a chance. *((B
          chuckles, MA joins in))*

          (7.0)

87 B: do you drink a lot of coffee,

88 MA: m:, sometimes. I don't miss that. if I (have) it's alright. I don't, still alright.
          (2.0) only one thing, I don't like to lose. (what.)

89 B: water?

90 MA: what, you don't know what I don't like to lose, (1.5) <u>eat</u>. *((both chuckle))*

          (6.0)

91 X: *(unintelligible)*

92 MA: I don't know you. (1.5) na- I don't know you, let me tell you somethin.
          ((intercom:)) (xxx) you come over there, (1.0) (three months.) *((ends))* three
          months.

93 B: three months?

94 MA: if you (don't x come) crazy, you're a good man. *((chuckles, B joins in))*

95 B: {LV oh yea. }

          (9.0) *((loud voices in background; continued quiet chuckle from B))*

96 B: is this in your way at all,

          (2.0)

97 MA: oh that's alright.

98 B: okay,

          (3.0)

99 MA: oh lord.

          (8.0)

100 B: have you had any other visitors,

101 MA: huh?

102 B: have you had any visitors,

103 MA: uh?

104 B: any vis- anybody come and visit you lately? or,

105 MA: over there? oh ya,

          (12.0) *((11:40–11:59; intercom; X: i'm cold.; silence))*

106 MA: you (want come) B some time?

107 B: (go to) B?

108 MA: ya,

109 B: haven't been there yet.

110 MA: before you cross the bayou. on your right. 'bout (.) two mile. that's my place.

111 B: that's your place?

112 MA: ya, (2.0) I (started, with) nothing. (1.5) and I take credit, and I work, I take
          credit, long time ago, you don't buy no gas. (there's) wood,

113 B: wood?

114 MA: there's wood. (1.5) so I work, I work (1.5) I take credit, give me credit, (2.0) 'bout six months, (2.0) I got all the (thing paid. d'you know how come?)

115 B: how come.

116 MA: if I can make a dollar for you, I make a dollar for me. and I pay my bill.

117 B: that's right.

118 MA: yea, (.) because, (.) a dollar's nothing to it. let me tell you. it take a good mind to save it.

119 B: {LV yes. }

120 MA: that's right eh,

          (2.0)

121 B: yep,

122 MA: a- and that's not right?

123 B: no that's very right.

124 MA: oh ya.

125 B: no. anybody can make a dollar but it takes a smart man to keep it.

126 MA: ya. (1.0) all the time you got a big pocket.

127 B: [yea?*

128 MA: [(that's true.)* (1.5) that's true eh,

129 B: mhm?

130 MA: put it in your pocket and close it.

131 B: {LV yes th-}=

132 MA: =i- i- if you don't do that, it go out. ((B chuckles))

          (14.0) ((talk between other residents nearby))

133 B: so. your farm's right (.) when you get over the bridge?

134 MA: eh?

135 B: your farm's right when you get over the bridge? into B?

136 MA: that? if I (want do it)?

137 B: {forte your farm?}

138 MA: if I farm?

139 B: {?uncertain yea.}

140 MA: for my work?

          (3.0)

141 B: tha- you're a dairy farmer. correct?

142 MA: yea. but yea. (2.0) [(x hard)*

143 B: [(that) must be* difficult work,

144 MA: y- tha- that's a good job, but you (don't see, n- no light,) you got to go to work. (2.0) because you know how come? all the cow, you got to milk. (1.5) twice a day.

145 B: twice a day?

146 MA: I start at one o'clock in the morning, (2.0) 'bout (2.0) six o'clock, (1.5) I got the milk all ready. (2.0) and they give me credit, (.) for my ([fɛd]) that's all. I got nothing. 'bout half a- (.) 'bout six months, (.) I don't owe nobody. you know how come? I do the right thing.

147 B: {LV yea?}

148 MA: {LV if you do the wrong thing you goin be wrong all the time.} ((*both chuckle*))

149 B: {LV oh yes.}

150 MA: oh ya. (3.0) a:h you know the- the love, nothing to do. (xxxXxx) you got to be safe to save a few dollar. (1.0) that not true?

151 B: that's very true.

152 MA: oh ya. (3.0) oh ya. an- I'm- I'ma tell you the truth. (2.0) anybody can make a dollar. (1.5) got to be a smart man to save it. (.) that not true?

153 B: that's very true.

154 MA: oh ya. (6.0) oh well.

(5.0)

155 B: where were you born.

156 MA: eh?

157 B: where were you born.

158 MA: me?

159 B: yea.

160 MA: o:h, (1.5) born (.) right there, and I stay right there. I'm ((*intercom announcement starts*)) {LV (on [dætɹɪgɪnt]).} ((*both chuckle*)) ((*ends*)) oh no cher.

161 B: so you've always been here.

162 MA: eh?

163 B: you've always been in this area?

164 MA: heh?

165 B: you've always been i- around this area?

166 MA: no:, ([lorʌʃ],(1.0) [lorʌʃ].)

167 B: so there a- (.) it's a very <u>pretty</u> place.

168 MA: yea- oh yea, (2.0) oh ya. (8.0) the love is a- a funny thing. eh cher? the love is a funny thing.

169 B: {LV yea.}

170 MA: (take) anybody can make a dollar. got to be save- smart (.) to save the dollar. (1.0) that not true?

171 B: it's very true.

172 MA: oh ya,

173 B: yea, (3.0) I try to save as much money as I can.

174 MA: eh- a- y-you save it,

175 B: I try to save it.

176 MA: well eh- that's good. you're young. after a while y-you goin be old. if you don't hold it, when you goin be old, you goin to <u>suffer</u>.

177 B: mhm,

178 MA: that's true eh,

179 B: yea.

180 MA: oh ya. (3.0) oh well. (10) oh well (13.0) love, (2.0) young (child we would) do, and got more tax.

181 B: more tax?

182 MA: not much, (1.5) but (I ain't) got much money to. (that lot of different eh,)=

183 B:　　=yea,

184 MA: the day you got plenty money. but you got plenty tax,

185 B:　　lots of taxes.

186 MA: oh ya.
　　　　(2.0)

187 B:　　makes it very difficult to save money when you have so many taxes.

188 MA: eh?

189 B:　　makes it hard to save money when you have lots of taxes.
　　　　(2.0)

190 MA: you got to close your pocket.

191 B:　　{LV yea, put it into pockets} ((both chuckle))

192 MA: oh ya. (4.0) oh well. (8.0) you stay around here?

193 B:　　yea I stay around here, (.) I live over at the university (.) right now.

194 MA: uhum,

195 B:　　yea.
　　　　(5.0)

196 MA: oh well.=

197 B:　　=yea I'm working on getting my doctorate currently,

198 MA: eh?

199 B:　　I said I'm working on getting my doctorate.

200 MA: uhum.

201 B:　　yea.

202 MA: we:ll:, look. (1.5) ((creak)) you're young. you're young.

203 B:　　yes.

204 MA: but if you don't save your dollar, (.) when you be old (.) you ain't goin have
　　　　it. that not true,

205 B:　　that's very true.

206 MA: you got to close your pocket {LV and lock it.}

207 B:　　{LV yes,}

208 MA: oh ya. (5.0) oh lord. (6.0) but everything now, (.) e: everything now, let me
　　　　tell you. it don't go old. (.) up. up. anything you bought. up. buy it today and
　　　　it (is a) price, tomorrow a different price. but (.) (that for you,) that up. up. up.
　　　　that not {LV true? } ((chuckle))

209 B:　　{LV that's very true.}

210 MA: oh ya. (3.0) oh well.

211 B:　　yea even in the twenty years that I've been alive I've seen the prices go up.

212 MA: huh?

213 B:　　even in the twenty years that I've been alive I've seen the prices go up quite a
　　　　bit.

214 MA: ((laughs)) yea. ((both chuckle)) oh ya.

215 B:　　I'm sure you must have seen a lot of changes in the prices.

216 MA: oh ya. (2.0) let me tell you, (1.0) you got a good pocket,

217 B: oh ya,=

218 MA: =put your money in that and lock it. *((B: chuckles))* if you don't lock it you (won't) find it. *((both laugh))*

219 B: {LV yes, (2.0) gotta make sure you don't have any holes in your pockets either.}

220 MA: ah ya. (1.5) oh well. (6.0) long time ago. remember ([edəta:t], ain't) goina renumber w- remember that?

221 B: yea.

222 MA: (ain't goina) renumber w- ga-, (.) that got (a) job. one day, they start, a- (rain rain) (and you can't) say stop, (.) that's true,

223 B: {LV yes.} *((chuckles))*

224 MA: you know how come?

225 B: how come.

226 MA: god is the best thing, god- god (loves you both).

227 B: yes.

228 MA: {piano yes,} ain't goina (rain) no more, (rain) no more, when (you) start (rain he just say <u>stop</u>.) {LV it stop.} *((chuckles))* (the rain?) *((B chuckles))* no. cher. look. (2.0) don't play with god. that the boss.

229 B: yes.

230 MA: oh well.

231 B: definitely the boss.

232 MA: oh well. (7.0) oh ya. *((unintelligible utterance from C; B chuckles))* (5.0) oh well.

((21:28–22:12: untranscribed; brief conversation between C and B))

233 MA: how old are you.

234 B: I'm twenty-one.

235 MA: twenty-one?

236 B: twenty-one.

237 MA: o::h. (3.0) (xx god,) you got plenty time to (seek a) woman.

238 B: {LV yea,}

239 MA: eh?

240 B: plenty of time to see what?

241 MA: the women.=

242 B: =yes.=

243 MA: =you got plenty time.

244 B: ah plenty of time.

245 MA: let me tell you. (1.5) you got plenty. (xx one) if you- take you a good one. (1.0) that not true?

246 B: very true. I got to find myself a good one.

247 MA: ya, (1.5) but you got to take (x you) save, let me tell you. don't (count yourself. think how you) pocket, *((laughs; B joins in))* {LV that's true,} *((both laugh))* o:h I can joke ya.

248 B: {LV yea, (.) joking's good.}

249 MA: eh?

250 B: it's good to joke.

251 MA: mais ya.
       (2.5)

252 B: you got to keep yourself happy.

253 MA: mais yea. (2.0) and you know, i- if I don't joke, (.) I'm lonesome.

254 B: you're lonesome,

255 MA: I got to joke for somebody?

256 B: yea.

257 MA: oh ya. got to have somebody.

258 B: oh you can joke with me anytime you want.

259 MA: oh ya. (2.5) oh yea you got to joke. (.) sometime, (.) I'm lonesome, (.) but I take everything. when you old (there's) nothing. (.) you know how come,

260 B: how come.

261 MA: (when you're young) you don't (wait) for nothing, ([laɪ-]) you old, you got to (wait) (.) {LV for nothing. } ((chuckles; B joins in))

262 B: {LV that's nice.}

263 MA: {LV oh ya.} ((B chuckles)) oh ya.
       (2.0)

264 B: now how old are <u>you</u>.

265 MA: eh?

266 B: how old are <u>you</u>.

267 MA: me?

268 B: yea.

269 MA: sixty-two.

270 B: sixty-two?

271 MA: ((chuckles)) no:. ((B joins chuckle)) I'm sixty-seven.

272 B: sixty-seven?

273 MA: ya. (1.5) oh ya. {CV (ehh- } I passed plenty time) let me tell you. my first wife died with bone cancer.

274 B: really.

275 MA: (she suffered plenty.) you understand? (.) my first wife died with bone cancer.

276 B: that's horrible.

277 MA: {CV a::h }(stayed with her) (.) night and day.

278 B: {piano I understand.}=

279 MA: =because is good for me. (2.0) oh ya. (3.0) you know? (1.5) an- and the love is something. (.) but you got to watch w- what you doin. that not true?

280 B: very true.

281 MA: oh ya. (2.0) oh ya. and you see over there? (x plenty thing.) sometime you see don'- he don't see. that's bad. sometime you got not legs. that's somethin. (2.0) and plenty people uh goin la- laugh with that. (what to god.) that not true?

282 B: that's very true.

283 MA: oh ya. (1.5) oh ya. (3.0) oh well.
       (3.0)

284 B: have you seen this area change a lot since-=

285 MA: =eh?

286 B: this uh B. (.) has- uh have there been a lot of changes in it since when you were there and now,

287 MA: (for on the) dairy?

288 B: yea.

289 MA: before you cross the bridge (.) to go to B. you turn to y:: the right, (.) that's my place.

290 B: that's your place?

291 MA: a:I started, a:I take credit, (.) yet, that's my face ((or: faith))

292 B: that's your face?

293 MA: you take my word for it. so (.) I work, (.) and say (.) I got the old man, he called it (A B). he said I'm go'll, I'm 'll hep you. he hep me, (1.5) give me credit, (.) one year, I got everything (.) u:h I don't (owe) nobody. you know how come?

294 B: how come.

295 MA: {LV I do the right thing. }

296 B: {LV yea?}

297 MA: oh ya,

298 B: saved your money,

299 MA: ([ɛlo:]) (2.0) anybody can save money. you got to be smart to <u>save</u> your money.

300 B: mhm,

301 MA: that not true?

302 B: very true.

303 MA: oh ya. (2.0) oh well, (7.0) you know everything (change years). (2.0) you know that, for ten years and that, everything (change) [tʃeːn]. you know how come?

304 B: how come.

305 MA: it don't go down. up.

306 B: it goes up?

307 MA: up. everything go up, up. and (it's) good for a (.) rich man. but the poor man, they got nothing.

308 B: yea.

309 MA: that's true huh?

310 B: that's very true.

311 MA: oh ya. (3.0) oh well, (10) ([ləˈloˈdɑʊn]), du- du- everything change. I remember, a long time ago, the- the- the (crazy people), say {singing ain't gonna rain no more.} remember that?

312 B: yea,

313 MA: {LV ain't gonna rain no more,} when it starts rain, it rain, (four times).

314 B: four times.

315 B: y-you can't- a-a god is the (job). (.) that god job. that not me and you, that god job. {LV that's not true?}

316 B: {LV that's very true.}
(2.0)

317 MA: oh ya, (5.0) oh lord.=

318 B: =we can't change what he wants.

319 MA: eh?

320 B: I said you can't change what <u>god</u> wants.

321 MA: oh no. (8.0) oh well, (2.0) when you old- when you young i- it's a good life.
       (1.0) and when you get old that's a different life. that's true huh?

322 B: it's very true.

323 MA: oh ya, (.) let me tell you. I don't know you (.) much. (.) you got to save your
       money, for (dirty) people. (save) it for you.

324 B: mhm,

325 MA: long time (w- when you may) need that. (1.5) because you know, your dad
       and you mamma, ain't goin be alive for long time. you got to try to hep {LV
       yourself. that not true?}

326 B: that's very true.

327 MA: oh ya,

328 B: I hope my mom and dad are around for a long time.

329 MA: eh?=

330 B: =said I hope my mom and dad are around for a long time,

331 MA: oh ya.
       (6.0)

332 B: do you have any kids?

333 MA: yea I got two boys,=

334 B: =two boys? ((light cough from M)) are they both=

335 MA: =eh?=

336 B: =are they both here?

337 MA: yea, I got one, (.) (you know uh), R,

338 B: R,

339 MA: R, (.) that's my grandson,

340 B: yea?

341 MA: he's a strongman,

342 B: strongman?

343 MA: he got the belt.

344 B: he got the belt?

345 MA: oh ya. he makes plenty money, but (don't know he should) save it. (1.0) that
       not true?

346 B: yea,

347 MA: any credit can make money, you got to be smart to save it.

348 B: {LV yes,}

349 MA: MA:?

350 C: are you okay, (x). ((in background))

351 MA: I-I'm alright cher, I'm alright. (1.0) I'm <u>al</u>right.

352 C: you're not cold (xxx).

353 MA: no cher, m:m, oh no. (3.0) oh well.
       (3.0)

354 B: are you having a good day,

355 C: no. not too good. {LV I don't like it.}

356 B: {LV you don't like it,}
357 C: no. nobody don't talk to me, I don't know what they think I am.
358 B: {LV I'll talk to you,}
359 C: yea, you alright,
360 B: yea.
361 MA: oh lord.=
362 C: =(XXx*xx, ((B chuckles))
         (7.0)
363 MA: {CV e::h yu-} (where you stay)? (to) U? that's what you say, you (.)
         ([wεn]- where you stay)?
364 B: what did I say?
365 MA: eh,
366 B: I said. (.) I enjoy talking with you,
367 MA: huh,
368 B: yea.
369 MA: I said um {emphatic (<u>where</u> <u>you</u> <u>stay</u>)?} (.) U?
370 B: yea. U.
371 MA: it good for you?
372 B: very good for me. (.) I enjoy it (.) quite a bit.
373 MA: mhm, well, (2.0) (they) try to hep you huh,
374 B: yea,
375 MA: (well, man,) what- you want to tell you somethin,
         (2.0)
376 B: what's that.
377 MA: (he) try to hep you, but you got to hep yourself.
378 B: yep,
379 MA: eh?
380 B: that's what I'm working on doing right now is helping myself.
381 MA: oh ya. (1.5) I like to talk with you, (and [wɪl'gɪvɪlgo'plɛntɪ'sɛn]) (1.0)
         anybody can save money. you got to be smart to <u>save</u> it.
382 B: {LV yup,}
383 MA: you know how come,
384 B: how come.
385 MA: everything uh not go down. up, up, that not true? up?
386 B: that's very true. everything goes up.
387 MA: oh ya. oh well.
388 B: yea,
389 MA: the best thing y-you can say. when you go to the bed, thank you for the day I
         pass. I hope pass a good night. (.) that's not true?
390 B: that's very true.
391 MA: oh ya. (3.0) oh ya- oh well.
         (6.0) ((10 s unintell.; Ms C; background voices))
392 MA: eh cher, that's sad. that poor man he don't see.
393 B: yea?

394 MA: that poor man he don't see. that's sad. you can't talk, can't do nothing, but you got to see. (.) that poor man, he don't see.

395 B: no,

396 MA: that's sad.

397 B: that is sad,

        (4.0) ((loud coughing in background))

398 MA: and he (suffer) plenty. (.) he suffer plenty that poor man.

399 B: it is,

400 MA: ((creak)) he suffer plenty from his stomach, (.) that's that.

401 B: he saw plenty,

        (5.0) ((violent coughing continues))

402 MA: sometimes his stomach hurt- hurt. mais that's sad.

        (3.0) ((violent coughing continues))

403 B: yea.

        (5.0) ((violent coughing continues))

404 MA: oh lord. (2.0) all the time we (think about) god. (1.5) mais et j'(x) god, (x that's the) the <u>church</u>.

405 B: yea, (2.0) do you go to church every week,

406 MA: eh?

407 B: do you guys have church every week,

408 MA: me?

409 B: yea.

410 MA: he come (give) the church over here.

411 B: that's awesome.

412 MA: ya.

413 B: that's very nice.

414 MA: ya. (1.5) ya, (2.0) but you know, (1.5) ((creak)) let me tell you you're young. make anybody love you. somthing, someday, you gona ((creak)) anybody. I don't (X) not (xx) call (x). god is the best.

415 B: yes.

416 MA: oh ya.

        (8.0)

417 B: how long have you two been married,

        (2.0)

418 MA: 'bout forty years,

419 B: about forty years?

420 MA: my first wife died.

421 B: yea,

        (2.0)

422 MA: and my first wife suffered plenty. bone cancer.

423 B: wow.

424 MA: ((background coughing resumes)) (I- I stay (.) work x day,) at night I sleep by her. (1.5) well, (2.0) he suffer plenty. but the doctor give me something, to relieve him (x) suffer much, (1.5) but (.) one day pass (on), one day pass (on)

o::h, ((comment on violent coughing?)) ((coughing stops; 9 s background
voices; coughing resumes)) if (xxx) over there six months. if you (don't come
crazy), {LV you's a smart man.} ((MA & B chuckle; coughing continues))

425 B: {LV easy to go crazy?}

426 MA: (it's okay, (.) six [months,*

427 C: [{piano (unintelligible)}*

428 MA: if you (x) six months, (.) if you don't come crazy, you're a good man.=

429 B: =yea,

430 MA: =because m-me, I (.) {LV (in the seventh month), now I'm crazy.} ((MA & B
          chuckle))

431 B: {LV you're crazy, } ((both chuckle))

          (7.0) ((violent coughing and shouting continues))

432 MA: let me tell you. let me tell you something. (you heard the dog holler)?

433 B: what was that? ((violent coughing continues))

434 MA: {LV sometime you heard the dog holler,}

435 B: yea?

436 MA: {LV (it's like a dog.)} ((MA and B laugh))

          (9.0) ((violent coughing continues))

437 MA: oh lord. ((coughing stops; same person now shouts)) (8.0) well you know,
          (1.5) let me tell you. you're young. it's goin be a big difference when you
          goin be old yea. get like that. turn like that.

438 B: yea?

439 MA: oh ya. (2.0) oh ya. oh well. put that on god job.

440 B: mhm, ((shouting stops))

441 MA: that the best. (1.5) oh ya. that the best. (5.0) if you (tell / take) over there,
          (xxx) there for me, I used to be smart. now I've come crazy {LV; allegro too
          much too much too much} ((laughs, B joins in.))

442 B: {LV you say they became crazy, }

443 MA: (xx over there six months, (2.0) you got to hold yourself,) (2.0) oh yes, oh ya.
          (.) oh ya. (xxx that six months, xx come) crazy. because I know that
          (for/from) me, yea, ((deeper voice:)) I know I come crazy. ((laughs))

444 B: {LV I don't think so,} ((both chuckle))

445 MA: oh lord. (2.0) long time ago. I don't know (if you) remember that, ([dɪ pɪf]
          say) {singing: (I don't goina rain no more),} remember that, ain't goina rain
          no more. when it starts rain(ing), it rain (.) three days. like I say stop, {LV
          that's god job. } ((both laugh)) {LV you remember that?}

446 B: {LV yes.}

447 MA: oh lord.

448 C: ((in background:)) ain't goina rain no more,=

449 MA: =yea,=

450 C: ((3 s unintelligible))

451 B: {LV yea?}

          (2.0)

452 MA: oh lord.

          (2.0)

453 C: goina rain no more no more no more. ((B chuckles))

(6.0)

454 MA: but a long time ago, (.) I used to be a good cowboy.

455 B: you used to be a good cowboy?

456 MA: oh ya, I can rope any cow, (.) I got a good horse, I got two (whole) but I got one. I can rope 'em, I- I called it [te:p], I said (tip) hold it. (.) don't hold it, I'm go ho- go over there and I (tie it). I said (x) come on you come with me, (1.0) I said (tip) hep me, ((two clicks)) you (know an' tie yourself). ((B laughs)) I- I don't want, I can't make you jump (on it), eh if you can't get down, (xx goin) take you back. (it goin) bite you.

457 B: really.

458 MA: I said (tip) lay down (.) you lay down by me, but, you can't come. ((B chuckles)) oh no you can't come. (2.0) {WC oh well} well, ((clears throat)) (['ɔːnəmə] if you training, you got plenty (sense).

459 B: you got plenty of (sin)?

460 MA: yea. (['ɔːnəməs], if you got to trainin do. (.) oh ya. (7.0) oh well.

461 B: that must have been difficult. when [you were* a cowboy,

462 MA: [eh?*

463 B: must have been hard when you were a cowboy, (.) ropin the animals,

464 MA: you like to be like that?

465 B: I don't know. I've never ridden a horse before.

(3.0)

466 MA: oh ya. (1.5) me (.) I- I rope, (.) plenty cow. and (xx) long time ago, (I) got the eh eh- cow all the way i-in town, (1.5) and I'll go over there. and I called him- my horse tip. I rope 'em, and I put that e-eh. I go tie them, and I said (tip let go. you goin bring me to the [bæn]), you goin follow me,

467 B: yea,

468 MA: oh ya. I said tip let go. oh he fooled that cow. (1.0) let (it) down. said tip that's alright. you know what he want?

469 B: what,=

470 MA: =a little bit sugar.

(2.0)

471 B: {uncertain? yea?}

472 MA: you kno:w, he like sugar.

473 B: sugar?

474 MA: ((background voices)) (sometime sweet. I xxx I give some to him.) I said tip that's alright, (2.0) you do that, (with yourself). but lu- all the time I talk with that. I got it trained just like a people. {sigh: oh well,}

475 B: yea.

(3.0)

476 MA: oh well.

(9.0)

477 C: where are you from.

478 B: I'm (.) living over at the university.

479 C: (unintelligible)

480 B: yes.

481 C: (find a good place there,)

482 B: very good place. (1.5) I enjoy it. but I'm from uh (.) N, way up north,

483 C: oh yea?

484 B: yea,

485 C: (that's nice, xx)

486 B: it's very nice up there. actually, (.) they got snow yesterday up there.

487 MA: not snow eh,

488 B: yea, I talked with my mom yesterday and they got snow up there.

489 MA: it's cold over there,

490 B: <u>very</u> cold already.

491 MA: *((dysfluent struggle))* y-you got to have a good coat,

492 B: {LV yea a <u>very</u> good coat. } *((laughs; MA light chuckle))* I haven't even had to wear a jacket down here yet.

493 C: you have some brothers and sisters?

494 B: yea, I have uh three brothers.

495 C: three brothers.

496 B: yea.=

497 MA: =you you're one (the little) one?

498 B: I'm the youngest.

499 MA: yea,

500 B: yea.

501 MA: oh well,
        (3.0)

502 B: all my brothers are older than me.
        (2.0)

503 MA: oh well,

504 B: {LV I'm the little baby of the family. } *((laughs; M light chuckle))*

505 MA: oh well. I like to talk with you, and uh we will plenty ([sɛn]). before you marry, before you marry. (watch what x you) get to marry, if (xx) you got plenty, (.) but choose the good one. that's the hard job.

506 B: yea, it's a very hard job. *((MA laughs; B joins in))* {LV I have yet to find a really good one, }

507 MA: eh?

508 B: I have yet to find a really good one. (2.0) I'm still searchin for her. (2.0) *((C in background; unintelligible))*

509 MA: {LV maybe you goin dream that.}

510 B: { LV yea, } *((both chuckle))*

511 MA: {LV my wife, (.) you go dreamin about one, (1.0) bon- don't dream the bad one.}

512 B: {LV na: definitely not a bad one. }

513 MA: ya. oh well. (oh let me tell you) what you got to do. (pretty one one).

514 B: pretty woman?

515 MA: p-pray to <u>god</u>. that- that the best thing. god.

516 B: yes.

517 MA: oh ya. (4.0) oh lord.

(4.0)

518 B: what were you saying before?

519 C: heh?

520 B: what were you about to say,

521 C: ((unintelligible))

522 B: oh okay,

523 C: ((unintelligible))

524 MA: oh lord. (9.0) but, (2.0) over there, ((shouting in background begins)) (2.0) over there you see plenty thing. sometime (xx). sometime you see some don't see, sometime see don't hear. that's sad. ((shouting stops))

525 B: yea,

526 MA: that's sad. (2.0) you know what you got to do,

527 B: what's that.

528 MA: pray for the poor people.

529 B: pray for the cruel people,

530 MA: mais they don't see, don't hear, that's sad, (2.0) oh ya.

531 B: yea,

532 MA: oh ya. (4.0) th- that old man over there? that's sad. (1.5) he don't see, but he holler all the time. ((imitates shouting?)) (xx a dog die) he holler just a like a dog die, {LV yow yow, } ((B laughs)) ((shouting resumes))

            (6.0)

533 B: that's too bad.

            (3.0)

534 MA: oh well.

535 B: yea,

536 MA: if you stay there (.) six months, and you don't get crazy, you good.

537 B: really.

538 MA: good. (2.0) but you see plenty thing. (1.0) plenty thing plenty thing. and the only one you got to (see). (.) pray to god, that-that-that the winner.

539 B: that's the winner,

540 MA: god is- that's the winner. that not true?

541 B: that's very true.

            (10.0)

542 MA: {WC oh well,}

            (7.0)

543 B: the people here seem like they're very nice.

544 MA: eh?

545 B: said the people here seem like they're very nice.

546 MA: oh ya. ((loud voices in background)) (and you know, that not xxx. (.) all xxx come and stay over there. the poor thing I got no place to stay. he come over there, give me some place to sleep, give me something (.) to eat, that- that's good.

547 B: yea.

548 MA: you know how (they) pay that,

549 B: how.

550 MA: me and you,

551 B:　me and you?

552 MA: yea. (it) tax. tax.

553 B:　yea.

554 MA: tax. (1.0) oh well.
　　　　(14.0)

555 MA: that poor man, (1.5) he don't see.

556 B:　don't see? *((shouting resumes briefly))*

557 MA: that's sad. (2.0) that's sad. (2.0) oh well, (2.0) *((coughing resumes briefly))*
　　　　that's sad when you don't see ya.

558 B:　oh yea.

Appendix F

Conversation Between FM, MH, and R

The setting is FM's room in the nursing home. The three participants are seated in a triangle formation with FM in her wheelchair and MH and R in comfortable chairs. The tape recorder and microphone are placed on the floor close to FM.

```
1   R:    have you been to C?
2   FM:   huh?
3   R:    have you been to C before?
4   FM:   ye::s. if- oh if I-, (.) been there,=
5   R:    =yes?
6   FM:   (.) yea I've been there. but I didn't you know (1.0) didn't stay (but a day),
7   R:    you have been to C?
8   FM:   yes,
          (1.0)
9   R:    wo:w, (1.0) so wonderful.
10  MH:   where did you visit. (.) in C.
11  FM:   huh?
12  MH:   where did you visit in C.
```

13	FM:	I visit (.) two of my friends. they were at H R. (3.0) and they had uh uh relatives or somebody (1.5) so I went w- I went to see <u>them</u> they took me there.
14	MH:	okay.
15	FM:	hmm,
16	R:	mhm,
17	FM:	and y'all doin' ok (honey) y'all lookin' well,
18	MH:	[((laughs))*
19	R:	[thank you. you too.* ((laughs))
20	FM:	a-ha-
		(5.0)
21	R:	were- were you a teacher before?
22	FM:	oh yes I've been teaching for years. (3.0) not around here you know.
23	R:	n-not in L.
24	FM:	it w- <u>yes</u> it wa- (.) it's in L.
25	R:	mhm,
		(3.0)
26	FM:	you know where H R is?
27	R:	no. I don't know.
28	FM:	{piano (xx) L.}
29	R:	is it far from here,
30	FM:	not too far.=
31	R:	{piano =not too far}
32	FM:	{piano it's not right- close- close, but ('dyou know what) not too far from L.} (1.5) where y'all from
33	MH:	O,
34	FM:	O. I used to have (.) relatives in O. (1.0) but I don't know if they still there. (2.0) I don't hear from them they must be gone somewheres else.
		(2.0)
35	R:	{piano mhm} you have been to O before?
36	FM:	yes I did go to O.
37	R:	how do you like that city.
38	FM:	I like it. I think O is fine. ((MH and R laugh))
		(2.0)
39	MH:	what school did you teach (.) at.
		(2.0)
40	FM:	u:h (3.0) well it was H R most of the time and that's where they wanted me you know, (1.0) so that's where I was at H R.
41	R:	{piano mhm,}(5.0) what kind of students do you teach.
42	FM:	huh?
43	R:	what kinds of students to you teach. (2.0) the primary school or the middle school.
44	FM:	what.
45	MH:	what grades [do y- you* teach.

46 R: [what grades* yea.
47 FM: oh. that was uh uh. at school?
48 MH/R: mhm,
                  (2.5)
49 FM: m:: first (1.0) until (5.0) the seventh I believe.
50 R: from first grade to [seventh*?
51 FM: [ye-* yes::.
                  (2.5)
52 R: do you like teaching?
53 FM: no.
54 R: no? ((MH chuckles))
55 FM: m:? I'm not doing anything now. (6.0) no I'm not teaching anymore.
56 R: {piano mhm,}
                  (3.0)
57 FM: because there's not much of {LV [a teacher's job*, you know?}
                                             [((MH/R chuckle))*
58 R: not an easy job,
59 FM: huh?
60 R: you mean tea- teaching is not a easy job?=
61 FM: =oh no, teaching is not a easy job. ((all chuckle)) ((indrawn breath)) (2.0) and
            I'm getting old, you know? ((all chuckle)) ((indrawn breath)) I'm old, sugar.
            (2.0) (xX,) (1.5) tryin' to take a little care of myself so,
62 R: mhm,
                  (2.0)
63 FM: where y'all from.
                  (3.0)
64 R: u- me? I'm from C.
65 FM: C?=
66 R: =yea.
67 FM: oh yea. you're not from here at all.
68 R: {LV yea. ((laughs))} a very different country.
69 FM: uh?
70 R: C, em. I mean-. it is very far,=
71 FM: =ye:s. and where you from honey.
72 MH: O.
73 FM: oh yes. O is not (.) not too far.
74 R: {piano yea.} have you been to C before,
75 FM: m:?
76 R: {lento have you been (.) to C before,}
77 FM: no:.
78 R: no,
79 FM: no. I haven't.
80 R: mhm.

81	FM:	but I know it's (.) fine.
82	R:	(mhm.)
83	FM:	(but I've uh (.)) I've had friends from C you know,
84	R:	oh. *((FM and R overlap; unintelligible))*
85	FM:	I promised I'd (xxx) but I never did get a chance,
86	R:	mhm.
87	FM:	to get enough money that I could=
88	R:	=*((chuckles))*=
89	FM:	=to go and come back when I got there. (2.0) but I still think (1.5) (xx late) I might get a chance (xx it) then.
90	R:	(Xx?)
91	FM:	mhm. (2.5) and that's where you live. m:?
92	R:	{*forte* yes.} I- I live in C.
		(4.0)
93	FM:	you're married?
94	R:	yea, I have got married.
95	FM:	got- got children?
96	R:	no,
97	FM:	uh?
98	R:	no.
99	FM:	oh that's good.
100	R:	how about you. have you got married?
101	FM:	I'm married but I don't have no children.=
102	R:	ah you have no children.=
103	FM:	mhm,
		(3.0)
104	MH:	you had enough children at school,
105	FM:	that's right. *((all laugh))* {LV that's right yea. I had enough (badsters.)} (2.0) fumble around with and teach them and-,
106	R:	mhm,
107	FM:	{*piano* (xxX,)} *((chuckles)) ((indrawn breath))* (3.0) yes:, (7.0) you have any children, huh,=
108	MH:	=n:o. no children [yet. *
109	R:	[m-m.*
110	FM:	*((chuckles))* and you don't have any either yet.
111	R:	no, I have no children.
112	FM:	{*piano* m-.} *((indrawn breath))*
		(6.0)
113	R:	(so- many beautiful bears.)
114	FM:	huh?
115	R:	so many beautiful bears.
116	FM:	yes I found that in here when I came.
117	R:	mhm,
118	FM:	and I'm no- I've been here just a while. (2.0) (X- x bears.) *((chuckles quietly))*

119 R: you have been here for (.) four days? how long have you been here.

120 FM: four days- about four days. not longer.

121 R: only four days?

122 FM: ye:s. it's about four days.

123 R: {piano oh.}

            (3.0)

124 FM: yes I haven't been in here long.

125 R: mhm,

126 MH: d'you mean you haven't lived here long?

127 FM: huh?

128 MH: do you mean you haven't lived here long?

129 FM: uh- who?

130 MH: {lento do you mean that you haven't lived here long?}

131 FM: oh no no. I haven't lived in here long. (2.0) just about ((announcement
            interrupts)) 'bout four days, ((announcement interrupts)) but I like it here you
            know it's nice, (.) the people is so- (1.0) nice, they come feed you 'n talk with
            you 'n everything, (1.0) they make it comfortable for you. (2.0) no I haven't
            been here (x: xxx), ((chuckles)) very short time. (10.0) y'all live around here?

132 MH: I do.

133 FM: you do?

134 MH: mhm,

            (2.0)

135 FM: not here.

136 MH: no.

137 FM: ((chuckles)) kind o' around.

138 MH: yea. O.

139 FM: O.

140 MH: mhm,

141 FM: and you honey.

142 R: I'm from C,-C.=

143 FM: =oh you don't live around here [(xx*

144 R: [{LV yea.}* ((chuckles))

            (4.0)

145 FM: and you like it around here?

146 R: yea. I enjoy everything here. (x very good [xx,*)

147 FM: [yea*

148 R: {piano mhm,}

            (6.0)

149 FM: I like it too but I'll be lea- leaving. next week. (.) I'm going back home. (2.5)
            I live here- d'you know where H R?

150 MH: it's in L,

151 FM: ye:s. I live near H- (.) near H R. (3.0) (that's why I go) to H R. (2.0) been
            teachin' there for good many years.

            (4.0)

152 R:	were you born (.) in L?
153 FM:	yes, I was born in L.
154 R:	and you grew up here.
155 FM:	{piano mhm,} (30.0) and I like it over here. it's (.) not far from L but-=
156 R:	=mhm.=
157 FM:	=L is right round, (13.0)
158 R:	are you tired?
159 FM:	m:?
160 R:	a- ar- are you tired? (2.0) you are tired, yes? or no.
161 MH:	are you tired?
162 FM:	oh no. I- I- I kind of like it over here. ((chuckles; R/MH laugh)) ((indrawn breath)) (1.5) ye:s. (1.5) but I don't- (1.0) I don't-I never lived (.) much (.) further you know. (.) I lived (.) in L, and that's right there.
163 R:	{piano mhm.}
	(4.0)
164 FM:	where y'all- where you live.
165 R:	I live in C. (1.5) C̲.
166 FM:	C̲.=
167 R:	=yea.=
168 FM:	and you honey.
169 MH:	I live in O?
170 FM:	oh you (x)- you live in O.
171 MH:	mhm,
172 FM:	that's not far from here.
173 MH:	no.
	(4.0)
174 FM:	and you live in C.
175 R:	yea!
	(6.0)
176 FM:	have any children,
177 R:	no,
178 FM:	you're married.
179 R:	yea.
180 FM:	{LV and you are married.}=
181 MH:	=no,=
182 FM:	=oh you're not married.
183 MH:	{CV no not yet.}
184 FM:	{LV you don't [have any-*}
185 MH:	[I'm only* twenty-one, ((R laughs))
	(31.0)
186 FM:	and y'all like it over here?
187 R:	mhm̲?
	(3.0)

188 FM:	((*indrawn breath*)) {LV been here just for a short while uh.}
189 MH:	we go to school in L.
190 FM:	oh y'all go to school.
191 MH:	mhm, (.) at UL, (.) at the University? (3.0) at the college?
	(2.5)
192 FM:	ye:s. (3.0) oh that's good. (12.0) and when you leave from there you're goin' home.
193 MH:	yea.
194 FM:	what is your home,
195 MH:	O.
196 FM:	O.=
197 MH:	=mhm.
	(2.0)
198 FM:	that's not too far from here,
199 MH:	no.
	(16.0)
200 FM:	{LV (they just got ev- <u>ev</u>erything in here)}
	(2.5)
201 R:	very lovely. (14.0) it's a nice day.
202 FM:	huh?
203 R:	it is a nice day.
204 FM:	huh?
205 R:	today it's very nice.
	(4.5)
206 MH:	it's pretty outside today.
207 FM:	oh that what she's saying.
208 MH:	mhm,
209 FM:	(just as well to-) (.) ye:s. (7.0) (x the truth an' everything) (24.0) where y'all from.
210 MH:	O.
211 FM:	O, that's not very far from here,=
212 MH:	=no.
213 FM:	I have (Xxxxx) up there. (3.0) yea they live in O.
	(6.0)
214 MH:	are you tired, do you want us to let you rest?
215 FM:	uh?
216 MH:	do you want us to let you rest? are you tired?
217 FM:	no I'm not tired sugar. (3.0) ((*background noise drowns out part of her utterance*)) (13.0) your hair looks so pretty.
218 R:	((*laughs*)) thank you,
219 FM:	long,
220 R:	uhuh.
	(2.5)

221 FM:	very pretty. yours long to, uh?
222 MH:	m:-it's ki- it's short.
223 FM:	oh d'you cut yours there. *((MH&R chuckle))* it's pretty too. *((MH chuckles))* (1.5) ye:s:.
224 R:	your hair is long, yea?
225 FM:	huh?
226 R:	your hair is also (.) long.
227 FM:	oh. *((indrawn breath))* yea mine all wrapped up to the back.
228 R:	{piano mhm,}
229 FM:	(xX) (.) longer. (13.0) and y'all's from (.) where.
230 R:	I'm from C.
231 FM:	C,
232 R:	yea.
233 FM:	an' you sugar.
234 MH:	not far from here.
235 FM:	not far from here,
236 MH:	mhm.
237 FM:	oh. you not far from here.=
238 MH:	=no. I'm about half an hour. (.) away from here.
239 FM:	ye:s:. (12.0) but you're at school? or what.
240 MH:	yes, we go- go to the college.
241 FM:	ye:s:. (7.0)
242 MH:	I'm going to be a speech therapist. (1.5) speech therapist? (2.5)
243 FM:	ye:s:.
244 MH:	mhm,
245 FM:	goo:d. (4.0)
246 MH:	they work a lot with school teachers.
247 FM:	ye:s:. (37.0)
248 MH:	do you know Ms B? down the hall? (3.0)
249 FM:	B. (2.0) yes I think I do.
250 R:	[yes,*
251 MH:	[right a*cross the hall,
252 FM:	yes I think I know her. (1.0) y'all know her too,
253 MH:	mhm,
254 R:	yea, (24.0)
255 FM:	where y'all from.
256 MH:	from- (.) about half an hour from (.) L.

257 FM: yes. (1.0) that's all?

258 MH: mhm,

259 FM: oh well you can almost see you from L eh,

260 MH: ((laughs)) {LV not quite.}

261 FM: {piano m::::.} (4.0) 'bout an hour from [L,*

262 MH: [half an* hour.

263 FM: about an hour from L?

264 MH: half an hour? you know?

265 FM: oh a half hour. (3.0) wh- what's the name of it.

266 MH: O?

267 FM: oh yes. I know where is O. (15.0) an' you live in O too.

268 R: no, (2.5) I live very far from here.

269 FM: huh?

270 R: far from here, I mean C. I'm from C.

271 FM: ((chuckles)) (xxx)

272 R: not- no, (xxxxx)

273 FM: (they moved xxxxxx xx) I'm talkin', ((light chuckle)) heh. (I don't know who're you) (10.0) where you say you're from,

274 R: C.

275 FM: <u>C</u>.

276 R: yea. ((female voice in background: 'you want some coffee B.' B: 'no,'))

277 FM: and you're over here just visiting,

278 R: ah here, (.) I go to the university.

279 FM: huh?

280 R: I go to the college. (3.5) I- I go to the U=

281 FM: =the college,=

282 MH: =U?=

283 R: =[yea*

284 FM: =[{forte ye:s.}* (1.5) oh that's goo:d.
          (2.0)

285 R: I'm a student.

286 FM: you're a student there.=

287 R: =yea,

288 FM: oh well that's good honey.
          (31.0)

289 R: today is the ha- ha- hal- Halloween,

290 MH: mhm, (.) Halloween?

291 R: Halloween,=

292 FM: =today is Halloween,

293 MH: mhm,

294 FM: ((indrawn breath)) {LV yea,}
          (14.0)

295 R: what did you do in Halloween (.) before.

296 FM: huh?

297 R: what did you do in (.) Halloween (.) before.

298 FM: honey I never was (.) too much *((light chuckle))* (4.0) (x down x) get together with those (.) young kids [(x) *

299 R: [uhuh,*

300 FM: an' me, so after a while (xxx) they went all over,

301 R: {*piano* uhuh,}

302 FM: but (.) not all the time. today I didn't- I didn't see (like or no x)=

303 R: mhm,

304 FM: *((indrawn breath; light chuckle))* (and I just X x)
        (4.0)

305 MH: do you wan'us to let you rest?=

306 FM: =huh?

307 MH: d'you wan'us to let you rest (2.0) d'you wan'us to let you rest?

308 FM: if I want y'all to do what=

309 MH: =to let you rest? (2.0) are you tired?

310 FM: m-mm.

311 MH: okay. I'm just makin sure.

312 FM: 'm not tired sugar. (3.0) just sittin round. doin nothin. (20.0) y'all not from here huh.
        (2.0)

313 MH: nn:,

314 FM: where y'all from.

315 MH: O,

316 FM: O. (2.0) that's not very far from here. huh,

317 MH: n:o,
        (35.0)

318 FM: I used to go to O. *((background noise))* (all the time) I had friends.

319 X: hello.

320 FM: how ya doin honey.

321 X: alright,

322 MH: (just visitin,)=

323 X: =(xx)

324 MH: oh your own (chair),

325 FM: thank you darling. (4.0) (xx they take) milkshake.

326 R: (xxx) thank you.
        (2.0)

327 FM: {*LV* yea. they always comin and bring me somethin.} *((MH & R laugh))* this is healthshake. (40.0) *((sound of drinking through straw))*

328 R: shall I put it (.) on the window?

329 FM: yes. just put it down there sugar. thank you.

330 R: here's ok?

331 FM: yea that's good. right there. (1.0) thank you darling.

332 R: you're welcome,

	(10.0)
333 FM:	where y'all from.
334 R:	uhm (.) very far from here, (.) C.
335 FM:	C?
336 R:	yea.
337 FM:	and who you (x) from here,
338 R:	u- uh, (.) sorry?
339 FM:	uh?
340 R:	sorry?
341 MH:	she said <u>far</u> from here.
342 FM:	o:h.
343 MH:	she's far- she's from (.) a faraway place.
344 FM:	where she's from?
345 MH:	she's from C?
346 FM:	C.
347 R:	{*piano* mhm.}
348 FM:	an' you sugar.
349 MH:	O.
350 FM:	O. oh you're not far from here. *((MH & R chuckle))* m::. (3.0) m::.
	(3.0)
351 MH:	it sure is not gumbo weather. (1.0) it's too hot.
352 FM:	ye:s, it's too hot that's right.
353 MH:	and it's almost November.
354 FM:	right. (5.0) and you like it here honey,
355 R:	mhm, I like here. (18.0) what did you do before.
356 FM:	m:?
357 R:	wha- what did you do before.
358 FM:	what did I do?
359 R:	mhm,
	(3.0)
360 FM:	{*LV* I didn't do (.) anything.} *((chuckles))* got out of bed, (2.0) talked walked round, *((announcement over intercom drowns out rest of her utterance))*
361 R:	mhm,
362 FM:	an' you sugar.
363 R:	I'm a student.
364 FM:	huh?
365 R:	I: I'm a student now,
366 FM:	you a student,=
367 R:	=mhm,
368 FM:	you went to school or somethin',
369 R:	yea.
370 FM:	o:h. (1.5) that's good. (9.0) well you're a student here.
371 R:	mhm,

372 FM:　an' you like it?

373 R:　yea, we like it.

374 FM:　where's your home.

375 R:　uh my home?

376 FM:　uhuh,

377 R:　my home is not here.
　　　　(2.0)

378 FM:　your home is not here. no I know where is it.

379 R:　ah, C.

380 FM:　C?

381 R:　mhm,

382 FM:　oh yes! (xx much)

383 R:　(piano mhm,)

384 FM:　you far from here. (4.0) ye:s:. (2.0) but you're here visiting.
　　　　(1.5)

385 R:　not visiting.

386 FM:　you goina be here a while?

387 R:　a:h I'm here to study.

388 FM:　a what?

389 R:　I'm a student (.) here.

390 FM:　oh you a student here.

391 R:　mhm,

392 FM:　oh ye:s:. you like it so far?

393 R:　mhm, yea,

394 FM:　((chuckles)) m::::. (2.0) but you- your home is (2.0) in whe- where.

395 R:　((laughs)) uh. my home is a v- very far away place.

396 FM:　it's a faraway place uh,

397 R:　yea.

398 FM:　where.

399 R:　C.

400 FM:　C?

401 R:　yea.

402 FM:　oh ye:s:. you're <u>far</u> away from <u>here</u>.

403 R:　yea.

404 FM:　and you like it to be around here,

405 R:　m, yea I do.

406 FM:　((chuckles)) (2.0) you enjoy wi- with all the younger children. (xx you away.)

407 R:　((light laugh))
　　　　(2.0)

408 FM:　ye:s:.
　　　　(10.0)

409 R:　there's no TV in your room.

410 FM:　m:?

411 R: there's no TV in your room. you're not watching TV?
412 FM: no.
413 R: no,
414 FM: ye:s I'm sittin in my room,
415 R: {piano mhm,}
416 FM: but my home is in L- L.
417 R: oh. your home.
418 FM: yes. my home. this is just (.) (xxx) visit. (3.0) a vacation I call it.
419 R: {LV vacation,} ((MH & R laugh))
            (2.0)
420 FM: ye:s,
            (4.0)
421 R: do you like here,
422 FM: huh?=
423 R: =do you like here?
424 FM: well- yea for a <u>while</u> you know fo-,
425 R: for a while it is okay,=
426 FM: =ye:s=
427 R: =uhuh,=
428 FM: =but I'd rather be home. ((chuckles))
429 R: uhuh, (4.0) when will you go home.
430 FM: when will I go home,
431 R: {piano mhm,}
            (2.0)
432 FM: next week.=
433 R: =next week.=
434 FM: oh ye:s. [ye:s:.* next week I'm goin home.
435 R: [wonderful*.
436 FM: (I'm not a x. but it didn't stop me, just x)
437 R: yea,
438 FM: m:, (.) oh yes I'm goin home next week, ((chuckles; announcement over intercom interrupts)) (4.0) where you live honey.
439 MH: I live in O?
440 FM: O,
441 MH: mhm,
442 FM: that's not far from here.
443 MH: no.
            (8.0)
444 R: how many family members are there in your home.
445 FM: huh?
446 R: how many family members (.) in your home.
447 FM: from here?
448 MH: how many brothers and sisters did you have.

	(3.0)
449 FM:	I have (2.0) three sisters. (1.0) MH, (4.0) B. (3.0) and FX. I have three sisters.
450 R:	mhm,
	(3.0)
451 FM:	an- and I'm FM.
	(5.0)
452 R:	do you have brothers?
453 FM:	yes, (2.0) I have two brothers.=
454 R:	=mhm,=
455 FM:	=(should have been xxx.)
456 R:	yea.
	(3.0)
457 MH:	do they live in L?
458 FM:	m:. (1.0) yes honey they both in school. (4.0) yea they went (x) L.
459 MH:	which school.
	(2.0)
460 FM:	what school they go to? (2.0) I don't know it's Catholic schools I know. (6.0) but they both in school.
	(3.0)
461 MH:	how old are they.
462 FM:	huh?=
463 MH:	=how old are they.
464 FM:	how old are [they,*
465 R:	[mhm,*
	(3.0)
	((knock on the door))
	(2.0)
466 MH:	{forte: come in.} ((sound of door opening)) yea you can come in.
467 R:	you can come in.
468 FM:	you can come in sugar.
469 X:	(X x back) I was just checkin on you.
470 FM:	huh?
471 X:	I was just checkin on you.
472 FM:	oh I'm still in here, ((chuckles; MH & R laugh))
473 X:	alright.
474 FM:	alright sugar. come back.
475 X:	okay.
	(2.0)
476 MH:	how old are your brothers.
477 FM:	my brothers.
478 R:	mhm,
479 FM:	o:h, (7.0) I'm tryin to think, (4.0) I'm older than them. (17.0) it must be like sixteen, (.) and a- (.) eighteen somethin like this. one must be sixteen the other

one eighteen. (3.0) they still in school they're not (1.5) out of school yet. (14.0) and where you live,

480 MH: O,

481 FM: O. that's not far from L,

482 MH: no. about half an hour,

(2.0)

483 FM: and where you live honey.

484 R: uh. C. ((clears throat)) C. very far from here.=

485 FM: C.=

486 R: =yea.=

487 FM: =oh ye:s that is very far from here. (3.0) ye:s you're right. that's very far from here.

488 R: yea,

(4.0)

489 FM: and you visitin too?

490 R: no. (.) uhm. I go to the (.) college here.

491 FM: you go to the college (.) school,

492 R: uhuh.

493 FM: in L?

494 R: yea.

(2.0)

495 FM: oh that's good. that's your first year?

496 R: yea. my first year.

497 FM: m:. and you like it sugar.

498 R: yea I like (.) I like everything here,

499 FM: uh?

500 R: I like here.

501 FM: you like it uh?

502 R: uhuh. (8.0) did you like your students, {forte, lento: did you like your students?}

503 FM: if I like what?

504 R: like uh- uh like a- the teaching job?

505 FM: teaching job?

506 R: mhm,

507 FM: a little. not much. (2.0) I don't like it too well. ((R and FM chuckle)) (I'll soon) be away from it.

(6.0)

508 R: how many years h- ha- had you been teaching.

509 FM: how many years I've been teaching,

510 R: mhm,

511 FM: honey it's about, (10.0) sure 'bout twelve years.

512 R: about twelve years?

513 FM: yes:.

514 R: that's a long time,

515 FM: that's a long time. (xx). I'm sure it's about twelve.
516 R: you are sure.=
517 FM: =m:,=
518 R: =you are sure (.) about it.
519 FM: yea I'm sure that that's about twelve, (12.0) what kind of work do you do
            honey.
            (3.0)
520 R: uh, you mean what? I'm sorry?
521 FM: uh?
522 MH: what kind of work (.) you do.
523 R: here? (.) uh (.) I didn't do any work. (3.0) I don't do any work here. I'm a
            student.
524 FM: ((chuckles)) oh you not doin any work over here.
525 R: yea. I'm just a student.=
526 FM: =student.=
527 R: =uhuh,
528 FM: at what school.
529 R: uh, the university of L,
530 FM: ye:s:. (7.0) and you like it over here?
531 R: yea. sure.
532 FM: ((chuckles)) m:. (2.0) and you like it too.
533 MH: ((laughs)) yea,
            (11.0)
534 R: are you married?
            (3.0)
535 FM: mhm. (3.0) yes I'm married. I don't have any children but I'm married.
536 R: how old were you. (.) when you (.) got married.
            (2.0)
537 FM: o::h about (13.0) {piano when I got married I was around} (5.0) {LV (xxx that
            long back)} ((chuckles)) just about (10.0) about ten years back I'm sure.
538 R: about ten years back?
            (5.0)
539 MH: where's he. (2.0) where's your husband.
            (3.0)
540 FM: my husband is dead. (3.0) yes. I buried him year before last. (16.0) and I
            haven't met nobody else. you know. that I (.) fell in love with. ((MH & R
            laugh)) if I do I'll marry again. somebody else can take care of me. (3.0) both
            of y'all married. huh,
541 MH: I'm not married.
542 FM: oh you're not mar[ried,*
543 MH: [no*
544 FM: you are.
545 R: mhm,
            (4.0)

546 FM: you live here?
547 R: I just study here.
548 FM: huh?
549 R: I study here.
550 FM: study here,
551 R: uhuh,
552 FM: where you live.
553 R: uh. uhm. I'm in C. I live in C.
554 FM: ye:s in C. (4.0) and you like it here?
555 R: uh, yea. *((laughs))* (10.0) how old are you.
           (2.0)
556 FM: I am (10.0) *{pianiss.* twenty (4.0) {WV nine.}}
           (5.0)
557 R: you are twenty-nine? you are twenty-nine?
558 FM: yes:. (22.0) and you honey how old are you.
559 R: I'm twenty-six. (2.0) twenty-six.
560 FM: twenty-six?

References

Alajouanine, T. (1956). Verbal realization in aphasia. *Brain, 79,* 1–28.

Albert, M. S., Naeser, M. A., Levine, H. L., & Garvey, J. (1984). Ventricular size in patients with presenile dementia of the Alzheimer's type. *Archives of Neurology, 41,* 1258–1263.

Althusser, L. (2001). *Lenin, philosophy and other essays.* New York: Monthly Review Press.

Alzheimer, A. (1907). Über eine eigenartige Erkrankung der Hirnrinde [On a peculiar disease of the cerebral cortex]. *Allgemeine Zeitschrift für Psychiatrie, 64,* 146–148.

Alzheimer's Association. (2005) Retrieved January 9, 2005, from Alzheimer's Association Web site: www.alz.org

American Psychiatric Association. (2000). *Diagnostic and statistical manual of mental disorders, 4th ed., Text Revision.* Washington, DC: Author.

Atkinson, J. M., & Drew, P. (1979). *Order in court.* London: Macmillan.

Atkinson, J. M., & Heritage, J. (1984). *Structures of social action.* Cambridge, England: Cambridge University Press.

Austin, J. L. (1962). *How to do things with words.* Oxford: Oxford University Press.

Austin, J. L. (1967). *How to do things with words* (2nd ed.) (J. O. Urmsson & M. Sbisa, Eds.). Oxford, England: Oxford University Press.

Bach, K., & Harnisch, R. M. (1979). *Linguistic communication and speech acts.* Cambridge, MA: MIT Press.

Bakhtin, M. (1981). *The dialogical imagination.* Austin: University of Texas Press.

Bakhtin, M. (1986). *Speech genres and other late essays.* Austin: University of Texas Press.

Ball, M. J., Esling, J., & Dickson, C. (1999). Transcribing voice. In R. D. Kent & M. J. Ball (Eds.), *Voice quality measurement* (pp. 49–58). San Diego, CA: Singular Publishing.

Ball, M. J., & Rahilly, J. (2002). Transcribing disordered speech: The segmental and prosodic layers. *Clinical Linguistics and Phonetics, 16,* 329–344.

Barkow, J. H., Cosmides, L., & Tooby, J. (1992). *The adapted mind: Evolutionary psychology and the generation of culture.* Oxford: Oxford University Press.

Bauman, R., & Sherzer, J. (Eds.). (1974). *Explorations in the ethnography of speaking.* Cambridge, England: Cambridge University Press.

Bayles, K. A. (1982). Language function in senile dementia. *Brain and Language, 16,* 265–280.

Bayles, K. A., & Kaszniak, A. W. (1987). *Communication and cognition in normal aging and dementia.* Boston: College-Hill.

Bayles, K. A., & Kim, E. S. (2003). Improving the functioning of individuals with Alzheimer's disease: Emergence of behavioral interventions. *Journal of Communication Disorders, 36,* 327–343.

Bayles, K. A., Tomoeda, C. K., Kaszniak, A., Stern, L. Z., & Egans, K. K. (1985). Verbal perseveration of dementia patients. *Brain and Language, 25,* 102–116.

Bell, A. (1991). *The language of new media.* Oxford, England: Blackwell.

Ben-Yishay, Y. (2000). A holistic perspective. In A. Christensen & B. P. Uzzell (Eds.), *International handbook of neuropsychological rehabilitation* (pp. 127–136). New York: Kluwer.

Berrewaerts, J., Hupet, M., & Feyereisen, P. (2003). Langage et démence: examen des capacités pragmatiques dans la maladie d'Alzheimer. *Revue de Neuropsychologie, 13,* 165–207.

Blessed, G., Tomlinson, B. E., & Roth, M. (1968). The association between quantitative measures of dementia and of senile change in the cerebral grey matter of elderly subjects. *British Journal of Psychiatry, 114,* 797–811.

Bliss, L. (2002). *Discourse Impairments: Assessment and intervention applications.* Boston: Allyn & Bacon.

Body, R., & Parker, M. (2005). Topic repetitiveness after traumatic brain injury: An emergent, interactive behaviour. *Clinical Linguistics and Phonetics, 19,* 379–392.

Boller, F., Boller, M., Denes, G., Timberlake W. H., Zieper, I., & Albert, M. (1973). Familial palilalia. *Neurology, 23,* 1117–1125.

Botella, L. (2004). *Constructivism and narrative psychology, p. 3.* Retrieved October 11, 2004, from http://www.infomed.es/constructivism/documsweb/andreas.html

Bourdieu, P. (1991). *Language and symbolic power.* Cambridge, England: Polity Press.

Brain, R. (1965). *Speech disorders.* London: Butterworth.

Brody, E. (1971). Excess disabilities of mentally impaired aged: Impact of individualized treatment. *Gerontologist, 25,* 124–133.

Brown, G., & Yule, G. (1983). *Discourse analysis.* Cambridge, England: Cambridge University Press.

Brown, L. (Ed.). (1993). *The new shorter Oxford English dictionary* (4th ed.). Oxford, England: Clarendon.

Brown, P., & Levinson, S. (1987). *Politeness: Some universals.* Cambridge, England: Cambridge University Press.

Buchan, R. J., Nagata, K., Yokoyama, E., Langman, P., Yuya, H., Hirata, Y., Hatazawa, J., & Kanno, I. (1997). Regional correlations between EEG and oxygen metabolism in dementia of the Alzheimer's type. *Electroencephalography and Clinical Neurophysiology, 103,* 409–417.

Bucholtz, M. (2000). The politics of transcription. *Journal of Pragmatics, 32,* 1439–1465.

Buckingham, H. W., Whitaker, H., & Whitaker, H. A. (1979). On linguistic perseveration. In H. Whitaker & H. A. Whitaker (Eds.), *Studies in neurolinguistics* (Vol. 4, pp. 328–352). New York: Academic Press.

Button, G. (1991). *Ethnomethodology and the human sciences.* Cambridge, England: Cambridge University Press.

Cameron, D. (1992). *Feminism and linguistic theory* (2nd ed.). London: Macmillan.

Cameron, D., Frazer, E., Harvey, P., Rampton, M. B. H., & Richardson, K. (1992). *Researching language: Issues of power and research.* London: Routledge.

Candlin, C. (1995). General introduction. In N. Fairclough (Ed.), *Critical discourse analysis* (pp. vii–xi). London: Longman.

Causino Lamar, M. A., Obler, L. K., Knoefel, J. A., & Albert, M. L. (1994). Cohesive devices and conversational discourse in Alzheimer's disease. In Bloom, L. K. Obler, S. De Santi, & J. S. Ehrlich (Eds.), *Discourse analysis and applications: Studies in adult clinical populations* (pp. 201–216). Hillsdale, NJ: Lawrence Erlbaum Associates.

Charniak, E. (1972). *Towards a model of childrens's story comprehension.* MIT Artificial Intelligence Laboratory Monographs (Tech. rep. TR 226). Cambridge, MA: MIT Press.

Cheepen, C. (1987). *The predictability of everyday conversation.* London: Pinter.

Chen, M., & Fernandez, H. L. (2001). Alzheimer movement re-examined 25 years later: Is it a "disease" or a senile condition in medical nature? *Frontiers in Bioscience, 6,* e30–40.

Chomsky, N. (1957). *Syntactic structures.* The Hague, Netherlands: Mouton.

Clark, A. (2003). *Natural-born cyborgs.* New York: Oxford University Press.

Clark, H. H. (1996). *Using language.* Cambridge, England: Cambridge University Press.

Clinical Linguistics and Phonetics. (2002). Volume 16(5).

Coates, J. (1996). *Women talk.* Oxford, England: Blackwell.

Coates, J., & Thornborrow, J. (1999). Myth, lies and audiotapes: Some thoughts on data transcripts. *Discourse and Society, 10,* 594–597.

Code, C. F. S. (1982). Neurolinguistic analysis of recurrent utterance in aphasia. *Cortex, 18,* 141–152.

Code, C. F. S. (1989). Recurrent utterances and automatisms in aphasia. In C. F. S. Code (Ed.), *The characteristics of aphasia* (pp. 155–172). London: Taylor and Francis.

Collerton, D., & Fairbairn, A. (1985). Alzheimer's and the hippocampus. *The Lancet, 2,* 278–279.

Coulter, J. (1989). *The social construction of mind.* London: Macmillan

Coupland, J., Coupland, N., & Robinson, J. D. (1992). How are you? Negotiating phatic communion. *Language in Society, 21,* 207–230

Creswell, J. W. (1997). *Qualitative Inquiry and research design: Choosing among five traditions.* Thousand Oaks, CA: Sage.

Critchley, M. (1970). *Aphasiology and other aspects of language.* London: Arnold.

Cummings, J. L., & Benson, D. F. (1983). Dementia of the Alzheimer type: An inventory of diagnostic clinical features. *Journal of the American Geriatrics Society, 34,* 12–19.

Cummings, J. L., Benson, D. F., Hill, M. A., & Read, S. (1985). Aphasia in dementia of the Alzheimer's type. *Neurology, 35,* 394–397.

Damasio, A. (1999). *The feeling of what happens: Body and emotion in the making of consciousness.* Orlando, FL: Harcourt.

Damico, J. S. (1985) Clinical discourse analysis: A functional language assessment technique. In C. S. Simon (Ed.), *Communication skills and classroom success: Assessment of language learning in disabled students* (pp. 165–204). San Diego, CA: College Hill.

Damico, J. S. (1992). Systematic observation of communicative interaction: A valid and practical descriptive assessment technique. *Best Practices in School Speech-Language Pathology, 2,* 133–143.

Damico, J. S., Oelschlaeger, M., & Simmons-Mackie, N. (1999). Qualitative methods in aphasia research: Conversation analysis. *Aphasiology, 13,* 667–679.

Damico, J. S., & Simmons-Mackie, N. (2002). The base layer and the gaze/gesture layer of transcription. *Clinical Linguistics and Phonetics, 16,* 317–327.

Damico, J. S., Simmons-Mackie, N., Oelschlaeger, M., Elman, R., & Armstrong, E. (1999). Qualitative methods in aphasia research: Basic issues. *Aphasiology, 13,* 651–665.

DeClercq, A. (2000). (Participant) observation in nursing home wards for people suffering from dementia: The problems of trust and emotional involvement. *Forum Qualitative Sozialforschung, 1*(1). Retrieved August 8, 2004, from http://www. qualitative-research.net/fqs-texte/1-00/100declercq-e.htm

DeLacoste, M., & White, C. L. (1993). The role of cortical connectivity in Alzheimer's Disease pathogenesis: A review and model system. *Neurobiology of Aging, 14,* 1–16.

Dennett, D. C. (1990). True believers: The intentional strategy and why it works. In W. G. Lycan (Ed.), *Mind and cognition* (pp. 75–87). Oxford, England: Blackwell.

Dore, J. (1979). Conversation and preschool language development. In P. Fletcher & M. Garman (Eds.), *Language acquisition* (pp. 279–308). Cambridge, England: Cambridge University Press.

Duchan, J. (1994), Approaches to the study of discourse in the social sciences. In R. L. Bloom, L. K. Obler, S. De Santi, & J. S. Ehrlich (Eds.), *Discourse analysis and applications: Studies in adult clinical populations* (pp. 1–14). Hillsdale, NJ: Lawrence Erlbaum Associates.

Duranti, A., & Goodwin, C. (Eds.). (1992). *Rethinking context: Language as an interactive phenomenon.* Cambridge, England: Cambridge University Press.

Edwards, D. (1997). *Discourse and cognition.* London: Sage.

Edwards, D., & Potter, J. (2001). Discursive psychology. In A. W. McHoul & M. Rapley (Eds.), *How to analyze talk in institutional settings: A casebook of methods* (pp. 12–24). London: Continuum International.

Edwards, J. A. (1993). Principles and contrasting systems of discourse description. In J. A. Edwards & M. D. Lampert (Eds.), *Talking data: Transcription and coding in discourse Research* (pp. 3–31). Hillsdale, NJ: Lawrence Erlbaum Associates.

Edwards, J. A. (2001.) The transcription of discourse. In D. Schiffrin, D. Tannen, & H. E. Hamilton (Eds.), *The handbook of discourse analysis* (pp. 321–348). Oxford, England: Blackwell.

Eggins, S., & Slade, D. (1997). *Analysing casual conversation*. London: Caswell.

Fairclough, N. (1989). *Language and power*. London: Longman.

Fairclough, N. (1995). *Critical discourse analysis*. London Longman.

Fasold, R. (1990). *Sociolinguistics of language*. Oxford, England: Blackwell.

Feil, N. (1982). *Validation: The Feil method*. Cleveland, OH: Edward Feil Productions.

Feiser, J. (Ed) (2004). *The Internet encyclopedia of philosophy*. Section 6. Retrieved October 2004 from NWW.iep.utm.edu

Fine, E. (1983). In defense of literary dialect: A response to Dennis R. Preston. *Journal of American Folklore, 96,* 323–330.

Firth, J. R. (1957). *Papers in linguistics 1934–1951*. London: Oxford University Press.

Foucault, M. (1984). The order of discourse. In M. Shapiro (Ed.), *Language and politics*. Oxford, England: Blackwell.

Fowler, R. (1991). *Language in the news: Discourse and ideology in the press*. London: Routledge.

Fowler, R., Hodge, B., Kress, G., & Trew, T. (1979). *Language and control*. London: Routledge & Kegan Paul.

Fox, P. (1989). From senility to Alzheimer's disease: The rise of the Alzheimer's disease movement. *Millbank Quarterly, 67,* 58–102.

Friedland, D., & Miller, N. (1999). Language mixing in bilingual speakers with Alzheimer's dementia: A conversation analysis approach. *Aphasiology 13,* 427–444.

Gaik, F. (1992). Radio talk-show therapy and the pragmatics of possible worlds. In A. Duranti & C. Goodwin (Eds.), *Rethinking context: Language as an interactive phenomenon* (pp. 271–289). Cambridge, England: Cambridge University Press.

Galtung, J., & Ruge, M. (1973). Structuring and selecting news. In S. Cohen & J. Young (Eds.), *The manufacture of news: Social problems, deviance and the mass media* (pp. 62–72). London: Constable.

Garcia, L. J., & Joanette, Y. (1994). Conversational topic-shifting analysis in dementia. In R. L. Bloom, L. K. Obler, S. De Santi, & J. S. Ehrlich (Eds.), *Discourse analysis and applications: Studies in adult clinical populations* (pp. 161–184). Hillsdale, NJ: Lawrence Erlbaum Associates.

Garcia, L. J., & Joanette, Y. (1997). Analysis of topic shifts: A multiple case study. *Brain and Language, 58,* 92–114.

Gardner, H. (1974). *The shattered mind: The person after brain damage*. New York: Random House.

Garfinkel, H. (1967). *Studies in ethnomethodology*. Englewood Cliffs, NJ: Prentice Hall.

Geertz, C. (1973). *The interpretation of cultures*. New York: Basic Books.

Gergen K. J. (1991). *The saturated self: Dilemmas of identity in everyday life*. New York: Greenwood.

Giddens, A. (1976). *New rules of sociological method: a positive critique of interpretive sociologies*. London: Hutchinson.

Giddens, A. (1991). *Modernity and self-identity*. Cambridge, England: Polity Press.

Giles, H., & Coupland, N. (1991). *Language contexts and consequences*. Milton Keynes, England: Open University Press.

Glasgow University Media Group. (1976). *Bad news*. London: Routledge & Kegan Paul.

Glosser, G., & Deser, T. (1990). Patterns of discourse production among neurological patients with fluent language disorders. *Brain and Language, 40,* 67–88.

Goffman, E. (1964). *Asylums: Essays on the social situation of mental patients and other inmates.* New York: Doubleday.

Goffman, E. (1967). *Interaction ritual.* New York: Pantheon.

Goffman, E. (1974). *Frame analysis.* New York: Harper & Row.

Goffman, E. (1981). *Forms of talk.* Philadelphia: University of Pennsylvania Press.

Golander, H., & Raz, A. E. (1996). The mask of dementia: Images of "demented residents" in a nursing ward. *Ageing and Society, 16,* 269–285.

Goodwin, C. (Ed.). (2003). *Conversation and brain damage.* New York: Oxford University Press.

Goodwin, C., & Duranti, A. (1992) Rethinking context: An introduction. In A. Duranti & C. Goodwin (Eds.), *Rethinking context: Language as an interactive phenomenon* (pp. 1–34). New York: Cambridge University Press.

Goodwin C., & Harness-Goodwin, M. (1992). Assessments and the construction of context. In A. Duranti & C. Goodwin (Eds.), *Rethinking context. Language as an interactive phenomenon* (pp. 147–190). New York: Cambridge University Press.

Goodwin, C., & Harness-Goodwin, M. (2000). Emotion within situated activity. In A. Duranti (Ed.), *Linguistic anthropology: A reader* (pp. 239–257). Malden, MA: Blackwell.

Goodwin, C., & Heritage, J. (1990). Conversational analysis. *Annual Review of Anthropology, 19,* 283–307.

Goodwin, J. S. (1991). Geriatric ideology: The myth of the myth of senility. In J. A. Gubrium & J. A. Holstein (Eds.), *Aging and everyday life* (pp. 331–339). Mahwah, NJ: Lawrence Erlbaum Associates. Reprinted from *Journal of the American Geriatrics Society, 39,* 627–231.

Gott, P. (2004). Ask Dr Gott: Alzheimer's devastates lives of patient, family. *Hammond Daily Star,* March 28, 2004, Section G, p. 4.

Gramsci, A. (1971). *Prison notebooks.* New York: International Publishers.

Grice, H. P. (1957). Meaning. *Philosophical Review, 66,* 377–388.

Grice, H. P. (1975). Logic and conversation. In P. Cole & J. L. Morgan (Eds.), *Syntax and semantics 3: Speech acts* (pp. 41–58). New York: Academic.

Grimes, J. (1975). *The thread of discourse.* The Hague, Netherlands: Mouton.

Grundy, P. (1995). *Doing pragmatics.* London: Edward Arnold.

Guendouzi, J. (2001). "You'll think we're always bitching": The functions of cooperativity and competition in women's gossip. *Discourse Studies, 3,* 55–77.

Guendouzi, J. (2003). Caregiver beliefs about communication in dementia. Unpublished data.

Guendouzi, J., & Müller, N. (2002). Defining trouble sources in dementia: Repair strategies and conversational satisfaction in interactions with an Alzheimer's patient. In F. Windsor, M. L. Kelly, & N. Hewlett (Eds.), *Investigations in clinical phonetics and linguistics.* Mahwah, NJ: Lawrence Erlbaum Associates.

Gumperz, J. (1982a). *Discourse strategies.* Cambridge, England: Cambridge University Press.

Gumperz, J. (1982b). *Language and social identity.* Cambridge, England: Cambridge University Press.

Gumperz, J. J. (1992). Contextualization and understanding. In A. Duranti & C. Goodwin (Eds.), *Rethinking context: Language as an interactive phenomenon* (pp. 229–252). Cambridge, England: Cambridge University Press.

Gurland, B., Copeland, J., Kuriansky, J., Kelleher, M., Sharpe, L., & Dean, L. L. (1983). *The mind and mood of aging.* London: Croom Helm.

Habermas, J. (1989). *The structural transformation of the public sphere.* Cambridge, England: Polity Press.

Hainsworth, S. (2000). *Gramsci's hegemony theory and the ideological role of mass media.* Retrieved October 11, 2004, from http://www.cultsock.ndirect.co.uk/MUHome/cshtml/contributions/gramsci.html

Hall, S., Hobson, D., Lowe A., & Willis, P. (1980). *Culture, media, language.* London: Hutchinson.

Halliday, M. A. K. (1978). *Language as a social semiotic: The social interpretation of language and meaning.* London: Edward Arnold.

Halliday, M. A. K. (1985). *An introduction to functional grammar.* London: Edward Arnold.

Halliday, M. A. K., & Hasan, R. (1985). *Language, context and text.* Geelong, Victoria, Australia: Deakin University Press.

Hamilton, H. E. (1994a). *Conversations with an alzheimer's patient: An interactional sociolinguistic study.* Cambridge, England: Cambridge University Press.

Hamilton, H. E. (1994b). Requests for clarification as evidence of pragmatic comprehension difficulty: The case of Alzheimer's disease. In R. L. Bloom, L. K. Obler, S. De Santi, & J. S. Ehrlich (Eds.), *Discourse analysis and applications: Studies in adult clinical populations* (pp. 185–200). Hillsdale, NJ: Lawrence Erlbaum Associates.

Hancher, M. (1979). The classification of cooperative illocutionary acts. *Language in Society, 8,* 1–14.

Harness-Goodwin, M. (1994). Social differentiation and alliance formation in an urban black children's peer group. In M. R. Stevenson (Ed.), *Gender roles through the life span* (pp. 31–43). Muncie, IN: Ball State University Press.

Harness-Goodwin, M., & Goodwin, C. (1992). Context, activity and participation. In P. Auer & A. di Luzio (Eds.), *The contextualization of language* (pp. 77–99). Amsterdam: Benjamins.

Harré, R. (1983). *Personal being.* Oxford, England: Blackwell.

Harré, R. (1991). The discursive production of selves. *Theory and Psychology, 1,* 51–63.

Harré, R., & van Langenhove, L. (1999). *Positioning theory.* Oxford, England: Blackwell.

Hays, S. J., Niven, B., Godfrey, H. P. D., & Linscott, R. J. (2004). Clinical assessment of pragmatic language impairment: A generalisability study of older people with Alzheimer's disease. *Aphasiology, 18,* 693–714.

Hecaen, H., & Albert, M. L. (1978). *Human neuropsychology.* New York: Wiley.

Heritage, J. (1984a). *Garfinkel and ethnomethodology.* Cambridge, England: Polity Press.

Heritage, J. (1989). Current developments in conversation analysis. In D. Roger & P. Bull (Eds.), *Conversation: An interdisciplinary perspective* (pp. 21–47). Clevedon, England: Multilingual Matters.

Hodge, R., & Kress, G. (1992). *Language as ideology* (2nd ed.). London: Routledge.

Huber, W., Poeck, K., & Weniger, D. (1982). Aphasie [Aphasia]. In K. Poeck (Ed.), *Klinische Neuropsychologie* (pp. 241–260). Stuttgart, Germany: Thieme.

Hunt, K. (1965). *Grammatical structures written at three grade levels.* Urbana, IL: National Council of Teachers of English.

Hustad, K. C., & Beukelman, D. R. (2001). Effects of linguistic cues and stimulus cohesion on intelligibility of severely dysarthric speech. *Journal of Speech Language and Hearing Research, 44,* 497–510.

Hustad, K. C., & Beukelman, D. R. (2002). Listener comprehension of severely dysarthric speech: Effects of linguistic cues and stimulus cohesion. *Journal of Speech Language and Hearing Research, 45,* 545–558.

Hyltenstam, K., & Stroud, C. (1993). Second language regression in Alzheimer's dementia. In K. Hyltenstam & Å. Viberg (Eds.), *Progression and regression in language* (pp. 222–242). Cambridge, England: Cambridge University Press.

Hymes, D. (1972a). Models of the interaction of language and social life. In J. Gumperz & D. Hymes (Eds.), *Directions in sociolinguistics* (pp. 35–71). New York: Holt, Rinehart & Winston.

Hymes, D. (1972b). Toward ethnographies of communication: The analysis of communicative events. In P. P. Giglioli (Ed.), *Language and social context* (pp. 21–44). Harmondsworth, England: Penguin.

Hymes, D. (1974). *Foundations in sociolinguistics: An ethnographic approach.* Philadelphia: University of Pennsylvania Press.

Hymes, D. (1981). *"In vain I tried to tell you." Essays in Native American ethnopoetics.* Philadelphia: University of Pennsylvania Press.

Jaworski, A., & Coupland, N. (1999). *The discourse reader.* London: Routledge.

Jefferson, G. (1973). A case of precision timing in ordinary conversation: Overlapped tag-positioned address terms in closing sequences. *Semiotica, 9,* 47–96.

Kafka, F. (1915/1988). *The metamorphosis* (Bantam Classics). New York: Chelsea House Publishers.

Kazui, H., Mori, E., Hashimoto, M., & Hirono, N. (2003). Enhancement of declarative memory by emotional arousal and visual memeory function in Alzheimer's disease. *Journal of Neuropsychiatry and Clinical Neurosciences, 15,* 221–226.

Kempler, D. (1995). Language changes in dementia of the Alzheimer's type. In R. Lubinski (Ed.), *Dementia and communication* (pp. 98–114). San Diego, CA: Singular.

Kent, R. D. (Ed.). (1992a). *Intelligibility in speech disorders.* Amsterdam: Benjamins.

Kent, R. D. (1992b). Introduction. In R. D. Kent (Ed.), *Intelligibility in speech disorders* (pp 1–10). Amsterdam: Benjamins.

Kent, R. D., Miolo, G., & Bloedel, S. (1994). The intelligibility of children's speech: A review of evaluation procedures. *American Journal of Speech Language Pathology, 3,* 81–95.

Kent, R. D., Weismer, G., Kent, J. F., & Rosenbeck, J. C. (1989). Toward phonetic intelligibility testing in dysarthria. *Journal of Speech and Hearing Disorders, 54,* 482–499.

Kitwood, T. (1988). The technical, the personal, and the framing of dementia. *Social Behaviour, 3,* 161–179.

Kitwood, T. (1990). The dialectics of dementia: With particular reference to Alzheimer's disease. *Ageing and Society, 10,* 177–196.

Kitwood, T. (1997). *Dementia reconsidered: The person comes first.* Philadelphia, PA: Open University Press.

Kitwood, T., & Bredin, K. (1992). Towards a theory of dementia care: Personhood and well-being. *Ageing and Society, 12,* 269–287.

Kress, G. (1988). *Linguistic processes in sociocultural practice.* New York: Oxford University Press.

Kress, G., & van Leeuwen, T. (1996). *Reading images: The grammar of visual design.* London: Routledge.

Kuiper, K., & Everaert, M. (2000). Constraints on the phrase structural properties of English phrasal lexical items. In B. Roswadowska (Ed.), *PASE papers in language studies* (pp. 152–170). Wroclaw, Poland: Aksel s. c.

Kurzweil, R. (1999) *The age of spiritual machines.* New York: Penguin.

Labov, W., & Fanshel, D. (1977). *Therapeutic discourse: Psychotherapy as conversation.* New York: Academic.

Labov, W., & Waletsky, J. (1966). Narrative analysis: Oral versions of personal experience. In J. Helm (Ed.), *Essays on verbal and visual arts* (pp. 12–44). Seattle: University of Washington Press.

LeDoux, J. (2002). *Synaptic self: How our brains become who we are.* Harmondsworth, England: Penguin.

Levinson, S. (1983). *Pragmatics.* Cambridge, England: Cambridge University Press.

Lincoln, Y., & Guba, E. (1985). *Naturalistic inquiry.* Beverly Hills, CA: Sage.

Lindsay, J., & Wilkinson, R. (1999). Repair sequences in aphasic talk: A comparison of aphasic-speech and language therapist and aphasic-spouse conversations. *Aphasiology, 13,* 305–325.

Linscott, R. J., Knight, R. G., & Godfrey, H. P. D. (1996). The Profile of Functional Impairment in Communication (PFIC): A measure of communication impairment for clinical use. *Brain Injury, 10,* 397–412.

Littlejohn, S. W. (1999). *Theories of human communication.* Belmont, CA: Wadsworth.

Lubinski, R. (Ed.). (1995). *Dementia and communication.* San Diego, CA: Singular.

Ludlow, C. L., Polinsky, R. J., Caine, E. D., Bassich, C. J., & Ebert, M. H. (1982). Language and speech abnormalities in Tourette syndrome. *Advances in Neurology, 35,* 351–361.

Luria, A. R. (1987a). *The man with a shattered world.* Cambridge, MA: Harvard University Press.

Luria, A. R. (1987b). *The mind of a mnemonist.* Cambridge, MA: Harvard University Press.

Lyman, K. A. (1989). Bringing the social back in: a critique of the biomedicalization of dementia. *The Gerontologist, 229,* 597–605.

Lyons, J. (1968). *Introduction to theoretical linguistics.* Cambridge, England: Cambridge University Press.

Machetanz, J., Schönle, P. W., & Benecke, R. (1988). Iterative Dysarthrie beim M. Parkinson [Iterative dysarthria in Parkinson's disease]. *Nervenarzt, 59,* 559–661.

Malinowski, B. (1972). The problem of meaning in primitive languages. Supplement to C. K. Ogden and I. A. Richards, *The meaning of meaning.* London: Routledge and Kegan Paul. (Original work published 1923)

Malmkjaer, K. (1991). *The linguistics encyclopedia.* London: Routledge & Kegan Paul.

McDermott, R. (1977). The ethnography of speaking and reading. In R. Shuy (Ed.), *Linguistic theory* (pp. 198–213). Newark, NJ: International Reading Association.

Mentis, M., Briggs-Whittaker, J., & Gramigna, G. D. (1995). Discourse topic management in senile dementia of the Alzheimer's type. *Journal of Speech and Hearing Research, 38,* 1054–1066.

Mey, J. L. (1985). *Whose language: A study in linguistic pragmatics.* Amsterdam: Benjamins.

Minsky, M. (1977). Frame-system theory. In P. N. Johnson-Laird & P. C. Watson (Eds.), *Thinking: Readings in cognitive science* (pp. 355–376). Cambridge, England: Cambridge University Press.

Molloy, D. W., & Lubinski, R. (1995). Dementia: Impact and clinical perspectives. In R. Lubinski (Ed.), *Dementia and communication* (pp. 2–21). San Diego, CA: Singular.

Müller, N. (2003). Intelligibility and negotiated meaning in interaction. *Clinical Linguistics and Phonetics, 17,* 317–324.

Müller, N., & Damico, J. S. (2002). A transcription toolkit: Theoretical and clinical considerations. *Clinical Linguistics and Phonetics, 16,* 299–316.

Müller, N., & Guendouzi, J. A. (2002). Transcribing discourse: Interactions with Alzheimer's disease. *Clinical Linguistics and Phonetics, 16,* 345–359.

Müller, N., & Guendouzi, J. A. (2005). Order and disorder in conversation: Encounters with dementia of the Alzheimer's type. *Clinical Linguistics and Phonetics, 19,* 393–404.

Obler, L. K., De Santi, S., & Goldberger, M. A. (1995). Bilingual dementia: Pragmatic breakdown. In R. Lubinski (Ed.), *Dementia and communication* (pp. 133–139). San Diego, CA: Singular.

Ochs, E. (1979). Transcription as theory. In E. Ochs & B. Schieffelin (Eds.), *Developmental pragmatics* (pp. 43–72). New York: Academic.

Ogden, J. A. (1996). *Fractured minds: A case study approach to clinical neuropsychology.* New York: Oxford University Press.

Pawley, A., & Syder, F. H. (2000). The one-clause-at-a-time-hypothesis. In H. Riggenbach (Ed.), *Perspectives on fluency* (pp. 163–199). Ann Arbor: University of Michigan Press.

Peccei, J. S (1999). *Pragmatics.* Routledge Language Workbooks. London: Routledge.

Perkins, L., Whitworth, A., & Lesser, R. (1998). Conversing in dementia: A conversation analytical approach. *Journal of Neurolinguistics, 11,* 33–53.

Perkins, M. (2000). The scope of pragmatic disability: A cognitive approach. In N. Müller (Ed.), *Pragmatics in speech-language pathology* (pp. 7–28). Amsterdam: Benjamins.

Perkins, M. (2002). An emergentist approach to clinical pragmatics. In F. Windsor, M. L. Kelly, & N. Hewlett (Eds.), *Investigations in clinical phonetics and linguistics* (pp. 1–14). Mahwah, NJ: Lawrence Erlbaum Associates.

Perkins, M. (2003). Clinical pragmatics. In J. Verschueren, J.-O. Ostman, J. Blommaert, & C. Bulcaen (Eds), *Handbook of pragmatics: 2001 installment* (pp. 1–29). Amsterdam: Benjamins.

Perkins, M. (2005). Pragmatic ability and disability as emergent phenomena. *Clinical Linguistics and Phonetics, 19,* 367–378.

Perkins, M. (in press). *Pragmatics and communication impairment.* Cambridge, England: Cambridge University Press.

Perkins, M., Body, R., & Parker, M. (1995). Closed head injury: Assessment and remediation of topic bias and repetitiveness. In M. Perkins & S. Howards (Eds.), *Case studies in clinical linguistics* (pp. 293–320). London: Whurr.

Pinker, S. (2002). *The blank slate.* New York: Viking.

Pomerantz, A. (1978). Compliment responses: Notes on co-operation of multiple constraints. In J. Scheinken (Ed.), *Studies in the organization of conversational interaction* (pp. 79–101). New York Academic.

Pomerantz, A. (1984). Agreeing and disagreeing with assessments. In J. M. Atkinson & J. Heritage (Eds.), *Structures of social action* (pp. 57–101). Cambridge, England: Cambridge University Press.

Potter, J. (2003). *A discursive psychology of institutions.* Paper presented at the BPS Social Psychology Section Annual Conference, London School of Economics, London.

Potter, J., & Wetherell, M. (1987). *Discourse and social psychology.* London: Sage.

Powell, J. A., Hale, M. A., & Bayer, A. J. (1995). Symptoms of communication breakdown in dementia: Carers' perspectives. *European Journal of Disorders of Communication, 30,* 65–75.

Prigatano, G. P. (2000). A brief overview of four principles of neuropsychological rehabilitation. In A. Christensen and B. P. Uzzell (Eds.), *International handbook of Neuropsychological rehabilitation* (pp. 115–125). New York: Kluwer.

Psathas, G., & Anderson, T. (1990). The "practices" of transcription in conversation analysis. *Semiotica, 78,* 75–99.

Pye, C., Wilcox, K. A., & Siren, K. A. (1988). Refining transcription: The significance of transcriber errors. *Journal of Child Language, 15,* 17–37.

Ramanathan, V. (1997). *Alzheimer discourse: Some sociolinguistic dimensions.* Mahwah, NJ: Lawrence Erlbaum Associates.

Ramanathan-Abbot, V. (1994). Interactional differences in Alzheimer's discourse: An examination of AD speech across two audiences. *Language and Society, 23,* 31–58.

Reisberg, B. (1983). *Alzheimer's disease: The standard reference.* New York: Free Press.

Reisberg, B., Ferris, S. H., de Leon, M. J., & Crook, T. (1982) The global deterioration scale for assessment of primary degenerative dementia. *American Journal of Psychiatry, 139,* 1136–1139.

Rempusheski, V. F. (1999). Qualitative research and Alzheimer's disease. *Alzheimer disease and related disorders, 13* (Suppl. 1), S45–S49.

Ripich, D. N., & Terrell, B. Y. (1988). Patterns of discourse cohesion and coherence in Alzheimer's disease. *Journal of Speech and Hearing Disorders, 53,* 8–19.

Ripich, D. N., Vertes, D., Whitehouse, P., Fulton, S., & Ekelman, B. (1991). Turn-taking and speech act patterns in the discourse of senile dementia of the Alzheimer's type patients. *Brain and Language, 40,* 330–343.

Roberts, C. (1997). Transcribing talk: Issues of representation. *TESOL Quarterly, 31,* 167–172.

Sabat, S. R. (1991). Turn-taking and turn-giving, and Alzheimer's disease: A case study in conversation. *Georgetown Journal of Languages and Linguistics, 2,* 161–175.

Sabat, S. R. (2001). *The experience of Alzheimer's disease: Life through a tangled web.* Oxford, England: Blackwell.

Sacks, H., Schegloff, E. A., & Jefferson, G. (1974). A simplest systematics for the organization of turn-taking in conversation. *Language, 50,* 696–735.

Salmon, D. P., Heindel, W. C., & Butters, N. (1995). Patterns of cognitive impairment in Alzheimer's disease. In R. Lubinski (Ed.), *Dementia and communication* (pp. 37–46). San Diego, CA: Singular.

Santo Pietro, M. J., & Ostuni, E. (2003). *Successful communication with persons with Alzheimer's disease: An in-service manual.* St Louis, MO: Heinemann.

Saville-Troike, M. (1982). *The ethnography of communication. An introduction.* Oxford, England: Blackwell.

Schegloff, E. (1987). Between macro and micro: Contexts and other connections. In J. Alexander, B. Gressen, R. Munch, & N. Smelser (Eds.), *The macro link* (pp. 207–234). Berkeley: University of California Press.

Schegloff, E. A. (2003). Conversation analysis and communication disorders. In C. Goodwin (Ed.), *Conversation and brain damage* (pp. 21–58). New York: Oxford University Press.

Schiffrin, D. (1994). *Approaches to discourse.* Oxford, England: Blackwell.

Schiffrin, D., Tannen, D., & Hamilton, H. E. (2001). (Eds.). *The handbook of discourse analysis.* Oxford, England: Blackwell.

Schwartz, J. M., & Begley, S. (2002). *The mind and the brain.* New York: HarperCollins.

Searle, J. (1969). *Speech acts.* Cambridge, England: Cambridge University Press.

Searle, J. (1975). Indirect speech acts. In P. Cole & J. L. Morgan (Eds.), *Syntax and semantics 3: Speech acts* (pp. 59–82). New York: Academic

Searle, J. (1979). A taxonomy of illocutionary acts. In J. Searle (Ed.), *Expression and meaning* (pp. 1–29). Cambridge, England: Cambridge University Press.

Shenk, D. (2001). *The forgetting. Alzheimer's disease: Portrait of an epidemic.* New York: Anchor.

Sherzer, J. (1994). Transcription, representation and translation: Repetition and performance in Kuna discourse. In B. Johnstone (Ed.), *Repetition in discourse: Interdisciplinary perspectives* (Vol. 1, pp. 37–52). Norwood, NJ: Ablex.

Shindler, A. G., Caplan, L. R., & Hier, D. B. (1984). Intrusions and perseverations. *Brain and Language, 23,* 148–158.

Shweder, R. (1983). Beyond self-constructed knowledge: The study of culture and morality. *Merrill-Palmer Quarterly, 28,* 41–69.

Silverman, D. (2000). *Doing qualitative research.* London: Sage.

Simmons-Mackie, N., and Damico, J. S. (1999). Qualitative methods in aphasia research: Ethnography. *Aphasiology, 13,* 681–687.

Simmons-Mackie, N., & Kagan, A. (1999). Communication strategies used by "good" versus "poor" speaking partners of individuals with aphasia. *Aphasiology, 13,* 807–820.

Sinclair, J., & Coultard, R. M. (1975). *Towards an analysis of discourse: The English used by teachers and pupils.* New York: Oxford University Press.

Sjogren, T., Sjogren, H., & Lindgren, A. G. H. (1952). Morbus Alzheimer and morbus Pick. A genetic, clinical and pathoanatomical study. *Acta Psychiatrica Neurologica Scandinavica, 82,* 1–152.

Snowden, D. (2001). *Aging with grace.* New York: Bantam.

Spender, D. (1980). *Man made language.* London: Routledge & Kegan Paul.

Strawson, P. (1964). Intention and convention in speech acts. *Philosophical Review, 73,* 439–460.

Stubbs, M. (1983). *Discourse analysis.* Chicago: Chicago University Press.

Tajfel, H. (1979). Social categorization, social identity, and social comparison. In H. Tajfel (Ed.), *Differentiation between social groups* (pp. 61–76). New York: Academic.

Tannen, D. (1984). *Conversational style: Analyzing talk among friends.* Norwood, NJ: Ablex.

Tannen, D. (1990). Gender differences in topical coherence: Creating involvement in best friends talk. *Discourse Processes, 13,* 73–90.

Tomlinson, B. E., Blessed, G., & Roth, M. (1968). Observations on the brains of non-demented old people. *Journal of Neurological Science, 7,* 331–336.

Tomlinson, B. E., Blessed, G., & Roth, M. (1970). Observations on the brains of demented old people. *Journal of Neurological Science, 11,* 205–242.

Trees, A. R., & Manusov, V. (1998). Managing face concerns in criticism: Integrating nonverbal behaviors as a dimension of politeness in female dyads. *Human Communication Research, 24,* 564–683.

Turner, R. (1974). *Ethnomethodology: Selected readings.* Harmondsworth, England: Penguin.

Tyler, S. (1986). Post-modern ethnography: From document of the occult to occult document. In J. Clifford & G. Marcus (Eds.), *Writing culture* (pp. 122–140). Berkeley: University of California Press.

Ulatowska, H. K. (Ed.). (1985). *The aging brain: Communication in the elderly.* San Diego, CA: College Hill.

Ulatowska, H. K., & Chapman, S. B. (1995). Discourse studies. In R. Lubinski (Ed.), *Dementia and communication* (pp. 115–130). San Diego, CA: Singular.

Van Dijk, T. (Ed.). (1985a). *Handbook of discourse analysis. Volume 1: Disciplines of discourse.* New York: Academic.

Van Dijk, T. (1985b). Introduction: Discourse as a new cross-discipline. In T. van Dijk (Ed.), *Handbook of discourse analysis. Volume 1: Disciplines of discourse* (pp. 1–10). New York: Academic.

Van Dijk, T. (1988). *News as discourse.* Hillsdale, NJ: Lawrence Erlbaum Associates.

Van Dijk, T. (1997). *Discourse as structure and process.* London: Sage.

Van Dijk, T. (2001). Critical discourse analysis. In D. Schiffrin, D. Tannen, & M. E. Hamilton (Eds.), *The handbook of discourse analysis* (pp. 352–371). Oxford, England: Blackwell.

Van Lancker-Sidtis, D. (2004). When novel sentences spoken or heard for the first time in the history of the universe are not enough: Toward a dual-processing model of language. *International Journal of Disorders of Communication, 39,* 1–44.

Verschueren, J. (2001). Predicaments of criticism. *Critique of Anthropology, 21,* 59–81.

Wallesch, C. W. (1990). Repetitive verbal behaviour: Functional and neurological considerations. *Aphasiology, 4,* 133–154.

Wallesch, C. W., & Blanken, B. G. (2000). Recurring utterances-How, where, and why are they generated. *Brain and Language, 71,* 225–227.

Watson, C. M., Chenery, H. J., & Carter, M. S. (1999). An analysis of trouble and repair in the natural conversations of people with the Alzheimer's type. *Aphasiology, 13,* 195–218.

Weismer, G., Jeng, J. Y., Laures, J. S., Kent, R. D., & Kent, J. F. (2001). Acoustic and intelligibility characteristics of sentence production in neurogenic speech disorders. *Folia Phoniatrica et Logopaedica, 53,* 1–18.

Wilkinson, R. (1999). Sequentiality as a problem and resource for intersubjectivity in aphasic conversation: Analysis and implications for therapy. *Aphasiology, 13,* 327–343.

Williams, A., & Guendouzi, J. (2000). Adjusting to the home: Dialectical dilemmas and personal relationships in a retirement community. *Journal of Communiction, 50,* 365–382

Williams, A., & Nussbaum, J. (2001). *Intergenerational communication across the life span.* Mahwah, NJ: Lawrence Erlbaum Associates.

Wilson, E. O. (1978). *On human nature.* Cambridge, MA: Harvard University Press.

Wittgenstein, L. (1958). *Philosophical investigations* (G. E. M. Anscombe, Trans.; 2nd ed.). Oxford, England: Blackwell. (Original work published 1953)

Wootton, A. (1989). The management of grantings and rejections by parents in request sequences. *Semiotica, 37,* 59–89

Wray, A. (2002). *Formulaic language and the lexicon.* Cambridge, England: Cambridge University Press.

Yorkston, K. M., & Beukelman, D. R. (1978). A comparison of techniques for measuring intelligibility of dysarthric speech. *Journal of Communication Disorders, 11,* 499–512.

Yorkston, K. M., Beukelman, D. R., Strand, E. A., & Bell, K. R. (1999). *Management of motor speech disorders in children and adults* (2nd ed.). Austin, TX: ProEd.

Zimmerman, D. (1988). On conversation: The conversation analytic perspective. In J. Anderson (Ed.), *Communication yearbook* (Vol. 11, pp. 406–432). Beverly Hills, CA: Sage.

Author Index

Subject Index